GROWING UP MUSLIM

Muslim College Students in America Tell Their Life Stories

EDITED BY

Andrew Garrod and Robert Kilkenny
Introduction by Eboo Patel

Cornell University Press
Ithaca and London

First published 2014 by Cornell University Press
First printing, Cornell Paperbacks, 2014

Printed in the United States of America

Library of Congress Cataloging-in-Publication Data

Growing up Muslim in America (Garrod and Kilkenny)
    Growing up Muslim : Muslim college students in America
tell their life stories / edited by Andrew Garrod and Robert
Kilkenny ; introduction by Eboo Patel.
        pages cm
    ISBN 978-0-8014-5252-9 (cloth : alk. paper)
    ISBN 978-0-8014-7915-1 (pbk. : alk. paper)
    1. Dartmouth College—Students—Biography. 2. Muslim
college students—New Hampshire—Hanover—Biography.
3. Muslim youth—Education (Higher)—New Hampshire—
Hanover. I. Garrod, Andrew, 1937– editor of compilation.
II. Kilkenny, Robert, editor of compilation. III. Ahmed, Zahra.
Far from getting lost. IV. Title.
    LD1435.45.G76   2014
    378.1'9828297—dc23   2013037424

Cornell University Press strives to use environmentally
responsible suppliers and materials to the fullest extent
possible in the publishing of its books. Such materials
include vegetable-based, low-VOC inks and acid-free papers
that are recycled, totally chlorine-free, or partly
composed of nonwood fibers. For further information, visit
our website at www.cornellpress.cornell.edu.

Cloth printing   10 9 8 7 6 5 4 3 2 1
Paperback printing   10 9 8 7 6 5 4 3 2 1

GROWING UP MUSLIM

In recognition of their courage, hard work, self-understanding, and inspirational life stories, this book is dedicated to the twelve student autobiographers whose essays are presented here.

Marzuq Muhammad
Harun Hasanagić
Abdoul Mujyambere
Jeannine Uwase
Mouhamad Nshimiyimana
Mokhless Bouzayen
AG

Contents

Preface

By presenting the personal stories of thoughtful, intelligent, and coura-
geous student writers, *Growing Up Muslim* celebrates the role of Islam in
their lives while hoping to challenge some of the unquestioned public perceptions of Muslims. With this book we also seek to enlighten the U.S.
reading public by introducing a group of bright and hopeful Muslim students who, in Eboo Patel's striking words, "strive to be true to the principles of their faith while living fully in the world." In short, we hope our
book will encourage both Muslim and non-Muslim readers interested in
the development of faith among this age group.

These autobiographical accounts by Muslim students, those born
inside and outside the United States, can offer extraordinary insights
into the writers' perspectives on the role of faith in their lives. The personal stories in *Growing Up Muslim* are essentially memoirs in which the
autobiographers—all but one a current student or graduate of Dartmouth
College in Hanover, New Hampshire—reflect on formative relationships
and influences, life-changing events, and the role their faith has played in
shaping their values and their personal identity. Dartmouth does not keep
records of how many students self-identify as Muslim when they enter
the college, but it appears that the school's Muslim population is very
small and that the majority of Muslim students come from South Asia.
Because there are so few Arab Muslims at the college, we were compelled
to recruit an Arab writer from a major Canadian university to complement the one Arab Muslim contributor from Dartmouth, bearing in mind
that foreign-born and second-generation immigrants from South Asian
and predominantly Arab countries constitute the majority of Muslims in
the United States. While Dartmouth does not recruit evenly from various

Muslim populations in the world, we made a conscious attempt to include Muslims of faith traditions and backgrounds that varied as widely as the campus population allowed.

The representation of Muslim students at selective U.S. universities is not high. Dartmouth's records of self-identified Muslim students who contacted the Al-Nur Muslim Student Association show the following membership numbers for each graduating class year: eleven for the class of 2011, ten for 2012, ten for 2013, thirteen for 2014, and eight for 2015. The number of those who actively participate in Al-Nur events is somewhat smaller than these already modest figures. It is quite possible, however, that a number of practicing Muslims do not join the student group and are thus not reflected in these figures. The contributors to this book are of Pakistani, Afghan, Indian, Turkish, Jordanian, Somali, Yemeni, and Nigerian heritage; one contributor is of British American heritage. Despite the very small percentage of self-identified Muslims at Dartmouth, they come from an impressively diverse array of backgrounds and national origins. Although we collected almost all of these narratives on the Dartmouth campus, this book does not focus on Dartmouth per se or on the educational impact this particular college has had on our contributors. It focuses, rather, on these young people's evolving Muslim identities and the role of Islam in their lives. It is our hope that readers of this anthology will be able to engage with the particularities and details of these stories while also connecting with the individual human experiences.

Almost all the essays in this book were written in the last four or five years. Only two, "A Muslim Citizen of the Democratic West" (chapter 5) and "My Permanent Home" (chapter 8), are older, dating back to 2002. Thirteen of the fourteen authors worked one-on-one with Andrew Garrod in weekly one-hour meetings over the traditional ten-week academic term at Dartmouth; work with the contributor from Alberta was conducted via e-mail. The essays contained here were written exclusively for this anthology project. Typically, a student would submit seven or eight pages to Garrod prior to each meeting, and these pages were the focus of discussion when they met. Teacher and writer also discussed how to proceed with the next portion of the narrative. Garrod did not assume that a story was already formulated in a student's mind, and he conveyed to the student that each story had to be uncovered piece by piece. Because the emphasis was on process—that is, on the complex task of helping writers find their voice—no editorial interventions were made during the generative stage. Although we, the editors, necessarily had established parameters, we encouraged the writers to develop their own themes and to make sense of their experiences in ways that had significant meaning for their own lives. Not infrequently, a writer was halfway through the process before he or she came to understand what the essay's central concerns and themes were. As William Zinsser writes, "Memoir writers must manufacture a text, imposing narrative order on a jumble of half-remembered events. With that feat of manipulation, they arrive at a truth that is theirs alone, not quite like that of anybody else who is present at the same events."[1]

In helping our authors articulate their stories, we offered the following guiding questions:

- What do you live for?
- What is of transcendent value to you?
- Have there been critical incidents in your life, after which nothing was quite the same?
- What relationships have been of major significance to you, both within the family and outside it?
- What have been some of the major struggles in your life?
- In school, were your best friends of the same race, religion, and ethnicity as you?
- When you were a child, was religion discussed at home? If so, in what way?
- Have you been the victim of religious intolerance? Did you come to terms with this intolerance or lack of understanding, and if so, how?
- Has this college provided you with a supportive community in which to practice your religion?
- Have you been active in organizations that are concerned with the issues of religion and faith?
- What is the role of religious identity within your total identity?
- Did being a Muslim student at Dartmouth help you understand religious dynamics in this culture in a more profound way than perhaps people of other religions did?
- Do you ever desire or feel pressure to mask your religion when in the presence of others?
- How do people of non-Muslim backgrounds relate to you spiritually?
- To what extent have you accepted or challenged gender roles in your religious community?

These questions were offered as prompts. Many of our writers chose to engage some of these questions, and others found their own inspiration. Even though we did not intentionally stress the need for the writers to discuss 9/11, consideration of this event emerged organically as a pivotal point in some of the essays as they were being developed. Thus, 9/11 became one of the recurring themes of the anthology.

The first finished drafts of these autobiographical essays usually ranged from thirty-five to fifty pages. After careful consultation and discussion over months, or occasionally even years, cutting and editing reduced and sharpened the texts to a manageable fifteen to twenty-four pages. Editors' changes to the text were in most cases minimal. Variations in tone, degrees of self-analysis, and styles of expression reflect our commitment to respect each author's story and life. It should be noted that only one of the authors, the convert from Christianity to Islam, is a native English speaker. All other contributors wrote in their second or even third language.

After a draft was reduced from its original length to approximately twenty-five pages, it was sent to Robert Kilkenny, who had not worked with the students and therefore could offer a more objective reaction to their essays. This was done to bring the essays to another level of psychological cohesion in the hope that themes that seemed to be underdeveloped or mysteriously unaddressed in the stories could be brought to each writer's attention. Kilkenny suggested how and why a story would be better understood if some of these lacunae were explored more thoroughly. He also aimed to push the writers to the edge of their ability to ponder their own life stories. It was not unusual for a writer to balk, or to claim that they were genuinely unable to reflect further about experiences still raw and unresolved.

Because of its focus on the acculturation process of mainly foreign-born Muslim students attending a highly selective college in the Northeast, the anthology does not pretend to be representative of the Muslim American experience. Our contributors grew up in circumstances in their home countries that allowed them enough educational opportunity to gain admission and perform well academically in a competitive U.S. college. A few of the students in this book were enrolled in Andrew Garrod's various Education Department classes, most of which were informed by a psychological developmental perspective. A few of them came to us recommended by faculty members or by the college's Muslim adviser, and still others were recommended by other contributors. The fourteen essays, eight by men and six by women, represent fewer than half of those started. Some students withdrew their essays because they did not have the permission of their loved ones to write about them in such personal terms; for others, the writing of the essay and the self-reflection it prompted was the primary reason they had embarked on the adventure and they had little interest in being published. Others hesitated to make the suggested changes or to engage in further self-exploration and editing. In such cases, we made an editorial decision as to whether a piece could stand on its own without further effort or whether it was insufficiently coherent to merit publication. For a few of the writers, life intervened, and they found themselves short on the time or inclination to continue working on this demanding project. Thus, there emerged a self-selection favoring the student writers most committed to being published. In spite of these limitations, the editors believe these voices need to be heard because they make an important contribution to the debate on faith and identity in the United States. For all of the essays so diligently worked on over the years, whether they are included in the finished book or not, we are deeply grateful.

To encourage the frankest possible exploration of their lives, relationships, and the role of faith in shaping their attitudes and behavior, we insisted that the writers be given the choice to publish anonymously. It was clear to the editors that many of the contributors would not have committed themselves to paper and to such a personal exploration had we not offered anonymity. While central aspects of the stories, such as countries of origin and family details, were not changed, names of schools, siblings, and friends frequently have been altered. In all cases, the writer was asked to sign off on the final version that went to print.

For many of the authors, the process of putting their experiences into words has acted as a catalyst for further self-reflection on their life history. In twenty years of encouraging this type of work, we have consistently observed that the process of autobiographical writing can have a profoundly transformative effect on the spiritual, moral, and emotional domains of a writer's life, and that a life is often changed by such deep introspection. We have found would-be contributors overwhelmingly open to the invitation to make sense of their childhood and adolescent experiences, which up to then have been inchoate and unintegrated. This opportunity to reflect can often reconcile a student to trauma they have experienced and bring emotional resolution and understanding to the primary relationships and vicissitudes in their lives. We feel deeply privileged to be guiding student writers through deeper levels of self-understanding to help them gain purchase on the world through self-analysis and articulation.

We are deeply grateful to many student researchers and assistants, friends, and associates for the realization of this book. Dawood Yasin, the adviser to Al-Nur at Dartmouth College, has been a particularly staunch supporter of our project, suggesting candidates for student contributors and providing vital demographic material. Professors Kevin Reinhart and Lucas Swaine, from the Religion and Government Departments at Dartmouth, respectively, were especially helpful and encouraging with readings, references, and information on experts. Dody Riggs offered essential editorial suggestions as the manuscripts achieved their final form. Also essential to the completion of this manuscript have been the organizational, administrative, and computer skills of the following Dartmouth students, past and present: Richard Addo, Ibrahim Aly, Justice Amoh, Alex Caron, Mirhad Grebovic, Trevor King, Lamar Moss, Andrew Nalani, Adnan Rahimic, Joshua Solomon, Richard Waitumbi and Dennis Zeveloff. All have helped to markedly improve the text, organize the editors, and prepare the manuscript. Of all our invaluable assistants, none played a bigger role in helping to edit texts and to prepare the manuscript for publication than Tien-Tien Jong. For her help, we are deeply grateful. A special thank you is also due to the two anonymous reviewers for Cornell University Press. Their insights and recommendations helped to improve the text.

Whether writing under one's own name or anonymously, it is not easy to open your life, and your reflections on that life, to public inspection. We wish to recognize all those students who have written with such courage and commitment in bringing their personal stories of faith into the public domain.

Note

1. William Zinsser, introduction to *Inventing the Truth: The Art and Craft of Memoir* (Boston: Houghton Mifflin, 1987), 6.

GROWING UP MUSLIM

Introduction   Eboo Patel

A few years back, I did an interview on cable television about Islam. When I returned home, my three-year-old son, Zayd, greeted me at the door and said excitedly, "Daddy, you were on TV!"

I smiled, ruffled his hair, and asked if I did a good job.

He nodded vigorously, and then, with a look of confusion on his face, said, "Why were they showing pictures of bad people when you were talking?"

"What does he mean?" I asked my wife.

"You must not have seen the tape yet," she responded. She pressed a button on the remote control and played the segment back for me. There I was, describing Islam as a tradition of mercy and Muslims as a community of people who sought to make positive contributions to their countries. As I was speaking, a series of images was rolling in the background—pictures of men in masks with automatic machine guns training at a terrorist camp in Afghanistan. Some staffer at the cable network must have seen "interview about Islam" on the schedule and pulled the first roll of film he could find: images of terrorists.

I was about to go through the roof—I wanted to call the cable channel, get the staffer fired, and complain about the incident all the way up the chain. And then I heard a word that interrupted my angry train of thought: "Daddy?" my son said. He must have seen my face darken; he wanted to make sure I was OK. Suddenly, anger was no longer my primary emotion. I was struck instead by a sense of deep, deep fear. This was the environment my son would grow up in. When Islam was talked about on the evening news, there was a reasonable chance that the accompanying pictures would be of terrorists. When the word "Muslim" was mentioned on the school playground or in the aisles of the local grocery store, there was a strong likelihood that the images going through people's minds would be of violence. Everything I was telling him about his religion and community at home would be contradicted by the broader environment. As the Muslim American scholar Dalia Mogahed observes, after 9/11, "the national conversation about Muslims went from a whisper to a roar." My son would be developing his Muslim identity while trapped in the teeth of that roar. Whom would he believe—me or the images on TV?

I was reminded of just how heavy that burden would be while reading the essays in this volume, precisely because these readings helped lift the weight. It is not that the writers here—all students or recent graduates of Dartmouth College, with one exception, from the University of Alberta—had an easy go of negotiating their Muslim identities after 9/11. It is because they faced the challenge with such courage and clarity that it gives me hope for the path my son might carve. On the evening of September 10, 2001, these were sensitive, intelligent young people experiencing adolescent identity issues typical of the children of immigrants who practice a minority faith tradition. Twenty-four hours later, an important part of their identity had been marked as the source of absolute evil. People who look like their uncles and pray in their holy language invoked that language and that holiness as inspiration to murder three thousand people and to poison the reputation of 1.6 billion more. One night they are arguing with their parents about wearing "Western" clothes, talking on the phone with members of the opposite sex, and having friends who are not Muslim. The next day, in the jungle of the American middle school, they have to face the roar. "So, do you help your brothers build bombs?" the essayist Sarah Chaudhry recalls being asked by two boys in her seventh-grade study hall. Their hectoring lasted the entire hour. Those who overheard remained silent, including those she considered her friends. She reported the incident, but the vice principal's reaction was blasé. Sarah realized that life as a Muslim in the United States would never be the same.

Sara L. aptly describes the change: "9/11 was the beginning of my struggle to make sense of what it means to be a *public* Muslim." In one way or another, 9/11 and its aftermath made an impact on just about every one of these young writers, giving a public dimension to what had once been a personal struggle. Sabeen Hassanali writes about the palpable fear she feels for her Pakistani-immigrant parents who own a grocery store in South Houston, and how her conversations with them now reflect that care and concern rather than being dominated by disagreements that once seemed so salient. Zahra Ahmed, a Somali immigrant, writes, "I always viewed myself as a racial minority, as my being black seemed most significant to others in American society. After the attacks, however, my being Muslim was the characteristic that was most openly challenged and discriminated against." Aly Rahim is shocked by the pervasiveness of anti-Muslim sentiment, especially within academic and policy circles (*Why don't these people know better?* he wonders), and he dedicates himself to educating people about the core principles of Islam and the diversity among the world's approximately 1.6 billion Muslims. In the face of the angry post-9/11 roar against Islam, these young Muslims are speaking with grace and compassion, seeking to advance a conversation that gives dignity to all identities, rather than trying to out-hate the hate or outshout the roar. In this way, they follow in the footsteps of the Prophet Muhammad, who said that the ink of the scholar is more sacred than the blood of the martyr.

While 9/11and its aftermath created a traumatic turning point for most of the writers in this book, it is telling that none of their essays begin with that moment. These young people were living, probing, and shifting their Muslim identities long before 9/11. In fact, one of the most delightful features of this book is the window it provides onto the pre-9/11 lives of young Muslims, an experience that had been largely overlooked by both scholarly and popular literature on U.S. religious and ethnic minorities (an obvious exception being *The Autobiography of Malcolm X*). There is a powerful essay from one young Muslim man, Abdel Jamali, about being gay and his deep concern for how his sexual orientation will disturb his mother: "Was she being punished for her unknown sins by having a gay son? They say that God is merciful and compassionate and never tests a person more than they can handle, but did He forget my mother in this instance?" There are several essays by Muslim women who struggle with their families about continuing their education rather than submitting to an arranged marriage.

I've heard it said that the second generation never asks the first about its story, but nearly all the essays in this book include long, intimate portrayals of Muslim family life, often going back generations. These young Muslims are constantly negotiating the differences between families for whom faith and culture were matters of honor—a straight path toward what Sabeen Hassanali calls an "unquestioned destiny"—and North America's youth culture, with its emphasis on questioning, exploring, and inventing one's own destiny.

"Where were these essays when I was growing up?" I found myself asking over and over as I read through these pieces. I know intimately many of the generational battles described in this book, because they happened at the kitchen table in the home where I grew up in suburban Chicago. What career path should I follow? Which major should I select in college?

Who should my friends be? How should I spend my free time? My mother had clear views on each of these topics. Her answers: accountant, business, Indians and Muslims, studying…She was shocked that I had ideas of my own and that I would insist on voicing them.

One of the defining narratives of America is this recurring theme of breaking from tradition and creating one's own identity. The United States, after all, broke from Europe and charted its own course. It is a prominent feature in the literature of U.S. immigrants and ethnic minorities, especially those in the second generation, who stand at the intersection of inheritance and discovery and try to look both ways at once. As a young person, I inhaled this literature—Chaim Potok's *The Chosen*, Amy Tan's *The Joy Luck Club*, Ralph Ellison's *The Invisible Man*, James Baldwin's *Notes of a Native Son*. I would translate in my mind, replacing the distinctly Jewish or Chinese or black features with the idiom and experience of my own Indian and Muslim life, wondering all the while why the mental exercise of translation was necessary. Wasn't the experience of young people who prayed like me worthy of a literature of its own?

If the aftermath of 9/11 has had any upside for Muslims at all, it would be the fostering of a powerful, emerging American Muslim narrative—a conversation, not a roar—a literature that ought to have a special personal meaning for the growing Muslim population in the United States while also being of interest to a broad range of students and scholars in our multicultural nation. This literature is growing too large to mention each milestone, but some of my favorites include plays like Wajahat Ali's *The Domestic Crusaders;* the multiauthor stage production *Hijabi Monologues* (conceived by Dan Morrison, Zeenat Rahman, and Sahar Ullah); Ayad Akhtar's novel, *American Dervish;* sketches by the Muslim comedian Azhar Usman; Sumbul Ali-Karamali's personal account called *The Muslim Next Door;* and essay collections edited by Saleemah Abdul-Ghafur (*Living Islam Out Loud: American Muslim Women Speak*), Maria Ebrahimji and Zahra Suratwala (*I Speak for Myself: American Women on Being Muslim*), and Wajahat Ali, Zahra Suratwala, and Keith Ellison (*All-American: 45 American Men on Being Muslim*). This volume enriches that list.

One important theme these essays share with the other material in the emerging literature on the American Muslim experience is an emphasis on diversity in two dimensions—diversity within the Muslim community and the diversity Muslims encounter in the wider world. The 2009 Gallup Report on American Muslims calls this community the most diverse religious group in the United States. The essays in this volume highlight some important dimensions of that internal Muslim diversity. We have

Muslims here who hail from cultures as different as Somalia and Turkey; some who grew up believing that consuming alcohol was the height of evil and others who saw it on a regular basis at their dinner tables. There are Muslims who were accustomed to seeing women in burqas on the streets where they grew up, and others who frequented country clubs where Muslim women regularly wore bikinis. There is the powerful story of a white convert to Islam, Adam W., who credits Thomas Merton's *The Way of Chuang Tzu* with inspiring the first step of his spiritual journey, which led eventually to Islam. An essay by Asyah Saif, the daughter of a Russian Christian mother and a Yemeni Muslim father, describes how she grew up in Yemen, spent summers in Russia, and attended a United World College for high school in Canada. I've heard it said that more Muslims from different backgrounds gather in the United States than anywhere else in the Muslim world, except for Mecca during the hajj. The Quran speaks of the holy dimension of experiencing diversity: it is a holiness that the Muslims in this volume have the opportunity to appreciate on a regular basis.

Fourteen essays from college students and recent graduates obviously cannot represent the entire North American Muslim community. There is an overrepresentation of Ismaili Muslims in this volume, a relatively small group within the larger Muslim community—which happens to be the one I belong to. There are also several essays by young people who attended United World Colleges during high school, a powerful but rare experience among young Muslims. Finally, there are no pieces by indigenous African American Muslims—that is, Muslims who trace their ancestry in the United States back to slaves rather than more recent immigrants from Africa—although this group makes up somewhere between one-fifth and one-third of all American Muslims. It also includes the majority of American Muslim public figures, including the congressmen Keith Ellison and André Carson, the entertainers Mos Def and Dave Chappelle, and the athletes Muhammad Ali and Kareem Abdul-Jabbar.

As one can infer from the large range given above for the number of indigenous African American Muslims, speaking about population statistics when it comes to American Muslims is a tricky business. Muslim groups like the Council on American-Islamic Relations say that the total number of Muslims in the United States is between 6 and 7 million. The 2005 *Britannica Book of the Year* says it is 4.7 million. A 2007 Pew study concludes that the population of Muslims over eighteen years old is 1.4 million. Getting an accurate count is challenging for a variety of reasons, ranging from the understandable distrust some recent Muslim immigrants have of official-sounding people who call to ask about their religious affiliation, to the difficulty of getting a read on the number of Muslim converts in U.S. prisons.

What is less controversial is that the number of American Muslims between eighteen and twenty-nine years old is impressively large, as much as 36 percent of the Muslim population in the United States, according to the 2009 Gallup Report. To put that number in some context, only 18 percent of all U.S. citizens are between the ages of eighteen and twenty-nine, and only 9 percent of all Protestants are in that demographic. The writers you are reading here are among the most talented and successful representatives of an outsize group within the American Muslim community. Their experiences, views, aspirations, and actions will shape the direction of Islam in North America for generations to come.

Demographics always make for heated arguments, but an even more interesting subject here is the definition of two related categories that I've been using frequently throughout this essay: American Islam and American Muslims. Many of the essayists in this book had their formative experiences elsewhere, including Turkey, Jordan, Canada, and Sudan. Some have graduated from college and subsequently settled in other countries. Can we call them American Muslims? Are they part of American Islam? This is a topic worthy of its own book, but as I've read through these essays, something has become clear to me: our conceptualization of the United States' religious communities has to take into account their global nature. Institutions like Dartmouth College, which draw international populations into temporary communities, are an important part of life in America. They are, in fact, a major strength of this nation. As you will read in these essays, these young authors brought pieces of Pakistan and Somalia to the United States with them; they happily shared those cultures in the student groups and courses they participated in in college; and, in light of their experiences here, they rethought certain dimensions of those cultures—especially those that intersected with Islam. In fact, the intertwining of culture and religion is one of the most interesting themes throughout these essays. One Yemeni student, Asyah Saif, writes about how hugs between opposite genders is considered way out-of-bounds in her home country but is perfectly normal here in the United States—like a smile would be back home, she writes. And so, hugging boys has become part of her life in America.

Perhaps the most American thing these young Muslims encounter is diversity, within the Muslim community and beyond. Unlikely friendships—between an Arab Muslim from a conservative religious background and his gay adviser, between Sunnis and Shias, between a working-class Ismaili and her privileged Jewish roommate—abound in these essays, each one causing the writer to rethink how his or her faith views "the other." Many of these young people will lead global lives; they will have jobs in several nations throughout their careers, their friendships and personal influence will span continents. Their American experience will stay with them throughout their lives, shaping their personal trajectories and making an impact on those they touched while on these shores. And so, yes, I do believe, wherever they may live and whatever passport they may carry, these authors are American Muslims who are learning from and contributing to American Islam, while at the same time retaining their identities as Pakistani, Sudanese, and Jordanian Muslims.

A final theme worth commenting on is the role religion plays in the lives of these Muslims while they are at college. A common perception of college students is that they leave faith behind when they arrive on campus to focus instead on partying for the next four years. An interesting thread across these essays is just how central a role Islam plays in the lives of these students, even when they are doing things that they themselves consider "un-Islamic." As Abdel Jamali writes, "I decided one day to leave my religion in rebellion against God. I didn't pray, and I went out of my way to just do what I felt like doing with total disregard for my religiously guided judgment." Abdel discovers that his Muslim conscience is constantly present; no matter how far he tries to run, it nags at and comforts him at the same time. Even as he struggles with traditional notions of Islam and his growing awareness of his homosexuality, he is comforted by a verse in the Quran in which God, speaking to the Prophet Muhammad, says, "God does not hate you. Did I not care for you while you were an orphan?"

In my own experience as the founder and president of the Interfaith Youth Core, an organization that works on issues of religious diversity with college students, the internal conversation that Abdel makes explicit in his essay is far more insightful than the popular *Animal House* depiction of campus culture. College students have a far richer private dialogue—in their own heads and with their close friends and roommates—about religion than their outward behavior, and certainly perceptions of that outward behavior, might suggest. I hope that this volume encourages staff and faculty to shift the narrative of college from framing it as a stage where religious identities are easily shed in favor of wild behavior to recognizing that college students' religious identities often remain a central dimension of their campus experience.

So now I come to the most difficult part of my task: to organize the fourteen essays into categories that can help orient the reader. It is difficult in part because all the typical ways of categorizing Muslims—Sunni and Shia, hijabi and non-hijabi, immigrant and indigenous, observant and nonobservant—are fraught with tension. Too often they are not simply descriptive categories but stark judgments about who is a better Muslim, or who is a Muslim at all. One of the most striking aspects of this volume is that the student writers make little of such distinctions, and none of them uses their belonging to a particular category to demonize someone from another category. That in itself is a sign of a profound evolution in American Islam. The mosques, social groups, and organizations of the older generations of Muslims in the United States are frequently split along lines of race, ethnicity, theological school (Sunni or Shia), and level of observance, with no small amount of tension among the various groups. This younger generation is shedding such divisions, creating something I call "Big Tent Islam"—a canopy that covers all Muslims who believe that there is no god but God and Muhammad is His messenger. There are different circles—ethnic, theological, and so forth—within the tent, and there is vigorous discussion among those circles, but the days of Sunnis denouncing Shias for not being "real" Muslims (and the other way around) seem to be fading as a new generation has a formative experience amid the diversity of other Muslims at institutions like North American colleges.

So how, then, to categorize these essays, especially given that many cover the same themes? As I've read and reread these pieces, the word that comes to mind most often is "struggle." These young people struggle, thoughtfully and authentically, with the role of Islam in their lives, as college students from immigrant families, and at a moment in history characterized by high-profile Muslim extremism and the hateful roar of Islamophobia. By and large, the struggle deepens their faith, although often in unexpected ways.

One of the words for "struggle" in Arabic is the overheated and highly abused term *jihad*. It is commonly understood to mean "holy war," but the Prophet Muhammad emphasized to his companions that the term should be understood primarily as an internal journey to improve oneself. In conversations with Muslim scholars such as Shaykh Hamza Yusuf, I've come to understand the idea of struggle in Islam less as a fight and more as a sort of striving, in the sense of striving to be a better person. Whether they are struggling with family, with sexuality, or with Islamophobia, I find these essayists to be striving constantly. They are meeting their various challenges head-on, working through them, and charting a unique course for themselves and their communities. I have grouped the essays under five themes: diversity, Islamophobia, relationships and sexuality, piety, and family. While many cover several of these themes, I've tried to categorize them in ways that highlight their most interesting stories and form the most creative clusters.

The first part of this book is "Struggles with Diversity." The various essays here respond to the question, What happens when you meet people who are not like you, whose ways of life challenge some of your most cherished ideas and rattle your comfort zone? The first essay is by Zahra Ahmed, who immigrated to the United States from Somalia when she was four and a half years old. One of eight children of a single mother who experienced a dramatic downward shift in class in the move from Mogadishu, Zahra talks about the distinct discomfort she feels walking into her high-school honors history class that is full of white students. It is a powerful tale of negotiating race, class, gender, and faith, spiked with questions about wearing the Islamic headscarf and how to respond to 9/11.

Ala' Alrababa'h grew up middle-class in Jordan and went to Pearson College, a UWC school in Canada (chapter 2). He brought with him an interpretation of Islam conditioned by a relatively homogeneous Sunni Arab culture, including a negative view of homosexuals. At Pearson College, Ala' meets Muslims who are different from him and finds that one of the most helpful staff members is gay. He wonders about his interpretation of Islam, knowing it continues to be important to him but that his interpretation must change because, as he writes, "the world has proved to be infinitely more complex than I thought."

Asyah Saif's mother left Russia at the age of thirty-one to marry a Yemeni Muslim and live in Yemen (chapter 3). She remained a Christian but supported her children's Muslim identity. Asyah grew up balancing Yemen's ethnically homogeneous and conservative Muslim culture (all girls wore the headscarf, some wore the burqa) with the anti-Muslim sentiment in Russia, where she spent many summers. Her encounter with diversity hit overdrive once she enrolled at Pearson. "Pearson had it all," she writes, "Mormons, Buddhists, Jews, Muslims, people from every other possible religion, as well as atheists. There were straight people, gays, lesbians, and bisexuals....Some drank and smoked....Some believed in sex only after marriage, while others slept in each other's rooms every night." She charts her personal faith journey as she encounters and processes this diversity.

Abdul Moustafa grew up in an upper-middle-class Turkish family, rarely went to the mosque, and saw alcohol consumed regularly at the family dinner table (chapter 4). Both at the United World College in Swaziland and at Dartmouth College, Abdul encounters Muslims much more devout than he is. These experiences catalyze a personal journey of reflection on faith for Abdul and broaden his idea of Islam. Abdul wonders if Turkey, a country split between staunch secularists on the one hand and devout Muslims on the other, might not benefit from the kind of experience he had at his schools, which humanized both communities.

Part 2 is "Struggles with Islamophobia." The first essay is by Aly Rahim, who writes about how "having an openly Muslim identity in an increasingly hostile public arena is a daunting experience" (chapter 5). He describes listening to respected academic and policy intellectuals who insist that being a Muslim and being a citizen of a democratic nation are incompatible. He decides to use his own life to prove that this belief is not true. He spends weekends giving public lectures on Islam, closing with the line, "I am not the enemy," and chooses a career in government in his native Canada.

The next essay in this section is by Shakir Quraishi, an immigrant from Afghanistan who was raised by a single mother in Lansing, Michigan, and Richmond, Virginia (chapter 6). Shakir feels so self-conscious about his poor English and strong, identifiably foreign accent and dark complexion in the climate of post-9/11 Islamophobia that he goes through much of high school in silence, refusing to read an essay aloud in class when he is called on by a teacher. Even as he grows more confident and takes significant leadership positions in his school, his awareness of how organized and pervasive Islamophobia is within his community unnerves him.

The third section is "Struggles with Sexuality and Relationships." The first essay is by Abdel Jamali, who realizes at a young age that he is gay (chapter 7). He describes his first crushes and his concern for his mother with novelistic poignancy. What is most striking is the way Abdel writes about Islam as a faith he feels both condemns his sexuality and provides him comfort in his loneliest moments.

Sabeen Hassanali, an Ismaili Muslim who grew up in South Houston, opens her essay with the story of a marriage proposal (chapter 8). Her parents are trying to set her up with a suitable match, and Sabeen, an undergraduate at Dartmouth who has never been in a serious relationship, wants nothing to do with it. This issue has been a constant tension throughout Sabeen's life. She recalls receiving a national honor for her academics while in high school, only to have it dismissed by her mother with the comment, "Now that you've proven that you're smart, you should concentrate on learning to cook." Sabeen's essay is about navigating the world of dating and relationships with her faith as her headlights, carrying her family's cultural issues in tow.

The fourth section, "Struggles with Piety," includes essays that describe decisions regarding levels of religious observance. As the eldest son of a

Bangladeshi Muslim immigrant family, Arif Khan feels that the weight of his parents' culture and expectations rests on his shoulders (chapter 9). Sometimes it is a burden too heavy to bear for Arif, the firstborn son, leaving him bitter and jealous of his younger brother, who seems free to do just what he pleases. All the while, Arif reflects on his commitment to Islam. Keenly aware that he doesn't make the five ritual prayers a day or fast through all of Ramadan, he calls his approach to religion "à la carte," even while he claims that Islam is an all-or-nothing faith. Arif quotes one of his Muslim mentors at the beginning and end of the essay: "The way of the believer is optimism." It is a sentiment this young writer tries hard to embrace.

Adam W. is a white convert to Islam who came to the United States from a nominally Christian childhood in southwestern England (chapter 10). His father gives him a copy of Thomas Merton's *The Way of Chuang Tzu*, a collection of Taoist sayings that sets Adam on a spiritual search. There are many things about Christianity that Adam finds dissatisfying. At Dartmouth, Adam searches for a spiritual community but comes up empty-handed until, as he puts it, "I heard the call to prayer, and everything else felt inevitable." From there, Adam follows a straight path into the heart of Islam, becoming a deeply observant believer and a leader of the Muslim community at Dartmouth.

Sarah Chaudhry describes her adolescence with strict, traditional parents who essentially forbid her from having friends outside of her religious circle (chapter 11). Her idea of Islam is equally severe. She remembers telling a fellow five-year-old in kindergarten that Islam is a religion that allows no dancing and no singing. Sarah's college experience at Dartmouth includes partaking in the "work hard, party hard" culture. She is overjoyed to discover that in college she can finally set her own boundaries, even as she realizes that some of her actions there contradict her understanding of Islam. Conversations with her Thai American friend and readings of Rumi help ground Sarah. She closes her essay by saying, "It is true that I do not pray five times a day, but I do believe in Islam, and when I pray, I pray to Allah."

The next essay is by Sara L., whose father moved their family to the United Arab Emirates from Colorado, in part because he believed that life in the United States was having a corrosive effect on his daughters (chapter 12). Sara and her sisters consider it one of the best things that happened to them. She learns more about Islam by living in a Muslim culture, and at the same time, counterintuitively, living abroad makes her more aware of her Americanness. Sara describes the reasons she wears the Muslim headscarf: "It protects me from *myself*, from easy infatuations, from becoming involved with someone with whom a long-term commitment is just a possibility and not a goal." Although Sara chooses the headscarf for herself, she finds herself furious with a male Muslim student who sends out an e-mail suggesting that only Muslim women who wear the head-scarf should be considered for leadership positions in the Muslim student group. The way Sara deals with this challenge says a lot about her under-standing of faith—of what is required and what is open to interpretation.

The final section is "Struggles with Family." Tafaoul Abdelmagid was raised in Massachusetts by a strict, traditional Sudanese family (chapter 13). She describes homework as "a way to evade my parents' interrogation and suffocating distrust." That distrust is directed at anything non-Muslim, even while Tafaoul is discovering that many people in the United States share her values, if not her faith. When she "ruptures the bubble" by going to Dartmouth, she is thrilled to find a group of friends from differ-ent backgrounds with whom she feels comfortable and who have much to teach her. And yet, while she is at college, the traditions of home reach out to her in the form of a marriage offer, something perfectly normal in her culture. As she reveals in an epilogue to her essay, written three years later, Tafaoul agrees to marry the man whom she originally describes rejecting in her essay.

Nasir Nasser is a Canadian Ismaili who describes his parents' differ-ences in rich detail (chapter 14). His father is from a provincial back-ground and attends congregational prayers twice a day. His mother is far more cosmopolitan and prefers watching foreign films to attending the Ismaili house of worship, called *Jamatkhana*. Religion plays a small role in Nasir's adolescence. He feels his faith doesn't even ask the right ques-tions, let alone provide good answers. His faith is expressed through the pen, and he is given an opportunity to practice it at Dartmouth, where he writes a play for his senior project. Nasir writes about his parents' journey, and he has the pleasure of seeing the play produced—with his parents in the audience. He is overcome by the debt he feels "to those who raised us, to those who educated us, to those who know us."

As you read these essays, remember one final thing: there is a holiness to the idea of struggle in Islam. As these young people face and overcome their various challenges, as they strive to be true to the principles of their faith while living fully in the world, they are accomplishing one of the most important tasks God asks of them, and charting a path for the gen-erations to come.

PART I

STRUGGLES WITH DIVERSITY

1

Zahra Ahmed   Far from Getting Lost

"Don't get lost. Remember, home is the best." These were the last words my grandfather said as he walked me toward the front door. At age eighteen, I was holding my luggage and saying final good-byes to my family, preparing to live on my own for the first time, five hundred miles away from home. I don't remember all that was going through my mind, but I remember that I knew exactly what my grandfather meant, and his words struck me. I began to wonder whether he thought I would get lost, disappear into a new society. I knew college would change me, but how?

I didn't expect it to happen, but living at a university, attended predominantly by privileged white students, enhanced rather than diminished my understanding of myself and where I come from. I am African, American, female, and from a low-income family. I am all of these things outwardly, but inwardly, being Muslim is the characteristic that is most central to my life. It goes beyond phenotype or something I was born into—it is a choice I made, and continue to make, that gets to the heart of who I am. My perception of the world and the actions I take in it are guided by my deep faith. How this faith manifests itself is different in every person, and for me it has been a long journey to reach the point where I feel best. I have an unconventional and at times difficult story, but my faith in God has helped me recognize every blessing and confront every challenge. I feel an overwhelming sense of gratefulness for all of my experiences and what I have gained from them.

I was born into a Muslim family from Somalia, an arid country in East Africa with more camels than people. Somalis are historically nomadic, known for their poetry and proverbs, but in more recent years they have come to be known as refugees. My family left this distant country when I was four and a half years old, so I certainly consider myself more American than Somali. However, my family retains many traditional and cultural values from Somalia, from religion to language to food, which I am grateful for. This is probably because, unlike some immigrants, my family did not leave Somalia voluntarily. They love their homeland and everything about it, and my grandparents in particular can spend hours talking about the fresh air, their great friends and neighbors, the fresh fruit they enjoyed, and the good times they had in Mogadishu. War, however, brought them to Virginia, our new home. Listening to my parents, grandparents, and guests in our home speak about their memories of Somalia has given my siblings and me an unusual love for a country we have either never seen or do not remember, and we are grateful for this awareness and connection.

Before arriving in the United States as refugees of civil war, my family lived in Mogadishu. My mother came from a wealthy family of politicians and businessmen; my father came from a large, poor family, and was orphaned at just seven years old. He worked his way up academically and earned a college scholarship, eventually becoming an important engineer in Mogadishu. My parents met after my grandfather insisted that my mother meet an up-and-coming young man. My grandfather is an impressive man, the former Somali ambassador to the United States, China, and many other nations. He speaks with such confidence that some might interpret it as arrogance. When he asked my mother to meet this impressive young man, she was at first reluctant; but when she finally did meet my father, it didn't take long for him to win her over. My father has a charming personality and is always the center of attention, with his commanding voice and great sense of humor. He never lets a meeting go by without telling a story that leaves everyone in the room crying with laughter, including himself. When my parents got married, they settled in Mogadishu to start a family. By all accounts, before the civil war broke out in Somalia, their marriage was ideal. There was economic prosperity in Mogadishu, and my father was able to build a successful construction company, while my mother found a job with the UN. My parents were well off, living in a large house with guards out front, a beautiful fruit grove in the backyard, two drivers, and cooks constantly working in the kitchen. The house was always bustling with life, as guests and family members came in and out, and slowly my parents brought children into their lives.

This was a great time for my family, and looking at pictures of my youthful parents posing, smiling with their firstborn child, I see a romantic and hopeful era. But I must admit that I don't remember much about that time and very little about Somalia in general. All I have is a fuzzy memory of yellow dirt paths lined with houses and stores, and for some reason I have a most vivid memory of a bicycle store, full of new and seemingly gigantic bicycles. I am disappointed that I don't have clearer memories of Somalia. Unlike many African Americans, I can point on a map to where my origins are, and yet I feel removed from it because I haven't been there in so long—I do not even know the daily sights, sounds, smells, and life of the country. Someday, God willing, I hope to go back to Mogadishu and experience this place that is so murky in my imagination, and hopefully clarify the image of where I come from. But I know that I'll never fit in in Somalia—with my weak grasp of the language and American mannerisms, I'll stick out like a foreigner.

By the late 1980s, the Somali government began to disintegrate and a civil war broke out. My parents feared for the safety of our family, so in 1989 my mother, along with her four children and a fifth unborn child in her belly, boarded a plane to the United States. My mother fully expected to return to Somalia in a few months, or perhaps a year, when things settled down. But the civil war dragged on, and then intensified as outside parties intervened in the conflict. It eventually dawned on my mother that we would not be leaving the United States for some time, and eventually my father came to join us.

Our first home in the United States was a mansion, complete with lion statues on each side of the front door. I guess my parents thought our standard of living shouldn't go down, but they realized soon enough that the large house was not affordable. During this time, I was too young to grasp all the difficult decisions my parents were facing. My father was traveling back and forth between Mogadishu and Virginia, trying to maintain his construction company and provide for the family. My mother spent most of those years on her own in a new land. She eventually got a job as a phone operator for a taxi company—her first job in the United States—when my father's company collapsed.

At this time of transition, I was about five years old, and was trying to make sense of my new environment. I remember sensing that our new home lacked color—probably because of its emptiness and the stark white walls. Getting used to a new language and different-looking people was also an adjustment, but at my age, it didn't take long before it all felt normal. My siblings and I quickly learned English, and soon we could barely remember how to speak Somali. I wish we had been able to maintain our Somali as we grew up, and if she could do it all again, I'm sure my mother would have made an effort to help us do so.

When my grandmother and grandfather joined my family in the States, my mother was relieved—she now had help at home. At one point, though, our financial situation became so desperate that my mother asked my grandmother to work as a Salvation Army bell ringer. It's hard for me to imagine my grandmother doing this work, and it was probably much harder for her to come to terms with doing it. All her life she had been the ambassador's wife, beautiful and tall, always wearing fashionable dresses and lots of jewelry. Above all, my grandmother was now an old woman, and it was a tough decision to have her work. As it turned out, before my grandmother began her new job, my family was forced to leave our house and find a more affordable home. Her first decade in the United States was incredibly difficult for my mother. She regularly worked multiple jobs, and although we eventually saw the fruits of her labor, we didn't see very much of her.

My father came to the States from Somalia every couple of years to check on his family, but this situation was not acceptable for my mother. She couldn't handle his living in Somalia while she worked day and night to keep the family afloat. She was physically and psychologically exhausted, and she gave him the ultimatum that he either stay in the United States or get a divorce. My father was not happy about this, but he nevertheless agreed to attempt to live here with us. He found a job at an American construction company and lived for nearly a year with the family. Unfortunately, my father had so much pride that he couldn't handle his new life, going from being the boss of his own company in Somalia to working for an "incompetent man" at another construction company. He also had issues with his pay and his treatment at work. He once told me privately that in this country he is "just another black man," and no one knows him or gives him the respect he deserves. He claimed that he was aware of the clear inequality between whites and nonwhites in Virginia from the moment he stepped off the airplane, and he refused to be subordinated by American whites, including his boss. Ultimately, my father couldn't handle leaving his mansion in Somalia for our small, crowded town house in the United States, even if it meant leaving his wife and children. It's a tragic story that would never have occurred if my parents hadn't been caught between two countries, divided by war.

After my father split, my mother was left to provide for her now eight children (three that were born in the States) and her elderly parents all on her own. I'm not completely sure how she did it, but she managed to keep things afloat. Throughout all of their struggles in a new country, my mother, grandparents, and extended family set an example for me and my siblings. No matter how stressful and exhausting their lives were, they always maintained a strong faith in God and always appeared hopeful for a better future. When I ask my mother about her first few years in this country, she refuses to think back on that period and only says, "Thank God we survived."

I always knew the value of work. Most of my siblings began working as soon as we hit the legal age, fifteen. In my first job, I was a telemarketer for a charity. I was never too sure whether it was a legitimate business; I was just grateful they were willing to hire me at such a young age. For me, working was a huge step. It took me longer, however, to discover the value of education. Until middle school, I thought school was a thorough waste of time and rarely did any homework assignments. Strange as it sounds, I remember the moment that I began to take school seriously. I was in the sixth grade and I saw a Somali friend of mine, Sadia, listed on the A-B honor roll. I was surprised by this, and thought to myself, if she can do it, I can do it too. It was a simple conclusion, but very meaningful in terms of my outlook on school. From that point on, the honor roll was my target and I was going to get on it, even if it meant completing useless homework assignments. I succeeded in this goal, but the best thing about achieving good grades was seeing my mother's reaction to my report cards. She understood the importance of doing well in school a lot more than I did, and could not hide her excitement at seeing her daughter excel.

When I started middle school, to my delight, my mother enrolled my siblings and me in a Quran school (called a *Dugsii* in Somali). We went to the Quran school every Saturday and Sunday, from two o'clock to seven o'clock p.m. It was a free school for Somali youth between four and fifteen years of age, where we memorized chapters from the Quran, learned how to read and write in Arabic, and heard stories about the prophets, from Adam to Jesus to Muhammad and everyone in between, peace be upon them. I loved going to the Quran school. It had a thoroughly Somali environment; the students and teachers were all Somali, we spoke—or attempted to speak—the Somali language, and we were there to learn about Islam, a religion integral to our lives and our culture. After our classes, we would get together in a large carpeted room for a congregational prayer.

I loved the whole experience. I didn't know how to pray very well, but, for as long as I can remember, I was certain that God, *Allah* in Arabic, created me and listened to my prayers. I still remember analyzing different events in my life as a young girl and trying to understand God's reasoning.

During my last year of middle school, my eighth-grade English teacher passed out a form that allowed students to sign up for high school honors classes. All she said was that the classes were more challenging, which did not sound appealing to me. My middle school was very diverse, with no clear majority among whites, Hispanics, Africans, and Asians. It didn't take a scientific test to realize that the white students seemed to be the only ones interested in the honors courses, and my teacher certainly didn't do much to sell the value of the classes to the other students. I didn't give it much thought and stuffed the paper away. That evening, tired after a long day of work, my mother somehow saw the paper and asked me why I didn't want to take honors classes. I told her that there was no use in taking harder classes as long as I made good marks. All she had to do was make her "disappointed mom" expression—an expression I never wanted to be responsible for—for me to take my words back and ask her to sign the documents. I filled in "yes" for honors English and "yes" for honors history, but I didn't feel confident enough to apply for the math and science classes. Starting off in these two courses would change my high school trajectory dramatically.

I was shocked when I walked into class on my first day in honors history. Almost all of the students were white. This caught me off-guard and made me a bit uncomfortable; I still don't fully know why. I was friends with some of the students, but I still felt out of place. At the end of the class, I told the teacher, an elderly man named Mr. Mitchell, that I wasn't ready to take such a difficult class and asked to be switched out. He refused to let me drop out and insisted that I stay at least one week to see if I was sure I wanted to leave. By the end of the week, I felt confident enough to stay in the class, partly because of Mr. Mitchell's kindness and partly because I realized the course wasn't all that difficult.

High school was a whirlwind and I had a great time. Unfortunately, I found that the more advanced classes I enrolled in, the fewer of my friends would be in class with me. I never understood why my minority friends didn't bother to join me in the honors classes, and what it was that gave white students the confidence or desire to take the courses. My mother told me a story that showed me that the racial divisions in the classroom are sometimes reinforced by schools. When my younger sister Aaliyah was accepted into a school for gifted middle-school students, the school counselor held my mother and sister in the main office for half an hour because she felt certain that there must have been a mix-up. She couldn't believe that an African girl with her immigrant-looking mother wearing traditional clothes could be placed in the class for gifted students. My mother, much to her credit, didn't show her anger at the situation. I think race is a very artificial thing, and I don't understand why racial stereotypes and inequalities are still so strong in the United States. I believe in the ideals of this country, and I really hope that someday we can move beyond these arbitrary divisions.

I was in my sophomore year of high school on September 11, 2001. It has become a memory existing outside of time, and it's hard for me to describe that day. What I clearly remember is crying whenever patriotic songs would play on the TV as news footage showed the planes crashing into the World Trade Center. I knew something huge had happened in terms of lives lost, and I was moved by the feeling of tragedy that hung over everything. One of my close friends, Helen, lost her mother in the Pentagon. Even from my limited interactions with her, I knew she had been a very loving mother, and I was shocked and saddened to hear that she had been killed in the attacks. Helen, however, seemed to be very strong about the whole matter, at least outwardly. High school life eventually went back to normal, for the most part.

After 9/11, I gradually began to notice people criticizing Islam for the attacks—news personalities calling the bombers "Islamic" and conflating my religion with the criminal acts of the bombers. My family would sit around the living room and discuss, with outrage, what such-and-such personality had said or what the government was doing to some Muslim Americans. We became afraid and angry at the same time.

We knew that ignorance and bigotry were making some Americans demonize Muslims, but we had never realized how vulnerable we were as minorities until 9/11. I always viewed myself as a racial minority, as my being black seemed most significant to others in American society. After the attacks, however, my being Muslim was the characteristic that was most openly challenged and discriminated against. What is most frustrating is that while Islam is talked about so often, there is so much ignorance surrounding it. Few people know the difference between the religion, the cultural influences, and the diverse actions of the billion Muslims worldwide. I was turned off by the misinformation in the media, particularly the depiction of Muslims as homogeneous and prone to violence. More people were interested in discussing my faith following the attacks, and even those who were well-intentioned sometimes annoyed me with questions such as, "What is Muslim food like?" Nevertheless, these questions and the wider critical environment post-9/11 encouraged me to understand my own faith more fully.

When I was accepted at Dartmouth, I was both shocked and incredibly happy. It was the only Ivy League school I applied to, and I had little expectation that I'd be accepted. When I was, my mother was incredibly proud and let the whole Somali community in Virginia know about it. My siblings were also happy for me, but one day, while we were sitting in the living room watching the news, my older sister said, "I hope you know the average student at Dartmouth is a conservative Republican." Then my youngest brother said that I'd "become a white Republican" by the time I came home. Their conception of the Ivy League was of a condescending bunch of privileged wealthy whites who would never relate to a black Muslim Somali girl like me. I told them not to worry, that the school was diverse, but inwardly I was nervous about living for four years in an isolated college environment.

My mom then said something that will stick with me forever. She said that, yes, the people there are probably privileged whites, but that is where all the power and opportunity is located. I could either suck it up and deal with that environment for a few years, or I could pass up my opportunity to get ahead in life. She pointed out that wealth and power are racial issues in the United States, and to achieve either, an African girl like me would have to enter white culture for a while. I was turned off by this reasoning, but felt she spoke some truth. But I didn't want to change at all—I wanted to be me. I accepted my admission to an elite college knowing that I had worked too hard to back down from the opportunity, but I promised myself that I wouldn't change who I was.

Dartmouth did end up changing me, and I'm tremendously grateful for it. I made a lot of friends in my first year, found that the classes weren't as difficult as I had expected, ate great food in the dining halls that I didn't have to cook myself, and enjoyed my dorm room—my own space for the first time ever. As soon as I got a college e-mail account, I began getting a barrage of messages from every black, African, or African American organization on campus, all asking whether I wanted to be in the Black Business Association, Association of Black Engineers, Afro-American Society, African and Caribbean Students Organization, and so on. I joined the black student scene because that appeared to be where I was pushed. Given the number of clubs and associations, the black community was surprisingly small. I also joined the Muslim student association early on. I didn't receive an e-mail from them, but sought them out on my own because I was curious about what the group would be like. When I arrived at the first meeting of the year, I was dismayed by how few Muslims I saw in attendance, only about twenty. I was, however, impressed by the quality of the students, who struck me as extremely intelligent and confident. I was also impressed by my new friends in the black community. One of my best friends throughout my time at Dartmouth was Amina, a Cameroonian Muslim from New York, and we straddled diverse communities together.

Eventually, like most college students, I moved away from clubs and associations and started to find the individuals and movements that interested me most. I had friends from all sorts of backgrounds, but my closest friends—the ones I spoke to about serious and personal topics, whom I expected to meet for dinner without having to schedule it, whom I related to as if they were family—were three Muslims. There were many reasons why I grew closer to them, but I think the main thing was that we shared similar worldviews that shaped our decisions. We all believed in God and the importance of acting morally, and this guided our actions. So on an isolated campus where most students spend their free time playing drinking games in frat-house basements, I could count on my Muslim friends not to push me into that scene. I also found I could relate to my non-Muslim religious friends, including an Orthodox Jewish friend and a Catholic friend.

I had been struggling with whether to wear a headscarf for a long time. My mother wears one but never forced her daughters to do so; she just told us to wear modest clothes (i.e., we never wore shorts or sleeveless shirts). She did, however, encourage us to strive to be good Muslims. I always felt that the headscarf was a public expression of being a practicing Muslim. Unfortunately, especially since 9/11, there are many stereotypes of Muslim women in the United States, and wearing the hijab can lead to social discrimination and prejudice. I had wanted to start wearing a headscarf since middle school but never had the courage to take that step. What would my teachers say? What would my friends who were not Muslim think? I didn't want to mess up the social position I had, so for years I continually put off the day I would begin wearing the hijab.

It wasn't until I began to study my own faith and understand the significance of the hijab that I began to wear it. Growing up in a Muslim household, I had learned the acts of worship and had some knowledge of the faith, but had never really studied it on my own. College gave me the isolation and free time I needed to sit, read, and reflect on my faith.

During the spring term of my freshman year, I began to read a lot about Islam, and I became overwhelmed with a sense that I was discovering myself and God at the same time. I began to read the Quran for the first time with moral seriousness—not to memorize verses as I had in the past, but to hear the words of God. Reading the Quran made me feel nearness to God, as if He were speaking to me personally. In the Muslim tradition, when you are facing God directly in prayer, he responds to your supplications. I began to feel God's presence as I prayed, and my prayers became a more spiritual experience. I studied scripture and philosophy, trying to understand the nature of God, and the more I learned, the deeper my faith grew.

As I became stronger in my faith, I also became increasingly disappointed in my college's culture and how much energy I put into fitting in, when in reality I didn't want to be a part of it. There was a "Dartmouth norm" that many students fell into: they worked hard academically and partied hard on weekends. One night I saw a young woman, apparently wasted, being carried by a male student. I shivered at the sight, wondering where he was taking her and what he was planning to do. The experience made me disappointed in the college.

In the fall of my sophomore year, I took a sudden big step. On the first day of Ramadan, I woke up with excitement for the month of fasting that stood ahead of me. Ramadan always inspires me to be a better person and to be more conscious of God, and fasting humbles me and helps me put my priorities in order. When I got up that morning to get ready for my first class, I decided right then that I was ready to start wearing the headscarf. I knew the only thing holding me back was a fear of how people would react. But by then, my caring about people's judgments of me was at an all-time low, and my desire to fit into the "Dartmouth norm" had long since faded. I decided to wear the scarf proudly, and that anyone who would treat me poorly because of it was not the type of person I wanted to be around anyway.

I remember my first day of wearing the hijab vividly. As I walked out of my dorm and into the bright autumn morning, the sun felt like a spotlight. I began walking briskly to my first class of the day, trying not to look to the left or right. I stared at the ground in front of me and watched my sneakers kick up the piles of red and brown autumn leaves that crackled beneath my steps. The wind began to blow, and I folded my arms tightly against my chest, hoping to hold in some warmth. I suddenly imagined how I must appear: hunched over and looking down, a submissive and oppressed girl playing right into the stereotypes many hold of Muslim women. My face tightened with anger at myself, and I released my arms and straightened my back. Why was I acting so strangely? Was this not the same campus I had attended for over a year now? But in fact it wasn't the same campus, because I wasn't the same girl: I now had a thin navy-blue cloth wrapped around my head, my hijab, and this set me apart from the others.

As I walked across campus, I tried to avoid looking people directly in the eye, afraid of their reactions to me. I was afraid of being judged, stereotyped, discriminated against, or isolated by those around me. The first day of wearing the hijab was the hardest for me, as all my assumptions about other people's reactions were put to the test. Eventually I began to realize that not much was changed by the addition of an extra piece of clothing to my daily wardrobe; my life had not been turned upside-down, as I had imagined it would be.

Essentially, my decision to start wearing a headscarf in the middle of sophomore year was due to a combination of my growing religiosity and faith in God, decreasing interest in pleasing or conforming to those around me, and a desire for people to know and recognize my religious background. My assumptions and fears about how people would react turned out to be false. A few people distanced themselves from me—I'm still not completely sure why—but most of my friends and colleagues behaved just the same as they always had in their interactions with me. Some students asked me immediately why I started wearing the hijab, and I usually responded that I felt it was a spiritually beneficial thing for me to do. One friend didn't feel ready to ask me about my hijab until months later, which was interesting. She probably thought the decision was too personal and that I wouldn't want to talk about it. Surprisingly, things were pretty much the same as they had been before I wore the scarf, and my classes went on as usual.

Attending Dartmouth was an incredible experience. Far from getting "lost," as my grandfather had warned against, I believe I used my time in Hanover to find myself, and I'm indebted to the school for facilitating that process. As a member of a refugee family from East Africa, I was very different from most of my classmates, but I nevertheless developed friendships that I believe will last a lifetime, and I found professors who have had a meaningful impact on my intellectual growth. As I prepared to graduate, I realized that with my new degree, I would forever be in a social class that was different from what I had known most of my life. I would enter the largely white and privileged class that my mother had told me about years earlier. She was right, for the most part, but she was wrong to think I would have to conform to some norm that was foreign to me in order to succeed within this new class. On the contrary, I believe that the more I discovered who I am and what my relationship is with the world around me, the stronger I became academically and professionally. I could be me—African, American, Muslim, a woman—and earn my way into a great career. I get my strength and energy from my faith in God, my family, and the people I love, and it took all the life experiences I have had thus far to bring me to this point, where I am feeling most content.

After Dartmouth, Zahra went on to earn a master's degree in African Studies and to work as a U.S. diplomat—posted first in Kenya, and next in China. Although her post takes her far from home, she continues to have a very close relationship with her family.

2

Ala' Alrababa'h   A World More Complex Than I Thought

This story explores my development from an extremely religious and somewhat naive boy from Jordan to a nineteen-year-old man with a more nuanced view of religion and its role in my life. At age seventeen, I left my home and family in Jordan to attend Pearson College, which is located on Canada's Vancouver Island. The school's curriculum is the rigorous International Baccalaureate Diploma Program, and its mission, reflected in the school's international faculty and student body, is to foster internationalism and respect for other cultures. For me, going abroad meant diverging from my planned life in Jordan and having my religious beliefs put to the test. As I stepped out of my familiar environment and comfort zone into an alien culture, I experienced severe culture shock. In the process, I realized that, despite all the different nationalities, cultures, and religions I encountered, people around the globe are not so different from one another.

I arrived at Pearson College, one of thirteen United World Colleges, to attend its two-year program. Up to this point, I had lived in Jordan all my life and grown up in the capital city, Amman. I attended mosque for as far back as I remember. When I was only four or five years old, I always enjoyed going with my father, uncles, and grandpa to *Jum'ah* (Friday) prayers. Before I actually knew how to pray, I would make the same movements I saw my father making. I would watch as he put his hands up to his ears and said, *"Allahu Akbar"* (God is the greatest), and then do exactly the same thing myself. I would then bow down with him and put my forehead on the ground, always repeating, "Allahu Akbar."

During my childhood, my family put great emphasis on academic excellence. If I lost even half a mark on an exam, I would be worried about showing the grade to my father. My mother was more flexible, but she still cared that I got high marks. Reflecting on it now, I can see why my parents valued academic excellence so much, both being well educated themselves: my father has a bachelor's degree in agricultural engineering and my mother has a master's in the same field. Their education, however, did not allow us to live comfortably, and our family ranks only in the Jordanian middle class. Buying our modest apartment and two cars put my parents into debt for decades, and although they tried to provide everything my siblings and I wanted, we always felt their financial constraints. Thus, my parents wanted my siblings and me to be able to survive in a society that valued only two fields, engineering and medicine. In order to be able to study either of those, I needed either top grades in high school or lots of money. With the latter option ruled out, my parents had always emphasized the need to earn good grades, and my siblings and I never failed to be among the top students in our classes.

The year I completed seventh grade, my private school increased the tuition, so my father placed me in a public school. After spending my eighth-grade year in a very tough and underresourced public school, I was admitted into Jubilee School for gifted students. Coming from a public school where fighting was frequent into a school filled with smart kids who had withstood a tough selection process filled me with anticipation. The program began with a summer camp aimed at preparing us for the school's rigorous academic demands. The teachers at Jubilee were much more engaged and accomplished than those at my public school. Many of them had graduate degrees, and they were clearly eager to teach and give students individual attention.

Jubilee School was the first institution outside of my family that helped shape my thoughts about politics and religion. Because of its competitive selection process, Jubilee had many students who were knowledgeable and intellectual. One of my friends, Hasan, was a socialist agnostic. Even though I was extremely religious, I enjoyed his company because he was well-informed about numerous topics. When we discussed religion, although I disagreed with him, I found his existential ideas intriguing. He insisted that there is no way to prove God's existence. While I do not remember all his arguments, I do remember that he doubted everything.

My Islamic religion classes also raised a lot of fascinating questions. Our teacher once started the class by writing two Hadiths on the board. The first said, *"Al-Ajr 'la Qadr Al-Mashaqa"*—"The reward corresponds to the amount of effort done"—meaning that the harder you work for something, assuming it is for God's sake, the more greatly rewarded you will be. The other Hadith was *"Ma Khoyera Rasul Allah Bayna Tareeqayn, Ella*

Ekhtar Al-Tareeq Al-Aysar"—"Whenever the Prophet of Allah would be given the choice between two ways, he would choose the simpler one"—in other words, we should choose the simplest way to accomplish our tasks, especially when doing work for the sake of God, like worshipping. Our teacher asked, "What do you think about the apparent contradiction between the two Hadiths, one telling you that you'll be rewarded if you do more work, while the other urges you to do less work by taking the simpler path?" We discussed the two Hadiths for the whole class period and finally reached a conclusion, which our teacher summarized: "Although seemingly contradictory, the two Hadiths do not disagree with each other. If you are given the choice between two paths, you should choose the simpler, more manageable one. However, if you are facing an issue that requires hard work, like fasting in the month of Ramadan by not eating or drinking during the hot summer, then you will be rewarded more, as the reward corresponds to the effort. Hence, there is no contradiction between the two Hadiths." I was glad to realize that the two Hadiths demonstrated that radicalism is not part of Islam, that it is a religion of *yusr*, ease and simplicity.

I came to embrace such discussions and intellectual debates, and while I enjoyed talking to Hasan about different issues, I found our religion teacher's arguments more compelling. Before going to Jubilee School, I did not have many questions about religion, but once there, I started to question Islam more often. Contradictions in the Quran and Hadith and questions about the nature of Allah often entered my thoughts.

While in eleventh grade, I saw a poster on the cafeteria wall that promoted the United World Colleges, including details about how to apply. I applied, but with little confidence that I would be successful. I was extremely surprised when I passed the initial written test, and I began to take the application process more seriously after that. The interview was the final step; only eighteen people received interview invitations, and only six of them would be selected to attend the United World Colleges. I knew that the interview would be conducted in English and would probably be about international issues, so I began to work industriously on my English. My mom bought me the *Jordan Times*, a Jordanian newspaper written in English, which I read daily while thumbing through the dictionary to learn words that might prove useful to me. I had the support of my family and school friends and teachers.

When the day of the interview arrived, my topic was the crisis in Lebanon. I spoke about the situation as well as I could, while also praying to God for the opportunity to attend one of the United World College campuses scattered around the globe. A few weeks later, my mother called with the news: "Congrats, *habibi* [my darling], you were accepted to United World College in Canada!" I screamed with joy and excitedly told my friends and teachers, who were all pleased for me.

On a clear summer night the following year, my family sat in silence as my father drove us all to the airport. Only the words of advice my parents gave me—"Focus on your studying, don't let anything distract you!"— broke the tension. They knew that my time at Pearson College would open me to new ideas and a new value system, but they trusted that my religious education and the values they inculcated in me would protect me.

As the plane lifted off the tarmac, fear replaced my excitement. Making the trip to Canada had seemed like an adventure, but now I thought, what if I see people drinking alcohol? (I used to think people would get drunk after just a few sips.) What if students pressured me to drink or date girls? Even worse, what if they feared or hated me because I was an Arab? Would they think that I was a terrorist just because I am Muslim?

Later, walking up to the ferry that was to take me out to Vancouver Island, I saw a young East Asian youth. With my thick Arab accent I asked him, "Are you going to Pearson College?" He replied, "Yes," and then turned to a group of students he was walking with: "Guys. We have another student going to Pearson." They all were very friendly as they introduced themselves—Hieu from Vietnam, Rinus from the Netherlands, Eva from Finland, Nancy from Germany, Amber from New Zealand, Timo from Estonia, and Marko from Ukraine. When I introduced myself and told them I was from Jordan, I worried that they might judge me for being an Arab and was relieved that they did not.

That day and all the subsequent days I spent at Pearson would alter my life forever. Before going to Pearson, I had my future already planned out. I was going to finish school in Jordan, study engineering at a Jordanian university, find a job, get married, and then pay my debts for the next twenty years, after which I would send my own children to university, and the cycle would repeat itself for my kids. This trip took me out of that cycle. It had its risks, I knew, as my future became an unknown. I had no idea what or where I would end up after Pearson—after my life in "the West"—but I preferred an unknown future to the planned lives I could see of many of the people around me.

Katarina, a second-year student from Serbia, walked me around the college campus on the first day, answering my questions about teachers and courses. As we were making the tour, a man who was running with his dog stopped to say hi and to introduce himself as David. After he left,

I asked Katarina who he was, and she told me he was the director of Pearson College. That was another nice surprise about Pearson: that when students would see the director, wearing shorts and running around campus with his dog, they could call him by his first name. This informality made everybody feel they were part of the same community.

After our walk, Katarina and I spoke about politics. I did not know much about the Balkan Wars, but I knew that Muslims had been brutally killed by Serbs. While Katarina was an amazing person who was really friendly and helpful, she still was a Serb. Her people killed lots of Muslims—my people. How could I become friends with her? Then I remembered that she was a good friend of my Croatian roommate, Filip, and I wondered how that could be possible, as they were on different sides of the conflict. She deepened my confusion by saying, "All the students from the Balkans are close at Pearson—Vanes from Bosnia-Herzegovina, Jordan from Macedonia, and Filip and I are very good friends." I later saw them meeting regularly for meals. They were close indeed. At Pearson, students seemed to move beyond the conflicts between their countries.

During orientation I met many other people, including the other Arabs; we numbered thirteen out of the two-hundred-person student body. I also met the Israelis, whom I had not looked forward to meeting. I wondered, should I shake hands with them? Their people are killing Arabs all the time in the West Bank and Gaza. They are going to become soldiers in the future and kill my people. They created their "state" by murdering and displacing Arabs; I believed theirs was definitely an illegitimate state. When I eventually did meet an Israeli student, I was very nervous, but the meeting was casual. Thankfully, we did not discuss politics.

I did not wait to get myself into trouble as school started. Three main levels of English are taught at Pearson: A1, A2, and B, A1 being the most advanced. I was assigned to take English A2. After the first few classes, I felt it was too hard for me, so I dropped to English B. But level B felt too easy and I wanted to go back to A2. However, I was nervous that the registrar and teachers would be angry about my indecisiveness. I met my adviser, Christian, for the first time while trying to figure out how to get back into the English A2 class. Christian was from Germany, and other students told me he was gay. The idea of having a gay adviser was repugnant to me. As a religious Muslim, I considered homosexuality an enormous sin and did not want to interact with him—I thought of gays as dirty people.

Christian brought a cake to that first meeting with his advisees, and although I was nervous the whole time, I could feel that he was a warm person with a generous spirit. He seemed to care a great deal about his students, encouraging us to talk and paying close attention to what each person had to say. At the end of the meeting, Christian said if anyone had a problem, he could stay to talk about it. I decided to tell him about my need to switch back to English A2. I felt that I had made a big mistake, and one teacher was already mad at me for "shopping" for classes. When I explained the situation to Christian, he suggested we go for a walk. I was already concerned about my classes and feeling lost at Pearson, and now a gay man wanted to take me for a walk in the woods. I had had better days in my life!

Christian and I strolled up to the observatory, where the view was spectacular. We looked out over the trees and the buildings, and beyond them to the distant Pedder Bay, the Pacific Ocean, and the mountains of Washington State. The view made all the tensions in the world seem so silly, and I forgot about my problems at Pearson. For an instant, I even forgot that I was sitting beside a gay man. Christian told me it was normal for students to switch classes in the beginning of the year. He even told me that I was smart for doing so early in the year, before it was too late. It was great, he said, that I was trying to find a class that fit me most appropriately. Though comforted by his talk, I was still nervous, as I did not want him to touch me or put his hand on me. I was ready to run at any sign of harassment. That did not happen, of course. He promised he would do his best to solve the problem, and would talk to the registrar and the teachers to explain the matter. Far from harassing me, Christian proved to be a very helpful adviser and a very nice person. But at the time, even his friendliness disturbed me. Didn't he know that I was a Muslim and that Muslims do not accept gays? Didn't he know that in some places Muslims kill gays? I was sure he knew that, yet he really wanted to help me! His attitude and behavior puzzled me.

During the month of Ramadan, Muslims fast from dawn till sunset. We usually have *Suhur* before dawn—basically a time to eat and drink before the day's fasting begins. Before Ramadan started during my first year at Pearson, the second-year Muslim students posted a sign-up sheet to see if any students wanted to fast, and those who did would be woken up for Suhur. On the first day of Ramadan, the organizers woke me up and told me to go to the common room. When I arrived there, I found around thirty people, the majority of whom were non-Muslims. Although I wondered why non-Muslims would fast with us, I really liked the notion of them supporting us. Many of them were doing it to take part in the experience, and I found that strongly encouraging.

Before we started eating, some students gave speeches. I still remember parts of the speech given by Vanes, a Bosnian second-year student. He told a story of two people from two different religions who worshipped different gods. One said to the other, "You will go to hell, as you are worshipping the wrong god." The other person replied, "No, you will go to hell. My god is true and yours is fake." Then God spoke to the two people: "Why do you say he will go to hell, I am God and I have many forms, people can worship me in many different ways and none of them is incorrect." I did not agree with the story because there is only one God, as explained in Islam, but I liked it nevertheless. I did not want any of the non-Muslims in the room to go to hell, I wanted them all in heaven, and I wished the story were true. But I knew it was not.

When the term ended, many students could not afford to go home to their countries, so they spent the winter break with host families around Victoria. Abdullah, who was from Iraq, and I were among them, and we stayed with the same host family. Our host father, Wally, was a rotund man with a long white beard that matched the color of his hair. He was an Anglican priest who also worked in real estate. Sharleen, our host mother, had black hair and was taller than Wally. Both smiled and expressed their pleasure in hosting us, as they escorted us to their house in an old BMW.

As Abdullah and I were walking with two school friends, Jennifer and Amber, through the streets of downtown Victoria one evening, Amber asked, "What gifts are you guys buying for your host family?" We were surprised, as we did not know we had to buy them something. "Why should we buy the gifts? Is there anything special?" I asked. Jennifer and Amber seemed puzzled. "It's Christmas," they replied, "and at Christmas people buy gifts for each other." So the four of us wandered around the shops, hunting for gifts for our host families. On Christmas Eve, Wally came to our room. "Tonight is Christmas Eve," he said, "and every year we go to service on this night. You guys wanna join?" We answered, "Definitely." We thought he was referring to community service. It seemed like a good chance to help the community and see some friends.

The old BMW drove us to a church. I thought, "Oh, we will be serving in a church. So that's how it works here. Poor people go to church on Christmas and Canadians serve them." But instead of serving the poor, I found myself relaxed on one of the seats, listening to the hymns and preparing to stand up to repeat the psalms whenever the congregation did so. The ceremony went on for a few hours. Afterward, I asked the family, "So, are we going to do service now?" Wally replied, "What do you mean? We just came from the service." Abdullah and I were even more puzzled and I said, "We did not do any service. We did not clean the streets, prepare food for the homeless, or anything like that." The family then began laughing. Wally replied, "I'm sorry. We did not mean community service.

We call this event we just had in the church 'service.'" We, too, found the situation funny. I had enjoyed my first time in a church. People seemed happy as they were praying, and I liked the ritual when the priests moved among the crowd, smoke rising from their pots.

Christians pray differently from Muslims; their prayers sound more like singing. They all sit while the priests walk around and recite from the Bible. Sometimes the congregation repeats what the priests are saying, and sometimes they do not. I found it tricky to figure out when to repeat and when not to. I also felt that the way Muslims pray to God is easier, with a much shorter prayer that is led by the Imam.

After we went back to the house, Abdullah and I wondered where to put the family's gifts. We recalled from watching movies how Santa would come through the fireplace in the night to give gifts to the children. We wondered if we should just leave them next to the fireplace, but finally decided to put them in front of each person's room. Later that night we were watching a movie, when Abdullah stood up and said excitedly, "I found it!" I had no idea what he was talking about. He explained, "I found where to put the gifts." He took the gifts and ran down the stairs, and I followed him. I found him staring at the golden ornaments that twinkled in the dimly lit room, as did the gifts that lay underneath the Christmas tree we had decorated a few days earlier.

One night during the second term, my Palestinian friend Ghassan, whose father and cousins had recently been arrested by Israeli soldiers during a military action in Ramallah, said to me, "Ala', I don't know what I'm doing here in Canada, living safely while my people are being harassed and killed every day. I should be back in Palestine, fighting for my country, rather than sitting here doing nothing." I tried to calm him down: "Ghassan, maybe now you are not benefiting your country, but in the future you will be educated and you will be invaluable to your people....If you go back and fight now, what would you do? You'd be throwing stones at the soldiers, but would that change anything on the ground? Would throwing a stone save the Palestinian cause?"

He answered, "Ala', what you say makes sense, but I feel useless. I feel paralyzed. I cannot do anything." I sympathized with him. He was sitting on his bed in Canada, living securely, his worst fear being that he would fail an exam or not get an A on a paper. At the same time, in Palestine his father and cousin had been arrested and his people were being killed. I could not imagine what I'd do if my father were arrested, and my feelings encouraged me to support Ghassan. I did not want him to feel he was going through the ordeal by himself.

Middle Eastern politics occupied a lot of my thinking during my second term at Pearson. Earlier I had believed that because Israel had occupied Palestine without any legitimate reason, they must leave the land and return to the Arabs all they had taken. But after meeting Israelis at Pearson College, I began to see the conflict from a different angle. I continued to believe that Israel had illegitimately occupied Palestine, but I saw that the people who made that mistake were different from the people living in Israel now. My Israeli friends at Pearson were born in Israel and had lived there all of their lives; thus, it was not surprising that they felt it was their homeland. Still, millions of Palestinians continued to live in refugee camps around the world, and they desperately wanted to go back to their homes. To me the conflict seemed unspeakably complicated. I struggled with these thoughts and shared them with Ghassan, Katarina, Christian, Mohamad (a Shiite from Lebanon), and my other friends at Pearson. They were supportive of my questioning and available to help me at any time, and they urged me to keep thinking about it. I did not find an answer, but I felt that questioning the situation at least had made me more mature.

Going back to Jordan for the summer break after a year at Pearson College was hard, as I realized how much I had changed. I tried to convince my relatives and friends not to dislike Shiites or Israelis, explaining that they were normal, just like us. But they would not listen and clung to their existing ideas: "Israelis are killing our siblings in Palestine." "They took our land and want more." "Shiites hate us." "Iran wants to make us all Shiites." My friend Mohamad did not hate me, I tried to tell them, and the Israelis are not inherently bad. But nobody would listen to me.

When I returned to Pearson after that summer, there were two new Israeli students, Einat and Itamar. When I got to know them better, I became more interested in achieving peace between us rather than in winning them over. We became close from the very beginning of the year. During Ramadan, they sometimes fasted with the Muslims. Later, some Muslims fasted with the Jews during Yom Kippur. It was a remarkable experience—Jews and Muslims, Arabs and Israelis, not only living peacefully together, but also celebrating each other's ceremonies and religious observances.

Watching students conduct their respective religious practices at Pearson made me reflect on my own. Islam is linked to many ugly things going on in the world. Many terrorist groups use Islam to justify their actions and to manipulate people into carrying out terrorist attacks. I knew that Islam is against all of these violent actions and I was annoyed at how it was being abused. My other Muslim friends were thinking a lot about Islam at the same time. They were still Muslims but they were questioning some Islamic practices, like stoning people who committed adultery and capital punishment in general. Such punishments may have made sense at the time Islam began, but my friends felt they seemed outdated now. Observing non-Muslim believers made me feel that Islam is not as unique as I thought, and eventually I began to have some doubts about Islam too.

During the winter of my second year at Pearson, my Palestinian friend Ghassan started dating Lorena, a Paraguayan friend. I was quite shocked. Ghassan was very religious, so I was surprised to see him in a relationship. However, he seemed to think even more about religion while in the relationship, and we had a lot of talks about it. One night we walked around the campus while discussing religion. Ghassan began: "Ala', I really don't understand our religion." I asked him, "What is it now?" He replied, "Religion is trying to put many limits on us. I do not understand why there are many things that we can do in life, but then religion tries to stop us from doing them. If God doesn't want us to do these things, then why did he give us the option in the first place?" I was about to answer, but he interrupted me: "I know that God wants to test us, but why? Why should He test us? Why does He need to do that?"

I could not answer him. I did not know why God wants to test us. We stood for a minute in complete silence; the sky was very clear, and we could hear only the sound of the wind buffeting the trees around us. Ghassan was looking down, clearly struggling, but I was confident about my religion. Ghassan broke the silence, saying firmly, "Ala', you are Muslim for one reason: you were *born* in a Muslim family. We have seen some very religious people here, students who are strong believers, and they are not Muslims. You see, Muslims are not the only very strong believers." He paused for a second, then he continued, "And how about gays, what if they were actually *born* gay, as a lot of the research suggests?" He paused once more. "Religion also devalues love in some cases. It does not recognize its existence, and it views any kind of a relation between a man and a woman outside of marriage as completely sinful." I understood him. These issues had occurred to me as well, but as I said, I was confident about my religion, or at least I thought I was. I waited for a while, then I started speaking quietly, trying to convince him: "Ghassan, it is not as complicated as you're describing. Think about it this way; you believe that the Quran is true, as it has much scientific evidence to support it. Allah told us to do some specific things through Quran; we don't have to question them, since we've already proven that Quran is true, we just do them, it's that simple." Ghassan did not seem convinced, and I was not totally convinced either. I had been thinking about these questions for a while, and I tried to persuade myself that they could be answered within Islam, that Islam was right. But I realized that I was trying very hard to convince myself—I was not sure.

As the year went on, I thought a lot more about religion. I was not convinced about many issues in Islam, or in any other religion. It did not seem plausible to me that any one religion is right, but I was scared to actually admit that. I was afraid of going to hell, so I kept finding more excuses for Islam and why it was right. At the end of the year, I decided to be honest with myself, to face what I really thought. I found that I was just very confused and not sure any more what my religious belief was. However, the thought of the remarkable journey I had made from a public school in Amman to Pearson College kept me believing; I was even accepted to Dartmouth College that year. How could that public-school kid, who had once been unable to speak any English, attend an Ivy League college? Such a thing could not have happened without God! The only thing I did to earn those honors was to pray. I asked God, and He answered my prayers. Simple.

Later in the year, as the final International Baccalaureate exams approached, students grew worried. We were not really afraid of the exams, although we did need to do a lot of work to prepare for them. What really kept us up at night was the thought of leaving all our friends at Pearson. I was scared of leaving. But the exams came and went, we made the traditional jump in the bay, and we had the last dinner, where the faculty and students said their last tearful good-byes. None was more emotional for me than my good-bye with my adviser, Christian, to whom I had become very close. As he hugged me, I thought of the first time he had walked with me to the observatory and how scared I was, and compared that moment to how much I cared about him now. Christian's sexuality seemed irrelevant to me now. To me, Christian was just an amazing person. I did not want him to leave. I finally let go of him and walked back to the college campus, where I stopped beside a tree. I saw his car leaving and I wept.

Pearson College opened my eyes to the whole world, and the world has proved to be infinitely more complex than I thought. After going to Pearson, I decided I wanted to do something different. I wanted to help people around me, to pay back for my scholarship. I wanted to make an impact, to change somebody's life the way somebody had changed mine by giving me the scholarship to attend Pearson. I had learned that some people actually believe in something and work hard for it. It was wonderful to see donors giving thousands of dollars to students they had never even met.

As my flight was circling over Jordan, getting ready to land, I was thrilled to see my beautiful country again. The plane flew over Amman, and I could spot familiar buildings from far above. I could also see the perpetual yellow sand in the deserts to the east of Amman. The city's modernity blended with the golden desert beyond, and highlighted by the rising sun, the view was spectacular. As I watched the splendid scene before my eyes, for a moment I forgot all my sorrow about leaving Pearson. Euphoria took over as my plane landed.

That summer, I wanted to keep myself busy so as not to get bored, and also to prevent nostalgia for Pearson from consuming me. I took driving lessons, planned an orientation for the Jordanian students going to the United World Colleges the next year, and taught English to Palestinian refugees. However, what occupied me most during that summer was thinking about religion, as my experience at Pearson had intensely challenged my faith. I never resolved anything that summer, and many questions continue to irritate and confuse me, even making me feel insecure and hypocritical in some ways. I am Muslim and I continue to be religious, but I also have huge doubts about Islam. Despite my insecurity, I am glad to know I am a skeptic. At least I am using my mind, thinking and criticizing, rather than simply accepting that all teachings are absolutely true. Just as my time at Pearson opened my mind to a world of new ideas and ways of thinking, I know that the coming four years of college in North America will help me figure out my path in life.

Ala' is a sophomore at Dartmouth College, studying economics and government. He continues to be surprised that he was able to switch from engineering to a major not valued in Jordan. After college, Ala' plans to obtain a graduate degree.

3

Asyah Saif My Expanding World

At the age of thirty-one, my mother took a leap of faith and left her home in Russia for a different country, language, religion, and traditions. She was traveling with me, only three months of age, and my fifteen-month-old brother. Her mother called her crazy, but she had heard that before: crazy for deciding to go to university in Moscow, crazy for falling in love and marrying an Arab, and now, crazy for leaving the country.

Even though my family lived in Yemen, my upbringing was very much Russian. We spoke Russian in our house, at first because my mother didn't speak Arabic, and later because she never took an interest in learning the local language properly. Having lived in Yemen for more than twenty years, she can speak Arabic now, though not well. The intricacies of the language are lost in translation, and her misuse of words and odd pronunciation are all so funny to listen to that my brother and I can't keep a straight face when our mother speaks Arabic. At home we generally converse entirely in Russian, switching to Arabic only when we want to be amused. Thus we became fluent in both Russian and Arabic—Russian from speaking it at home, and Arabic at school and everywhere else outside our home.

My mother never cooked Yemeni or Middle Eastern recipes, so we ate things like *borscht, pirozhki, kotleti, blini,* and *olivje*—Russian salad. We would all get excited when our dad cooked, because his Yemeni cuisine was spicy hot and deliciously different. At home we watched Russian TV and learned Russian fairy tales and lullabies, and our knowledge of popular Arabic shows, cartoons, or movies came from conversations with our peers. My brother and I knew we were different. Our mother was very white and had green eyes, and we had lighter skin than other kids, but we only started noticing how different our family was from others in Yemen after becoming aware of the way people stared and commented. These reactions made me angry, until my mother explained that they stared at us simply because they had never before seen anyone different. "You wouldn't look at anyone like that because you have seen people from different countries, but they have not. To them, it is something new, something exciting! That's why they stare. Not because they're bad. Just because they're pure of heart."

When I was six years old, I learned an important lesson about nationalism. I was sitting next to a girl on my school bus. She said she liked the color of my skin and how fair it was. I told her it was because my mother was Russian.

"Russia? Cool," she said. Then, after a pause, she added, "Have you been there?"

"Yes. We go there every summer to visit my grandmother," I said.

"Do you like it there?"

"Oh yes!" I said. And I did love it there. My grandmother lived in Omsk, a city in Siberia close to the northern border of Kazakhstan. It is a beautiful city, with wide streets and trees and parks, farmers' markets and little shops, big buses and traffic lights, where the people are smiling and welcoming.

"Is it better than here?" the girl asked.

"Yes," I said.

"Why?"

"I...I don't know. It's prettier. There are no trees here. No parks...it's just different."

"But we have mountains!"

"Yes...they do too."

"No! Yemen is prettier! Yemen is better!" the girl said, her voice angry.

"Well, I love Yemen but—"

"There's no place like Yemen!" the girl screamed, and then she turned away and looked out the window. I sat back in my seat and said nothing. That was when I learned not to tell people that I preferred Russia to Yemen, and that every person believes their country is better than others. I loved two countries, but learned I should keep my innocent opinion that one is prettier than the other to myself.

I also came to know that the Yemeni people are similarly protective and proud of their religion—of Islam. If I was confused about why people got angry if you did not think their country was the greatest, I was even more confused when the talk turned to matters of religion. Religion is such a big part of the Yemeni culture that it is integrated into all aspects of life: the calls to prayer, the clothing, the language and sayings, nearly everything.

I remember how I first came to know that there are different religions and that people believe in different gods. There are no buses in my city, but we do have little vans called *dabab*, which roam the city to provide transport but have no particular routes or set stops. Most dababs have two sets of seats facing each other, enough for six people to sit comfortably. Late one afternoon, my mother and I were in a dabab, heading to visit the home of a family friend. A woman was sitting facing us. She was dressed in a long black dress called an abaya, which covered her whole body except for her hands. She also had a burqa covering her face, so only her dark brown eyes were visible from behind the black cloth.

"*Masha-Allah*, you are so pretty! Where are you from?" the woman asked my mother.

"Russia," my mother said. "My husband is Yemeni."

"Oh Masha-Allah," the woman repeated, and then she asked, "Are you a Muslim?"

"Yes," my mother answered. The woman's eyes smiled, but a look of confusion was fixed on my face until the end of the trip.

Later I asked my mother why she did not tell the truth when asked about her religion. She explained to me that it is easier that way because people are not always accepting of difference. She said that some people might find it difficult to understand those differences and even try to change them. She told me the story of our Syrian neighbor—a respectful and intelligent man who taught at the university—who was an Arab Christian. "When people asked him, he would say that he was Christian. Then everyone was asking questions and telling him that his faith was wrong. Everyone was telling him how Islam was the right path. It would have been easier for him to just say he was Muslim to avoid all that."

Before coming to Canada to attend high school, I was afraid to tell my friends that my mother is Christian. I would tell them that she fasts during the month of Ramadan, that she prays five times a day, that she is just like everyone else. Today I am all for celebrating differences between people, both cultural and religious. I strongly believe in being proud of what you are, of the choices you make, the path you walk. I believe in sharing, in learning from others, in advancing and developing. However, if asked that question by someone in Yemen, my answer even today would be, "She is Muslim." Not because I am afraid of the debate that would follow about how Islam is superior if I told the truth, but because I know that debating with someone who is closed to new ideas is pointless. I would love to talk to Muslims about Christianity and other religions that I have come to learn about, but I do not want to hear any more about how my mother will go to hell. I heard enough of that in my childhood, and it still makes me angry to think how closed-minded some people are, even though I know it is not because they are intentionally malicious. It is simply because not everyone is fortunate enough to be able to learn about others, especially those who live in a monolithic culture and are confined throughout their lives to only one way of thinking, only one idea, a single perspective.

Ironically, the person who told my brother and me that our mother was going to hell was not a neighbor or teacher or friend—it was our sister. To put this in context, I must go back to the years when my father left Yemen to study in Russia on a university scholarship. At that time, he was married to his first wife and had two children, a son and a daughter. While he was in Russia, his wife and son were killed in an automobile accident. A few years later, my father met my mother at the university. They dated for a while and then got married. It is important to understand that, as I mentioned before, my mother was taking a brave step by following her husband to a country so different from her own. Not only was she going to face a different culture, religion, and traditions, she was also going to become the mother of an eight-year-old child who had nothing in common with her.

I never refer to Lamees as my stepsister, because that concept was never present in our family. However, people are sometimes surprised when they hear that I have a sister, because I talk about her much less frequently than I do about my brother, Emad. There is a reason for that. During the first year in Yemen, we lived as one big family. Members of our extended family often visited us from the village, staying from several days to a few months. My grandmother and sister stayed with us that whole year. Despite my mother's efforts, Lamees never got used to the different style of life. My brother and I only spoke Russian at that time, my mother knew only a few words in Arabic, the food was different, and the atmosphere too. Lamees never got used to it, and my mother could not change things quickly enough to accommodate her. Lamees also never opened up to my mother, never let herself get close, and she eventually went back to the village with my grandmother. She stayed there until my father brought her back to further her education a few years later. Even then she didn't like living with us and wanted to be with her grandmother, so she decided to live at my uncle's house instead.

When Lamees came to live with us again, Emad and I were older and spoke Arabic fluently. That was when she told us about hell. Of course we learned about religion in school, including good and bad, hell and heaven. Starting in first grade, we had Quran and Islamic studies classes three times a week. I remember enjoying these classes, although I always did very badly in them. I loved their story aspect, the narratives of the past, of the prophets. I remember particularly liking the story about the Prophet Mohammed's kindness to his abusive neighbors. My brother and I always ran back home after school and repeated everything we had learned to my mother.

We were sitting in Lamees's room one afternoon, telling her about one of the stories from school and how our Arabic teacher lost his temper because the class was inattentive again. Then, somehow, we ventured onto the topic of religion, and Lamees told us about hell. She told us of the fire, the pain, and described how several layers of skin grow on a person's body in hell so that it doesn't burn easily, which causes more pain. They can't drink anything but lava, she told us, or eat anything other than the spiky fruit that hurts and burns the throat and stomach. She described the spirits there who whip the condemned with sharp, blazing iron chains. There is nothing but suffering and pain, she assured us. But the most terrifying thing she told us was that *everyone who is not Muslim will be there.* "Yes, your mother will go to hell because she is not Muslim," she said while looking into our lost and desperate eyes. Emad, always the emotional and sensitive one, had tears in his eyes for days afterward. Mom asked him if anything was wrong, but he wouldn't tell her because he had given Lamees an oath of silence. A couple of days later, when his childish ability to keep emotions hidden finally gave out, he came to my mother and begged her over and over: "Mommy, please become a Muslim."

"Why should I?" Mom asked.

"Because I don't want you to go to hell."

Mom was taken aback. "What makes you think I'm going to go to hell?"

"Because you're not Muslim."

Of course he soon cracked and told her where he got the idea. Mom then sat us down and tried to explain the concepts of good and bad. I believe this was the first push toward making me open-minded about religion, about questioning what I believe and not blindly following anything. I heard many times from my peers and elders that anyone who is not Muslim will go to hell, but then I would look at the people I knew who were of other religions. I refused to believe they would all go to hell. I refused to believe that God is unfair, because, in my view, that is what my Muslim friends were advocating. I believe that it is a person's actions that classify them, not any mere label, whether of a religion, race, or class.

Back in school, arguments on this subject sometimes became heated. One of my most vivid memories of such an argument was with a Pakistani English-language teacher from Britain when I was in grade ten. Referring to people of other religions, he said, "You should never trust them. They have no strong morals, no principles. That's why you have to always side with Muslims." That comment blew my mind. If the man were in Russia, I thought, he would no doubt have been looked at as a terrorist. He even looked like a fundamentalist, and the truth wasn't far from it. The class was turned into a sermon about Islam, rather than a lesson on the past participle.

"So you're telling me we shouldn't trust them just because they're not Muslim?" I asked, interrupting one of his other nonsensical proclamations.

"Yes, you understood me correctly."

"Even if they're good people?!" I continued, quickly losing my temper.

"It's not about them being good or bad people. Unlike us, they have no morals, they will only think of themselves, deceive you in their own interest—"

"No morals?! So we shouldn't trust Ms. Amanda, for example?" I asked, referring to a non-Muslim woman we all respected.

"No, you shouldn't."

I finally gave up and ignored everything he said on the subject of religion from then on. My classmates didn't speak up, but I'm sure that at least some of them were glad someone else had. The difference between my classmates and me was that I didn't care about the consequences, about what others would think if I argued against someone preaching for Islam.

The fact that my mother was not a Muslim taught me a great deal and gave me the opportunity to weigh what people said rather than just believing their words. My mother is one of the purest souls I've ever known, has one of the kindest hearts. As the years passed, I came to realize that she and I essentially believed in the same god—she was simply taking a different path to the same destination.

My family's tolerant ideas about cultural and religious expectations were not reflected in the larger Yemeni society. For example, when I chose to wear the hijab, I was conforming to the traditions and culture around me. In Islam, girls who reach puberty are expected to cover their bodies, except for their faces and hands. In some Islamic cultures, women also cover their hands and faces. I knew that girls as young as five years old would wear a hijab, while others would start in middle school, where it was part of the school uniform. That was the case in my school, which was one of the few in Yemen that was coed. Although it was not officially part of our uniform, when a girl passed into grade seven she would put on the hijab, simply because everyone else began wearing one at that age. Every girl in grades seven through twelve wore it, and who wants to be the white crow?

The fact that we had boys in our class made things more complicated. They were our friends, yes, but that didn't change the fact that we didn't want them to know when we had begun getting our periods. Wearing a scarf was a way of announcing to the world that a girl had reached puberty, and most girls would not put it on before grade seven. There were of course exceptions. Some girls had more conservative parents who forced them to wear the hijab once they got their period, even if they were very young. That is why, when my non-Muslim friends ask whether wearing the hijab is a choice or an obligation, I always answer, "It depends." It was a choice for me—although who would choose to be different at such an early age?—but others have no choice.

My attitude toward the hijab has changed dramatically throughout my life. When I was a child, I believed that if a girl were a true Muslim, she had to wear the hijab as a symbol of her faith, her dedication, and, most importantly, her purity. Why would she not wear it? To show off her hair? To show off her beauty and attract the attention of men? That would contradict the teachings of Islam. Therefore, wearing the hijab made absolute sense. However, I never agreed with wearing the burqa, as I couldn't see the sense in covering the whole face. There is no mention of it in the Quran, yet people preached it as the order of God, and some even approached me on the street to say that I had to put on the burqa, that it was sinful to show off my beauty. That seemed the epitome of nonsense to me, a teenager with self-esteem issues. I just could not see the need for a burqa.

While I was developing a view of religion that was as open and tolerant as possible in my situation, Emad entered a phase of hard-core religious conservatism that I found a bit too extreme. He suddenly started praying five times a day, and would do so in a location in our apartment where it was inevitable that we would see him. I believe it was his way of proving himself, not to us as much as to himself. The more complaints we made about this demonstration of his piety, the more oppressed and righteously religious Emad felt, which gave him a sense of achievement. He also stopped listening to music and insisted we boycott it as well. I remember traveling by car to Aden, the beach city of Yemen. We usually listened to ABBA or Boney M in the car, switching to Russian singers once in a while.

To prevent us from hearing the music during the trip, Emad would try to argue with us, and then put his fingers in his ears and start humming. Eventually Mom would give in, and we had to endure the silence and tense atmosphere for the rest of the trip.

The worst argument about my brother's extreme views occurred during another trip in the car, while we were on our way to Sana'a, Yemen's capital city. Everyone was in a happy mood and had been excited about the trip. When we stopped by a friend's house to drop off a bag of movie cassettes, I volunteered to do it. I was gone for no longer than five minutes, but when I came back, war was raging in our van.

"Shut up!" Mom yelled at Emad as I was taking my seat. "Not one more word!"

"What happened?" I asked, confused.

"Nothing," Mom lied. Then, seconds later, she burst out in anger, "He was saying you should put the burqa on! What right does he have to say that?! That's the last thing we want happening!"

"Mom, relax, I'll never wear it," I said. "You know what I think about that."

"You should!" my brother said, and all hell broke loose again.

The argument had started because Emad saw some man staring at me as I walked into the apartment building. He stated his opinion, Mom got angry, and all went downhill from there. I think Mom was very emotional about the topic because I had worn the hijab in Russia the previous summer, against her wishes. I had never before thought of wearing the hijab on our annual summer trips to Russia, even though I had been wearing it in Yemen for a couple of years. One summer while I was in high school, I decided it was hypocritical to wear it in Yemen and then take it off in Russia, and that it was my duty to God to wear it everywhere. I was certain that I should act on my beliefs in the same way no matter where I was, and slowly started feeding the idea of wearing the hijab in Russia to my mom. But when I confronted her at last, the conversation did not go the way I had imagined it. My mother wore the hijab in Yemen, out of respect for the traditions and the culture and for my dad, although he never asked her to. They both worked at the university and, to avoid any gossip, Mom had started covering her hair. She was never fond of the idea, but she respected it. And yet, though open-minded, understanding, and accepting of others, she refused to listen to me.

"It's summer! It's going to be hot!" Mom argued.

"It's summer here too, and I'm all covered up! No difference!"

"But EVERYONE will be wearing tank tops and shorts..."

"And why should I be like everyone?"

"Why shouldn't you be?! You want to stand out, huh? What satisfaction does it give you?"

"I don't care what people think! I'm not taking it off!"

The fights continued all the way into July, when we finally came to a compromise: hats.

"The point is to cover your hair, so wear a hat then, not a hijab," Mom said.

Looking back, I understand her position completely. I would have stood out wearing a hijab, and people would have talked. Moreover, with a rise in racism and the presence of skinheads in Saint Petersburg at that time, it was not very safe to stand out. I also now understand why I fought so hard to wear the hijab. I risked being different and being looked at as the "other," but it also strengthened my feeling of belonging to a religion and a culture. I also wanted to prove to the world that I could do it, that I wouldn't break. At the time, I saw it as a test from God to assess the strength of my faith. However, in truth there was no test, only a teenage girl who wanted to fight for what she believed.

When we came back from Russia, I felt like a saint, a pure soul devoted to God. That was the academic year I was asked most often about what I wore in Russia, and, oh, with what pride I told my friends about it! Their disappointment in me for making the compromise of wearing a hat would disappear as soon as I explained how dangerous—vastly exaggerated, of course—wearing the hijab in Russia could be. They would nod their heads in approval, proud and accepting of my courage.

The following year I went to finish high school in Canada, and there I grew to be who I am today. I was accepted into United World College's Pearson College, an international school located on Vancouver Island that has an International Baccalaureate curriculum for the last two years of high school. After a long application, a stressful selection process, and an even more stressful period spent waiting for a decision, I finally learned I would be going to Canada. In Yemen the image of Canada is quite positive, and it had always been my dream to study there. It is a neutral country that doesn't discriminate and where people generally don't tolerate racism. Yes, Canada did turn out to be the friendly country I imagined, although it surely wasn't perfect.

One of the main things my college stressed was culture, and every student was, to some extent, seen as an ambassador of their culture. During the summer before starting at Pearson, I had to decide on many things, one of them being whether or not to wear a headscarf. Mom and I went shopping for scarves, and she bought me many different colorful ones, saying that she wanted me to "fit in." There was no need to "fit in" at Pearson, though, because everyone was different and that was what we celebrated about each other. At Pearson I met Muslim girls from other countries and other cultures, and one of them became a close friend. She was from Kazakhstan, a country whose population includes a large percentage of Muslims. She did not wear a scarf. She did not pray five times a day. She did not fast during Ramadan. Nevertheless, she was a Muslim who believed in what I believed and was true to the philosophy of Islam. There was a lot of indirect pressure put on those who did not "practice" the religion. Boys who prayed pressured those who didn't to join them at prayer, and some girls preached about the benefits of wearing the hijab. I avoided any such meetings because I had dealt with a great deal of preaching in my early years, and had had to listen as others preached the value of their religion over that of my mother. By the time I went to Canada, I had come to believe that one should not judge whose faith is true and whose is to be questioned.

What pushed me to question the hijab for the first time was not the Western view of it or any pressure from others. It was, ironically, the pressure one of our older peers at Pearson put on my close friend to start wearing the hijab that first put me off. We had a simple tradition at the college of exchanging gifts for Christmas. The residents of each house would gather for a little celebration called Secret Santa. Each student was assigned another to whom they were to give secret gifts throughout a week, with a small gift at the last dinner that revealed who each person's Secret Santa was. I don't remember what I received, but I remember my friend's gift. She ran into my room, excited that our second-year peer from Palestine was her Secret Santa. She had received an Arabic black-and-white scarf and a letter. She had waited to open the letter with me. She smiled as she held the white envelope. Inside were six folded pages containing articles from the Internet about the importance of wearing the hijab. I remember one titled "Why I Should Wear the Hijab."

My friend cried, hurt and offended. It was that night that I started thinking, "Why do I wear the hijab?" There are many reasons for it, one of which is not to attract attention or stand out. The hijab provides a way for a woman to conceal her beauty and prevent her from seducing men. At least, that is how it was explained to me in primary and secondary school. But is it really that? And hasn't it changed since then?

I drowned out those thoughts and forced myself to think of other matters. Whenever I started questioning it again, I would get mad at myself.

"You are disobeying God!" I kept telling myself. That way, I suppressed my thoughts for two more years, until I graduated from Pearson, went to university in Canada, and finished my first year of undergraduate studies. One day that summer I confronted myself, finally facing those questions and letting my mind consider them freely. I came to a decision that very day, and this is how my thoughts unfolded.

The supposed purpose of wearing the hijab is to avoid bringing attention to myself, but here in Canada I was doing exactly the opposite by wearing it! And if the purpose is to avoid seducing men, well, surely they are not so weak and stupid as to be seduced merely by the sight of women's hair! Moreover, doesn't creating a veiled sense of mystery by wearing the hijab increase a woman's seductive power? My internal debate went on for the whole day. Should I? Should I not? Whichever argument I made, I came up with a logical counterargument. That night, I talked to my parents.

My mother's position was predictable. Although she respected the hijab, she saw no need to wear it outside the Arab world. She had always been against the idea and was happy to hear I had decided to take it off. I also knew my father would support my decision. Although he was Yemeni and a Muslim, he was always open-minded about other religions and cultures. Perhaps spending more than six years in Russia had helped him distinguish between people and their religion. He had never asked my mother to convert, nor did he force me to wear the hijab; I had chosen to do so myself. He also never forced Islam on us; my brother and I chose it ourselves, although of course we were greatly influenced by our surroundings and society.

Looking back, I don't remember discussing religion at any time with my father. We talked of God, of the prophets. He told us stories from the Quran and helped me remember verses that I had had quite some trouble memorizing as a child. He took pride in Islam and admired its philosophy, but he never put down any other religions and beliefs. That is why I knew my father would be supportive of my decision. And he was. "Whatever you are most comfortable with," he said. Then he reminded me of the Arabic saying about Islam: "*Al-deen yosr, wa lais osr*," which means that religion should ease a person's life and not make it more difficult.

My brother, too, was supportive. That, to be honest, was a bit of a shock. Having changed from an extreme conservative teenager to an open-minded young man, Emad said, "Ah, at last. Good decision." His thinking had changed because he had traveled and seen much of the world. He also learned that the reasons for wearing the hijab, which are as much cultural as religious, might not apply in Western countries as they do in the Middle East. He, too, has learned to judge people by who they are, not by their religion.

It is sometimes difficult for others to understand how different the cultures of Canada and Yemen are. Most difficult to explain, I find, is the physical separation of men and women. I once spent an hour explaining to an Ecuadorian friend that in Yemen men and women don't hug, don't hold hands, and don't even shake hands when they meet. It was especially difficult to explain it to him because his culture is so different, one in which affection, respect, and caring are shown in physical ways.

Another major difference is that in Yemen, marriage between cousins is rather common and socially acceptable. I only came to know that it is considered wrong in many cultures and illegal in numerous countries after traveling to Canada. I was as shocked to learn that it is not permitted in North America as people were shocked to learn it *is* allowed in Yemen. Moreover, marriage ceremonies are very different in Yemen. Because there is no mixing between genders, two separate wedding celebrations are held at the same time—one for men and one for women. In the last two hours of the celebration, when the groom joins the women and unites with his bride, all the women put on their black abayas and hijabs. Of course this description is very simplified, but my point is that genders don't mix in Yemen, and physical contact is restricted to direct relatives.

When I came to Canada, I had to face the need many Canadians have to hug to show affection, which I found quite strange. Even though I had spent every summer in Russia, I still was not accustomed to any physical contact with boys, and I would tell them not to hug me. Living with this custom and observing it from a distance, I started to realize the different meanings of a hug in the two cultures. In Yemen, if a boy and a girl hug, they are considered mischievous and their actions suspicious. In Canada, a hug is nothing but what a smile would mean in Yemen, a way to show care and affection of the purest kind. I have grown to understand the meaning of a hug in Canada and accept it as a warm way to show that I am there for my friends, that I care for them and that everything is going to be all right when they need to be comforted. Having said that, I must emphasize that I will not hug or shake hands when I go back to Yemen—not because my beliefs change, but because I respect what a hug means in Yemen.

"But how do people meet?!" my Ecuadorian friend asked. "How do people get to know each other?" I explained that they meet each other in school, at the university, or through arranged marriages. The subject of love and marriage in Yemen is complicated because many factors play a role in it, such as arranged marriages, not having sex before marriage, and marriages within the family. Questions that often follow my explanation of Yemeni marriages are about whom I am going to marry—whether I will have an arranged marriage and if I can marry only a Muslim man. My reply is that I do not restrict myself to Muslim men. In fact, the only thing I know for certain is that I will never marry an atheist, simply because there would be too much difference between us. I want to share my life with someone who will understand and respect my spirituality and faith.

While I had my share of interaction with a different religion and culture in Russia, it was a big adjustment when I actually began to *live* in a different culture. I know that quite a few of my peers from Yemen who went to study in North America and Europe returned home after just a few months or a year. Those who went to other Arab or Muslim countries, such as Egypt, Malaysia, or Indonesia, didn't seem to have the same difficulty adjusting to a new environment. Those who went to North America for the first time alone particularly suffered from culture shock.

The culture at Pearson College—with two hundred students from a hundred countries—is such a mix of cultures, religions, and traditions that it provided the best transition into North American culture I could have asked for. Pearson had it all: Mormons, Buddhists, Jews, Muslims, people from every other possible religion, as well as atheists. There were straight people, gays, lesbians, and bisexuals. There were the very shy and those comfortable enough with their bodies to jump naked into the bay. Some drank and smoked, both cigarettes and weed. Some believed in sex only after marriage, while others slept in each other's rooms every night. Pearson was like a taster's choice of the world.

I of course had seen much of what I found at Pearson in Russia, and it was a more difficult adjustment for the Yemeni friend who came with me. But, over time, she, too, understood the differences and got over her culture shock.

What made my encounters with new ways of thinking and living easier was the concept of respect and cultural understanding that was pervasive at Pearson. One of my roommates, for example, had a boyfriend at the college, but she never invited him to spend the night in our room out of respect for my values and privacy. My room was also the personal space where I could take off my scarf; thus, all house members respected the "Please Knock" sign on my door, instead of just barging in, as was customary.

Pearson also matched each first-year student with a second-year student, whose task was to look after their charge and to be there for them. My second-year was from Egypt. We talked things out all the time, which made it much easier for me. In my second year, I had to sit down with my first-year from Yemen—mind you, he was a boy, which made the conversation especially complicated—and explain to him that his room-mate was gay and had a partner on campus. I feared he would make an inappropriate remark or joke if he saw them together, so it seemed best to talk to him about it. Of course he was shocked. Months later, though, he was as close to his roommate as anyone could get, because he was able to let go of the stereotypes attributed to homosexuals in Yemen and Islam. Pearson was where I became aware of all the stereotypes attributed to different nationalities, religions, symbols, and actions, and also where I realized how ridiculous and closed-minded the stereotypes were.

So, what made me who I am today was everything around me: my en-vironment, my community, and my parents. Although my parents didn't play a key role in my choosing a religion or adopting values, they have had a strong influence, especially through their support and open-mindedness. When I was enclosed within the culture of Yemen and Islam, I knew nothing but my own traditions, my own values. Many of the values I had thought it unimaginable to change have in fact changed. For example, I could never have imagined myself hugging a boy, but now I have many male friends and we always hug. I used to frown on the girls who took off their hijab while in other countries, but now I have been without my hijab for more than a year.

I ask myself if I have made good changes and whether I have liberated myself. I conclude that perhaps I am liberated in some respects, that it is normal to adjust to your environment and learn new skills, new ideas, and new ways of thinking. Have I given up my values? Perhaps in some ways, but I don't believe I have necessarily *given them up*—I prefer to think of it as expanding the scope of my values, beliefs, and traditions. I also know that when I go back to Yemen I will embrace the local values—for example, I will wear the hijab—as I still respect them and the traditions they repre-sent. But when I am in Canada I will follow other values and traditions.

I have changed. I know it. I feel it. I also know that, by definition, change is neither good nor bad. Change is simply change.

After graduating from the bachelor of commerce program at the University of Al-berta, Asyah is working as service manager for a local home-care company in Edmon-ton, AB. Her parents are now living in Russia, and her brother is pursuing his degree in economics in the United States.

4

Abdul Moustafa   The Novice's Story

One of my most vivid memories is of being ten years old and following my father through the massive crowd of men bustling into the mosque on a Friday afternoon, trying my hardest not to get lost as I glimpsed his back disappearing through the throng of worshippers. *Where am I supposed to take off my shoes? Where do I leave them? How am I to cross in front of the men if they have started praying? Where should I stand?* These questions puzzled me as I tried to follow the rules of communal prayer in a mosque. I was more than a little out of place—I was a novice.

My father took me to the Friday prayers only once or twice during my entire childhood, where I mimicked everything he did without actually knowing the prayers. I always felt like a novice and was plagued by questions: When do I have to start going to the mosque every Friday? Will I have to say the five daily prayers, or *Namaz*, as we say in Turkish? Do I really need to do this at all? I knew I should start learning the prayers if I wanted to practice our religion properly...and so on. Such questions were not unusual for a young boy who was growing up in an environment with a balance of secularism and religion. I tried to justify my ignorance when I became starkly aware of kids outside my group of friends who had more confidence and competence conducting the Namaz, but I was forced to ask myself, am I a bad Muslim?

But as quickly as these questions popped up, I could just as quickly ignore them because, although I was brought up in a family where I was taught about our culture and traditions, as well as spiritual ideas, religious doctrine or practice was never a central part of my upbringing. I knew that we were Muslims and we believed in One God and His Prophet Muhammad, but I was not expected to practice my faith until I was old enough to make my own lifestyle decisions. My grandmother did teach me a short prayer that she suggested I recite every night before going to sleep so that God and His Angels would protect me, which I occasionally did, but I was not expected or taught to practice Namaz.

My family's religiously liberal lifestyle can be explained by our family history. I am the only child in a very progressive family. Both of my parents are strong followers of Islam, and our everyday lives have been influenced by the values of our faith, such as goodwill, generosity, humility, and fairness. These values played an important role in my upbringing—much more so than religious rituals and practices. Many people will be surprised to learn that these values are in no way anti-Western; on the contrary, they are pretty much the universal values found at the core of many religious teachings. They are probably also taught by any good parents who happen to be nonbelievers. In any case, I liked the fact that my parents raised me not according to labels and fables that indoctrinate children into unthinking habits of being and behavior, but with universally positive values that relate to the collective welfare of all humanity.

I am not arguing that the rituals and other religious practices are unnecessary. For many, they are important tools for nurturing people's beliefs and for creating deeper bonds with the other members of a spiritual community. These practices are, after all, a part of Islam, maybe even an important part, and I have nothing against them. However, I have simply grown up in a community that upholds Islam for its esteemed values and deep spiritual philosophy without necessarily keeping up with all the prayers or other rituals.

My parents are flexible and their lifestyle is quite Western in terms of attire and everyday activities. My parents are longtime members of a local sports club in their upper-middle-class neighborhood in Istanbul, which is located on the beautiful coastline. For a time they showed an interest in playing tennis, but now they go to the club mostly to socialize with their large network of friends from all walks of life. My father is a huge football fan and he regularly watches games with his friends, while my mother goes to the gym to exercise. In summer they hang out at the pool with people wearing shorts and bikinis—a scene that could be set in many Western countries. To us it doesn't mean being less Muslim, and as much as my parents enjoy their liberal lifestyle, they also maintain a deep attachment to their spirituality. Every now and then, my father recites the morning prayers before he goes off to work, and he occasionally stops by the mosque for the communal Friday prayers. For as long as I can remember, he has stuck to his fasting during the month of Ramadan, while at other times his dinners will be accompanied by his favorite drink, Raki, a famous Turkish alcoholic beverage.

My mother, on the other hand, while also a strong believer at heart, is not as conservative in terms of the traditional rituals of Islam. Or to put it another way, she does not embody any of the stereotypes that Westerners attribute to Muslim women. With occasional exceptions, she does not fast during Ramadan and does not recite Namaz five times a day. She does pray, however, when visiting important sacred sites. From a young age, my mother enjoyed a moderate level of freedom, as my grandparents gave her the chance to make her own decisions in most aspects of her studies, career, and marriage. She was brought up as a Muslim, but that never excluded her from being given the freedom to decide how she dressed, where she worked, what she did, and whom she befriended or even flirted with. Yes, indeed, the concept of a Muslim who flirts may seem an oxymoron in most Islamic societies, but in certain parts of Turkey it was somewhat acceptable, and in my parents' case, it certainly was.

All this freedom was naturally passed on to me. My parents chose to have only one child, and they have always wanted the best for me, although they didn't ever spoil me. At any rate, my middle-class family's financial situation enabled us to live a modest lifestyle, and despite occasional bumps I was lucky to be given opportunities that many other children could only dream of. For example, I started to learn tennis at the local sports club when I was eight. It soon became a wonderful hobby, and then a serious commitment. From the age of ten I competed in national and international tournaments.

In fact, the local sports club and friendships with my teammates were what defined most of my childhood. While some traditional parents might think that sports or other extracurricular activities will undermine a child's studies, my parents believed otherwise. They taught me that, with some discipline and organization, one can do it all. They always boosted my self-confidence and helped me tap my potential. I'm extremely grateful for all the trust they had in me, for their letting me make my own decisions, and for always choosing to encourage rather than to pressure me unnecessarily in every aspect of my life. The sort of freedom and trust that I'm talking about included allowing me to travel with my teammates to tennis competitions in other cities and countries, under the supervision of our tennis coach.

Regardless of their liberal lifestyle and outlook on life, both of my parents are very spiritual and their belief systems are very dear to them as a private aspect of their personalities. In a similar way, then, they taught me from the very beginning that my spirituality was my own responsibility. Instead of being told to follow religious duties or rituals, my parents chose to leave it completely up to me and to my life experiences to develop my own spirituality, although of course they did encourage me to embrace certain fundamental values. As a teenager, my only religious ritual, besides my irregular reciting of prayers before bedtime, was fasting with my father during Ramadan, even if I only did so for a few days. My father, on the other hand, was quite disciplined in his fasting, avoiding any food or drink (including his favorite alcoholic beverage) during daylight hours for a whole month.

Although I admit that my family is far more liberal than the typical Turkish standard, it is crucial to point out that the average Turkish family is significantly more progressive than those in most other Muslim countries. The freedom to consume alcohol, for example, says a lot about the attitude of a significant portion of the Turkish public; in contrast, in some other Muslim countries it's not always easy to buy alcohol.

Turkey, a nation with an established democracy that is located at the crossroads between East and West, is home to a wide range of citizens, from strict conservative Muslims to its minority Christian and Jewish communities. Therefore, its population has diverse views about alcohol use, women wearing the veil, fasting, and even prayer. In other words, devout believers who have flexible lifestyles are not at all uncommon in Turkey.

However, there is another important reason for my personal reconciliation with spirituality that is rooted in Turkey's way of handling religion. Turkey is the only secular and democratic Muslim country, and the word "laicism" more accurately describes the true nature of the role religion plays in Turkish society. Laicism is a political system characterized by the exclusion of ecclesiastical control and influence. Secularism aims to eliminate religion from political affairs, but Turkey, like some other European countries, embraces laicism, which aims to eliminate religion from not just governance but from the greater social sphere. Therefore, in public places such as the Parliament, government buildings, and even universities, people are not allowed to wear headscarves or any other religious symbols. They can neither pray in public nor form religious associations. The pros and cons of that can be argued in another forum; here I will simply say that, under these circumstances, people generally confine religion to their most private spaces.

Having grown up within this system, then, seeking privacy for prayer was as natural as doing so for any personal act of self-expression, like crying or contemplating. For me, praying was a mundane experience that I could do anytime and anywhere I wanted to, but it was also quite personal, not a social or communal experience. Therefore, as I reflect on my first memories of attending the crowded Friday prayer in a mosque, it makes sense that I felt so out of place and isolated from the others at prayer.

Questions of faith and obligation began to crystallize in my mind as I entered adolescence and started noticing social divides. I realized that there were other reasons why I felt so isolated from the more devout worshippers. In Turkey, religion divides society, as do race, language, and income, but religion possibly more so than the others. But this divide is ironically rather intrareligious, as it occurs within one religion and is entirely based on different interpretations of rights and freedoms. These interpretations often involve a great deal of prejudice. On one side you have the "laical elite," and on the other the conservatives—or, rather, "the religious," as they like to say, to distinguish themselves from the elite.

The gap between the religious and secular groups has long polarized Turkish society. When our great leader Atatürk took a Western approach, founding Turkey based on secular values and introducing modern ideas, he put his country on the path toward modern progressive Islam. He introduced coed schools, raised the social status of women, and established a democratic regime that promoted the equal rights and absolute sovereignty of the people. But in the following periods, clashes between those who deemed religion and modernity incompatible increased, along with the gap in understanding. Unfortunately, there's a gross misunderstanding to this day between the two ends of Turkish society. The more liberal side blames the other for being "backward-minded religious people" eager to bring Sharia (Islamic law) to Turkey, while the more conservative element accuses the other of being "Atatürk-obsessed sinners/atheists" who will drive Islam out of Turkey and turn it into an atheist or non-Islamic European country.

My position, which lies somewhere between these two extremes, was so internalized that it was only after going abroad to study that I had the glorious chance to freely discover my own spirituality and to gain an understanding of the uneasy dynamics between the political and Islamic character of my country. Until the age of seventeen, I had seen very few young people who would openly question their religion, explore their spirituality, or even go so far as to deny any religious affiliation.

It was exactly this quest for different experiences and fresh perspectives that landed me at a United World College, an international high school in southern Africa. To this day, I remember the urge I had to discover new things. I had no reason to escape from Turkey, but with so much curiosity about the rest of the world, being there still felt like being stuck. With a routine life that revolved around home, school, and tennis, I was not getting any answers. So, when I heard about the national competition for a scholarship at an international high school abroad, my eyes lit up. I flashed back to memories of my first tennis tournament abroad. I was eleven years old, surrounded by competitors of my own age from many other countries: different people from different countries who spoke different languages, had different perspectives, sang and danced to different music—everything about them was just *different!*

All these differences were bliss, each of them a newly discovered treasure. The experience compelled me to question many of my fundamental beliefs instead of taking them all for granted. This is exactly what the United World Colleges do by bringing high-school students from all around the world to live and study under one roof, with the mission of "mak[ing] education a force to unite people, nations and cultures for peace and a sustainable future." There are twelve United World Colleges all around the world; I attended Waterford Kamhlaba in the Kingdom of Swaziland. Waterford Kamhlaba was established in 1963 by a small group of teachers as southern Africa's first multiracial school, a protest against South Africa's apartheid regime. Nelson Mandela, while still in prison, sent his daughters there, as did Desmond Tutu. Seretse Khama, the first president of Botswana, enrolled his son Ian, who is now the fourth president of their country. Brought to the world's attention during the struggle against the South African apartheid regime, the school was widely seen as a symbol of resistance and racial unity. To this day, it's impossible to attend this high school without the rest of your life being infused with ideas of equality, justice, and freedom. This experience was, indeed, compelling—the best thing that has happened to me in my life so far.

Located on a green hill on the outskirts of the capital, Mbabane, the school sat right in the heart of nature, close to and yet somewhat isolated from mainstream Swazi life. In this bubble populated by only a couple hundred students, our nationalities covered half the world. Words like "diversity" and "pluralism" were not just carelessly thrown around, as they often are in the United States; our reality at the school was actually based on these words and no closeted racism could survive. There was no segregation, just diversity, in part because there was no one else "of your kind" to congregate with. Nobody formed a majority there, and nobody set the rules. Students didn't come into a fixed, prevailing culture; they had to form the culture, first by finding a way to understand each other, and over time by bonding with and learning from one other.

It was at the school that I met a Muslim convert for the first time in my life. Daniel was from the Netherlands. Since he was from both a moderate Christian family and a country that has a long-held negative perspective on Islam, I was quite intrigued by Daniel's enthusiasm for Islam and wondered about the motivation for his conversion. Unlike me with my lax practices, Daniel wouldn't touch alcohol, was highly keen on fasting, and even tried to discipline himself to say the early morning prayers. Seeing a Western European, who had converted barely a year earlier, practicing Islam so much more strictly and enthusiastically than I did at the time gave me a guilty conscience. Ever since meeting Daniel, I have questioned whether I would have ever found my way to Islam and practiced it so enthusiastically if I had been born in some other part of the world. Truth be told, I do not and cannot know!

Despite his persistent encouragement, I was not able to join Daniel for prayers at five thirty in the morning—not even once! I have to admit that at that time I had not yet learned how to pray properly. I knew some prayers by heart, but the routine was still a little foreign to me and I could not bear the embarrassment of admitting my ignorance about my own religion. I did make the effort to print out some documents on how to pray, but it soon became clear that my busy academic schedule and active social life, in the engaging atmosphere of such an interesting international high school, took priority. While I was very much wrapped up in Islamic ideology and its morals, I was quite lazy—in fact rather apathetic—about practicing its ritualistic aspects. As I said before, Islam for me has been primarily a way of coming to terms with life, and I have adopted its major values.

The only time I did observe some Islamic rituals was in the process of bonding with the small Muslim community at the school. At a United World College, one's similarities to others become obvious just as easily as your contrasts. Through Islam, I could connect with others from all over the Middle East, as well as some from Asian and African countries. During the month of Ramadan, I realized that missing the very cultural essence of our traditional festivities back home had drawn me closer to the other Muslim students. I spent more time with them during that month, as we were fasting together during the daylight hours. During the Eid holiday, the celebration marking the end of Ramadan, I decided to make way for a new experience and to join our Muslim teacher from Ghana and many other Muslim friends on a visit to the biggest local mosque for this important religious service. I must say that I had quite mixed feelings; during the sermon before the prayer, I was the same ten-year-old kid feeling out of place in the mosque, but with a new intensity. You would expect that my profound experiences at the school would have made me immune to culture shock, but not in my case. I did not mind that the sermon started in Urdu, since most in attendance were from Pakistan, Bangladesh, and India, but I was shocked when the Imam began to yell as he preached, making overly dramatic gestures. The crowd responded simultaneously, and most started weeping hysterically. I did not know how to react as I observed the congregation with awe. A Pakistani friend later explained that this behavior was perfectly normal for the more conservative groups, but it was a phenomenon I could in no way relate to. However, I also discovered a rather pleasant social aspect of Islam that I had been isolated from in my home country. I saw how religion could bring people together as they practiced these otherwise unnecessary rituals. I was surprised to see strangers refer to each other as "brothers" and "sisters" and invite one another to their homes to celebrate religious holidays over a meal. This unconditional hospitality felt very genuine and inspiring to me at the time, although in retrospect I realize that this bonding could have been the result of there being a relatively small expat Muslim community in Swaziland. But whatever the reason, it was beautiful to see and to feel the sense of belonging, as it really lived up to the name of Islam, which means "peace."

The rigorous academics at UWC—we graduated with the International Baccalaureate diploma—and the college's commitment to students developing an international perspective and ways of understanding the world led me to a small college in New Hampshire. I was excited about coming to Dartmouth, particularly because of its diverse and talented student body. Despite its rather conservative reputation, Dartmouth felt like a safe haven compared to the rest of the United States, and I didn't struggle too much in trying to fit in, possibly because of my rather typical Western European-North American appearance. When questioned about my religion and beliefs, I would explain that I'm Muslim, but that in Turkey Muslims are rather secular. I realized only later that this diplomatic and somewhat elusive response was a subconscious attempt to distance myself from a much feared and isolated group. When I first arrived in the United States, the wounds of 9/11 were still fresh, and the wars in Iraq and Afghanistan kept the focus on the "war on terror"—which was pretty much understood to be a synonym for the "war on Islam." This rhetoric and the resulting stereotypes clearly damaged the country's social fabric, even among the United States' own citizens, as the line between Muslim and non-Muslim Americans was drawn more sharply than ever. As much as people in the United States might hate to face it, this line has always existed, just as it does between other ethnic groups. My exposure to the real United States that exists outside the Dartmouth bubble has shown me that the country's wonderful diversity unfortunately has not led to tolerant and integrated communities but to sharp ethnic and racial divisions.

At Dartmouth, however, I had a pretty easy time. Given the college community's above-average awareness and open-mindedness, I managed to form some strong bonds with people with whom I didn't have much in common. As I did at UWC in Swaziland, I felt at ease in connecting with many internationals, including some Muslims. I was involved in various groups and activities at Dartmouth, including the Multi-Faith Student Council, a group formed to promote interfaith dialogue on key issues.

Early in my freshman year, after having observed Ramadan with Muslim friends, I attended some Friday prayers in the tiny room allocated to Al-Nur, the Muslim student group. The group had a Muslim student adviser who took on the task of preaching *Khutba*, the Friday sermon, and it was fascinating to listen to sermons that aimed to bring together a group of very diverse individuals. Through this group I came to grasp the similarities and differences between my Muslim friends and me. I realized that my understanding of Islam was not only minimal, but also different, because of my Turkish origins. Despite any differences, I became quite close friends with a few impressive Muslims: Ahmed was from an Afghan family that sought asylum and gained U.S. citizenship right before 9/11; Ibrahim was a half-Egyptian, half-American friend who had spent all his life in New Hampshire; Adrian was a Muslim convert from a British Christian family living in the United States. These friends left deep marks on the progress of my faith.

While an average Turk might be a lot more liberal and culturally open-minded than an average Muslim living elsewhere, I would have to say that I am a lot more liberal than an average Turkish Muslim. Although I acknowledge the Quran as a holy text, I do not interpret it literally; I see it as a dense inspirational script that gives the reader much more than a mere list of tasks and duties. The idea of intention is central to all the duties and responsibilities dictated in Islam, so that everything an individual does is first and foremost evaluated according to his or her sincerity. For instance, attending a religious service will not be accepted if done with a lack of sincerity, but on the other hand, some mistakes are overlooked if the wrongdoing was not intended.

I have adopted the fundamental idea of good intentions in my own belief system; I keep my conscience relatively clean by at least trying to have the right intentions in everything that I do, even if I don't fulfill all the religious duties and practices suggested by the Quran or Hadith. In other words, for me, having the right intentions prevails over rituals, especially when I see Muslims who comply with all of their religious obligations yet lack a real understanding of what they do and why. For example, it's important to understand that the actual point of prayer is to take your time in silence to seek composure with God, to self-reflect and remember one's intentions, duties, and responsibilities. Similarly, some people break their fast at Ramadan with extravagantly rich meals and end up wasting even more food than normal, instead of making the fasting an opportunity to appreciate important blessings like food. When people practice their duties just because Islam has commanded them to do so, it defeats the whole purpose.

All in all, I like to approach religious teachings with a very open mind that will allow me to extract lessons and ideas, instead of making my religion about rituals without self-reflection. The former ten-year-old in the mosque no longer feels like a novice!

Abdul is working as a TV reporter in the Middle East, mostly based in Jerusalem, covering the Israeli-Palestinian news.

PART II

STRUGGLES WITH ISLAMOPHOBIA

5

Aly Rahim   A Muslim Citizen of the Democratic West

I drove up to the crossing in my month-old black Volkswagen Jetta. I had never been apprehensive or fearful about going back to college and crossing the Canadian border into the United States. Usually it was a largely perfunctory procedure: I would simply show my student entry forms with my passport, which would then be stamped without much scrutiny, and I would quickly be on my way to our little rural corner of New Hampshire.

But on this crossing the border agent opened the back door of my car and unzipped a duffle bag nestled in the back seat. In the bag, a traditional South Asian garment caught his eye. He looked up and asked, "What religion do you practice?" It was a simple question that I had answered countless times, but this time was different. This time I was afraid to say who I was. I did meekly provide the truthful answer, but the experience left me with the poignant realization that everything had forever changed for me. Regardless of my confidence and pride in who I was, a new emotion was now unavoidably attached to my identity—fear. Until that moment I had never feared answering questions about my religion, but now I could not help feeling this question was loaded—especially coming from an official of the U.S. government. I did not understand what consequences my answer would bring, or what the agent's intent was.

In fact, the agent did not harass me when I told him I was a Muslim. He merely commented in a sympathetic manner that he had assumed this because he had seen my "prayer clothes" in the bag, apparently unaware that a Hindu or Buddhist could have worn the same South Asian garments.

During a vigil a week later, I spoke to 250 of my peers about the post-9/11 backlash and about the fear experienced by a large segment of U.S. citizens ranging from Buddhist Tamils to Arab Muslims. Looking out over the diverse crowd, I reflected on my small but telling incident and what it meant for my life as a Muslim in North America. "As I crossed the border a little over a week ago, my heart was heavy with grief—for the innocent victims of a horrific attack, and for a world awaiting new and interminable cycles of violence." I paused, and then added, "There was another sort of emotion, however, that I harbored in my heart. An uneasy amalgam of fear, anxiety, and apprehension, for I knew my sense of identity was forever changed. I was and am no less confident of who I am; my confidence has not been shattered. But I cannot say the same for the society around me. It is a sad truth that many members of our society will forever see my identity as an irreconcilable contradiction."

Growing up in Vancouver, British Columbia, I never entertained the thought that my identity as a Muslim and a Canadian could be perceived as any sort of contradiction. Religion was always an important part of our family life, and we were very involved in the Shia Ismaili Muslim community, a closely knit, mostly South Asian community with a significant immigrant population in both Canada and the United States. My father had come to Canada in 1972 as a political refugee from Uganda following Idi Amin's expulsion of South Asians. He had arrived as an educated professional eager and willing to integrate himself into his new society. My parents taught me that my faith was no more of an impediment to my full participation in Canadian society than that of our Christian or Jewish neighbors. Granted, instead of going to church on Sunday mornings, we went to the Ismaili Jamatkhana (the mosque and community center) on Friday evenings. But religion seemed to be an important part of many of my non-Muslim friends' families, so I did not think its role in mine was unusual.

I never really experienced the proverbial second-generation "identity crisis." My family was intellectually progressive and deeply spiritual at the same time, and a strong sense of Indo-Pakistani culture imbued our home. This dualistic ideal in our family life finds its origins in the unlikely marriage of my parents. My father grew up amid the Ismaili South Asian diaspora in East Africa. The norms surrounding marriage there differed significantly from the norms in Pakistan. Having been under British rule for so many years, many East African Ismaili families adopted the Brits' more liberal customs and attitudes about dating and marriage. In fact, almost all of my father's brothers and sisters married partners of their choice. Two of his sisters married Hindus, and his younger brother married a Roman Catholic Italian—hardly traditional arrangements! For my mother's family in Pakistan, dating was an alien concept. Marriages among middle- and upper-middle-class families remained semiarranged. Such was my parents' marriage.

My father left Uganda in 1972. On his arrival in Montreal, despite being penniless, he secured the single spot available to a foreign student in Mc-Gill's dermatology training program, beating out over a hundred other candidates. By 1979 he was a licensed dermatologist with a private practice and a comfortable lifestyle. Consumed with providing for his family as they settled down in Canada, he had not given much thought to marriage. He was thirty-one years old, and most of his family had given up on his ever marrying. Unlike his siblings, my father was not particularly inclined to date or have girlfriends. He remained single and yearned for something more traditional. More than any of his siblings, he felt a strong affinity for Pakistan, South Asian culture, and Islamic values. In the summer of 1979, he decided to move to Karachi. He closed up his practice and made arrangements to sell his Montreal apartment, but this plan would not ultimately prevail. My father eventually returned to Montreal, but as a married man.

My father arrived in Karachi in every way a foreigner. His Urdu was barely passable, as his mother tongue was the north Indian language Kutchi. He spent his first month traveling—in the late 1970s it still was relatively safe to explore the beautiful northern expanses of the country—and he made his way to the verdant mountains of the Hunza and Gilgit. He delighted in the spectacular vistas and the simple but genuine hospitality of the mountain villagers. My father's dream was to purchase a jeep and administer medicine in these far-flung regions. He also wanted to find a well-educated, cultured Pakistani Ismaili wife. The ideal place to start was the Jamatkhana, the Ismaili place of worship and community center.

One evening my father went to the largest Jamatkhana in Karachi. Though not many African Ismailis came in search of Pakistani brides, there was a very structured network of matchmakers in the community. The head of the so-called marriage committee in this area of Karachi happened to be Noorjahan bhai, my *nanima* (maternal grandmother). My father was given her address and told to pay her a visit. After a long meeting with my father, my mother's parents arranged for my mother to return to Pakistan from Los Angeles where she was in a postgraduate training program at an accounting firm. After only a few meetings chaperoned by her nineteen-year-old brother, my mother, who had rejected several previous suitors, made her decision to marry my father.

My father had a very different background from my mother, having grown up in Uganda and spent seven years living in Canada. Yet he continued to feel a strong affinity for the subcontinent, particularly for the emergent aspirations of the new state of Pakistan and the South Asian Muslim culture it celebrated. Although his siblings had adopted more liberal marriage practices, my father felt that, by marrying a wife who was brought up directly in the traditional culture and with whom he shared a common foundation of Ismailism, he could create a family more in line with the values of the "homeland."

In many ways, therefore, the beginning of my family was not so much a continuation of tradition as it was a conscious return to tradition, if also a traditionalism infused with modernist intellectualism. Towers of books have always filled an entire floor of our home. The library shelves long ago reached their capacity, and new books find a place in some haphazard pile. Scanning the spines, you might see Herman and Chomsky's *Manufacturing Consent*, a book on Sufi mystical traditions, and a volume of Wordsworth's poetry all stacked together. Education is a common theme in immigrant families of any ethnic stripe—computer science, engineering, business, and premed are considered legitimate academic pursuits by many South Asian parents, and I observed this phenomenon with cousins and friends of my generation.

However, in my family the function and value of education differed from the norm. My brothers and I never felt any pressure from our parents to change our academic orientation, although such pressure is not unusual in immigrant communities. My eldest paternal cousin is a striking example. My father's success as a dermatologist has become a sort of model for our extended family, and my cousin's parents pressed him to pursue premed studies throughout his undergraduate career, constantly reminding him of the standard of living enjoyed by my father and our family. When the time came for my cousin to apply to medical school, his efforts, along with my dad's counsel, paid off. My cousin gained admission to the medical school at the University of British Columbia. It took him four years of undergraduate toil to get in, and another two and a half years in medical school to realize that he was living his parents' dream, not his own. He dropped out. I never confronted such pressure.

I sometimes reflect on why my parents' educational ideals were so different from those of many of my South Asian peers. Our economic comfort was not necessarily distinct; many of my friends' parents were successful in business or medicine, yet they still pressured their children to pursue an education in those fields. The Ismaili community has an especially strong bent toward success in business.

It was a crisp but sunny Vancouver afternoon. The spring rain, for which the city is famous, had abated for at least a day, and my parents and I were enjoying a walk along the seawall. On our left, the Pacific inlet lapped up against the concrete walkway, and on our right loomed the backdrop of the majestic coastal mountains of British Columbia. The last quarter of my junior year would begin in just a few days, and being home for spring break was a much-needed sojourn. My parents loved these walks and insisted I join them when I was in town. We'd inevitably cross paths with a few West Vancouver Ismailis. That day, we were chatting about my recent experience volunteering in Karachi when we ran into Zubeen Suleiman, who had attended school with my father in Kampala, and his son Rafiq, with whom I had graduated from school. "How are you, Uncle?" I asked, using the term of respect used by most Ismailis when addressing male elders.

Mr. Suleiman, a wealthy Vancouver hotelier and the quintessential Canadian Ismaili businessman, asked me, "So, Aly, have you decided what you will be doing after next year?"

I hesitated, knowing that Mr. Suleiman would be puzzled by my reply. "Well, I'm going to continue with my studies in international affairs. I'm hoping to get my master's degree before I start working."

"OK," he said uncertainly, "what will you do after that?"

I tried to explain as succinctly and confidently as possible. "I'm interested in international security, and want to work in foreign affairs for the Canadian government or for an international organization like the UN."

"There's very little money in that, you know," he retorted. "Malik Mansoor's son is graduating from Dartmouth," he said, referring to another Ismaili student. "He'll be working in venture capital in New York. Why aren't you doing something like that?"

I tried to explain why I wanted a career that reflected my intellectual passions and moral convictions, but Mr. Suleiman simply could not comprehend this: "Someone as smart as you could be earning so much. You must have some great ideas; why waste all the effort and expense of being educated at such an expensive school in America?"

Mr. Suleiman was not at all uncharacteristic of other immigrant Ismailis of his generation. As immigrants from one diaspora in East Africa to another in North America, the Ismailis distinguished themselves primarily by being savvy in business. The perception of Ismailis as dynamic businesspeople is a central part of the Ismaili identity in Canada's multi-cultural fabric. During the last recession, the prime minister Jean Chrétien joked that what his hometown of Shawinigan, Quebec, lacked was "a dozen Ismaili entrepreneurs." An enterprising and affluent entrepreneur epitomizes the Ismaili immigrant success story. Many members of the community are therefore baffled if a young Ismaili attempts to pursue something outside the realm of business or medicine. Education is undoubtedly considered vital, but most older Ismailis regard it as a means to an end—not as a time for intellectual and personal development, but as preparation for professional success.

My parents always stressed educational attainment, but I was never expected to conform to this conventional image of Canadian Ismaili success. They considered professional success important, but education was an end in and of itself. I was raised to see college as a time to engage the ideas that have animated civilizations, to grapple with the social, cultural, scientific, and political issues confronting societies in wide-ranging disciplines, to read great literature, and to unravel the lessons contained in the history of the world. Though politics was my passion from a young age, I was dedicated to the notion of a liberal arts education—a concept that has little currency in Canada, let alone in the Canadian Ismaili Muslim community.

Increasing numbers of Ismaili Canadians are turning to what they see as the next level of educational attainment by applying to Ivy League and other top-tier U.S. schools; most are applying to graduate schools, but more and more are also looking to U.S. colleges. An overwhelming number still focus on a narrow range of disciplines. As an Ismaili undergrad pursuing a liberal arts degree, with a major in government and no inclination to pursue a corporate career, I am not entirely unique, but my choices are contrary to the conventions of success in my community. My parents sometimes explain to their Ismaili friends that other Dartmouth students with the same major continue into investment banking or consulting careers, earning between $50,000 and $100,000 their first year out of college. While their friends are often puzzled as to why I would not immediately grab such an opportunity, my parents state this fact with pride and believe that I have made choices based on my convictions rather than on the conventions of success in our community.

My social experiences have also often diverged significantly from those of most of my peers. During my senior year, a professor invited me to join a discussion group of about ten seniors. Each week the professor assigned us literature that was to touch off a discussion. The objective was to examine life, following somewhat from the Socratic principle that the unexamined life is not worth living. The group met every Monday night for an hour or two to examine a topic that brought meaning to all our lives. The ten of us, who were varied in academic interests, gender, and ideologies, showed up simply to experience an unusual and sustained form of shared introspection.

One evening, when we were discussing choices we make in life, the professor posed a question: "If you could remove any incident from your life, what would it be?" This was a compelling question, and I racked my brain for an answer, trying to recall some childhood blunder, life-changing decision, or traumatic event.

Bill raised his hand and began, "Well, there was this time sophomore year…" His story began comfortably in the everyday trappings of Dartmouth life. Bill explained that he and his girlfriend had set a date at Ben & Jerry's, but that his friend e-mailed him to tell him to come by his room beforehand. When he got to his friend's room, a marijuana pipe was being passed around. Bill couldn't resist and got "really high." He forgot his date, she found out why, and the romance came to an end.

Where Bill left off, Danielle started eagerly into her story: "Well, I first started dating Michael during senior year in high school and then I left for Dartmouth…" She earnestly explained the story of her "hometown honey," recounting how she "was torn between my loyalty to Michael and all the new and interesting men I was meeting at Dartmouth." I clenched my teeth. If this theme persisted, I would have to say something.

Josh piped in next about an ex-girlfriend at Dartmouth who found out he had gotten back together with his high-school girlfriend. After each sorrowful admission about how some relationship was lost because of thoughtlessness or stupidity, the rest of the group would murmur in collective understanding. But I just sat there, nervously, trying to make my silence inconspicuous.

Nevertheless, my turn did finally arrive, and I mumbled rather inconsequentially, "I don't have much to offer on this theme, but—"

"Wait a minute," the professor interjected, interrupting me midsentence. He had remained silent up until then, but it seemed that he had picked up on something in my voice, something that betrayed the fact that there was a deeper issue at heart. Furrowing his brow, he looked at me intently and asked, "Is there something more here? What do you mean when you say you don't have much to offer on this theme?"

One requirement of the group was a high degree of openness, but I hesitated, not knowing whether my fellow students would understand. I tried to shrug off the probing, saying, "Well, it's quite complicated; I'm not sure I should get into it."

The professor did not relent. "There's enough time to explain. We'll hear it if you'll say it."

And so I began, "I have never had a romantic relationship in my twenty-one years..."

As a Muslim, I will not have sex before marriage. Issues of dating or physical intimacy have always been wrapped up in questions of my faith and culture. I never so much as kissed a girl during my four years at Dartmouth, a fact I'm reluctant to admit to any but friends. I'm not embarrassed, but I also don't want to have to explain. Unlike many Muslims, I anticipate having some degree of physical and emotional intimacy with women before marriage. But I see dating as something I will engage in only a few times and when there is sufficient reason, such as when I meet someone with whom I connect ethnically and religiously. This person must be emotionally and intellectually attractive to me, and there must be serious potential for her to be a life partner.

My decisions to remain a virgin and to date only if I see a potential life partner placed me on the margins of my campus's social scene. Because of my faith, I do not drink. Since sexuality and alcohol are cornerstones of the American collegiate experience, my time at college was pretty atypical. The Dartmouth I experienced over my four years is probably very different from what many of my peers will remember of theirs. I have no stories about sexual encounters with girls I met in frat basements, no nostalgic tales about that brilliant and beautiful girl I dated during junior year, no whimsical anecdotes about drunken escapades. Even my most mild-mannered friends can share at least something on one of these scenarios.

Despite my lacking in some typical social experiences, during my first three years at Dartmouth, I never felt particularly marginalized because I was a Muslim student. I had always been vocal on a range of political issues and prided myself on being a political liberal. While at Dartmouth, I headed a number of nonpartisan political-affairs groups, and never felt that my involvement or leadership was ever questioned because of my Muslim heritage. After 9/11, however, the comfort zone started to contract. Having an openly Muslim identity in an increasingly hostile public arena is a daunting experience. I have read virulent columns by tenured professors at elite universities attacking Islam as intrinsically violent and hateful. I have sat through lectures at Dartmouth at which my religion was derided as a dangerous ideology. These hateful currents are increasingly strong, and a growing interest in the Islamic world has created fertile ground for provocative and incendiary opinions. I find myself being more and more on the defensive, having to explain why I can be both a part of

North American society and a Muslim. It is draining to constantly feel that you have to be on the defensive and to justify who you are, which I am beginning to increasingly resent. These challenges seem relentless, and not always separate or impersonal.

A little more than four months after the terrorist attacks, I found myself at a luncheon with a visiting fellow at Dartmouth. This former U.S. intelligence officer was invited to share the insights he had gained during his extended activity in the Middle East. Fifteen of my peers were comfortably seated in a large, homey living room, while the visitor sat stiffly in an oversized armchair. The questions and discussion wandered through the quirks of Middle East history and U.S. foreign policy. I raised my hand and asked, "What can be done to support democratization in the Islamic world?"

By this time, the speaker was well aware that I was a Muslim. He looked at me sharply and answered pointedly, "Islam and democracy cannot co-exist. You cannot accept the principles of democracy and Islam at the same time." He went on to substantiate his answer with what he felt was relevant evidence drawn from his reading of Islamic doctrine.

I sat in shock at his answer, which affirmed the fear I had referred to in my speech a few months earlier. I was confronting head-on the sad truth that many members of our society will forever see my identity as an irreconcilable contradiction. Uneducated anti-Muslim rants I could handle, but hearing such a specious opinion expressed as scholarly "evidence" by a former member of the U.S. foreign-policy establishment was terrifying. I looked around at my peers. How did such words affect them? I sank into my seat, my stomach knotted with anger and confusion. I was immobilized by his stinging implication that I could not be a true member of this democracy if I am a Muslim.

I worried that his explanations would convince my peers that I was confronting some sort of epic decision where I would have to decide between Islam and democracy. Although no such decision has confronted me, or millions of other North American Muslims, the myth of divided loyalty has been perpetuated by hatemongers and buttressed by self-proclaimed Islamic experts. My loyalty is undoubtedly being called into question, and I cannot help but have a new and uncertain sense of vulnerability. I know that I do not feel a contradiction in my identity, that I do not consider myself a false Muslim or a false Canadian, and I am unsure how to respond to such ideas.

During the spring of my senior year, the former prime minister of Israel, Ehud Barak, visited Dartmouth. His visit coincided with heightened tensions in the Middle East, as troops were being mobilized in and around cities throughout the West Bank. After a speech that characterized the United States and Israel as kindred spirits in a war against terror, a theme that most of the audience seemed to embrace, I got up to ask Barak a question. I asked him why the number of settlers in the West Bank had increased by 100 percent after the 1993 Oslo peace accords if the Israeli government acknowledged a Palestinian right to sovereignty over the area.

After the lecture, a friend of mine overheard a comment outside the auditorium. A student said to his friend, "That Aly Rahim—if he was not Canadian and a bleeding-heart liberal, he would have a bomb strapped to his chest." When my friend told me this, I felt an intellectual insecurity for the first time. If I tried to voice a dissenting opinion about foreign policy that involves Muslims, would I be branded as a potential terrorist?

There is another dimension of my post-9/11 experience that I never expected. Visible and violent hatred is deplorable, but at least it can be easily identified. But the insidious workings of educated minds cause me great concern. Two months after 9/11, I was talking with two of my close friends, intending to highlight what I thought was unjustifiable ignorance. I innocently related an experience my brother had had a few days earlier as he flew from Toronto to New York. "My brother was flying back to Princeton," I started. "He was sitting a few seats back from two twenty-something Indian guys. The two guys happened to have beards, and were sitting next to each other. Some passenger told the flight attendant that these two seemed suspicious. In a few minutes the police showed up and escorted the two men off the plane, based simply on that tip. The plane was grounded for an hour as it was searched." I was indignant about what I felt was a ridiculous incident, but my friends' responses led me to realize I had not grasped the reality of my post-9/11 world. I discovered a type of visceral reaction that was shared by many more people than I had anticipated. I looked at the odd expressions my two friends wore and said, "Well, that could have been me. If you didn't know me, and you saw me on a plane, would you be scared? Would you report me as suspicious?"

My friend Adam looked cautiously at me. "I wouldn't report you, but..." and he stopped. It seemed he was too sympathetic to follow through with his answer.

Nevertheless, his "but" had already given me an obvious answer. If Adam did not know me, he would be afraid to see me on a plane. I was not willing to leave it there. "You know me, you have other South Asian friends—Indians and Pakistanis, Muslims and Hindus—but you'd still feel scared if you saw someone who looked just like your friends?" By now I was agitated. Brown skin does not redden easily, but I was probably approaching some shade of crimson. I prodded, "Does this seem rational to you?"

Adam's reply gave me remarkable insight, into not only what my friend was thinking, but also what I could expect to confront in the post-9/11 world. It was not malice, or ignorance, or hatred. It was something entirely different. "I know it's not rational," Adam explained. "In my mind I know it's nonsense and doesn't make sense. It's a fear I can't reason away. I feel miserable that I feel it, but I am being honest."

"But you would not act on your fear?" I asked.

"No," Adam replied. "That I can reason away. I know the fear is irrational."

Our friend Terence said he would react in the same way. Despite having close friends of South Asian descent, these two bright Dartmouth students said they would feel a visceral fear if they saw someone with my skin tone on a plane. At least they were aware that this had nothing to do with any rational processes, that it was an instinctual response, and they had the capacity not to act on what they knew was irrational. But what would happen with other people who could not recognize that their fear was irrational? I had assumed that such fears belonged to ignorant people I would not have to meet, but my friends' comments left me shocked at how pervasive such feelings were.

Since 9/11, I have not been beaten or been the target of racial epithets. My challenge has been a more subtle and insidious assault on my identity. I am far more fearful of educated intolerance than of sheer ignorance. The university professor who uses authoritative scholarship to explain why Islam and Muslims are anathema to the West terrifies me far more than the evangelical pastor preaching from the pulpit. I have always been proud of my distinct identity, and have never had a desire to be assimilated. Being considered a dangerous presence in my own society was not part of the picture, but it has been since 9/11. I am not going to feign assimilation to gain security, although I have found myself considering this option.

I know that educating the people around me is the most effective thing I can do to help them understand who I am. With that in mind, I chat openly with friends or acquaintances about how I live with Islam every day as an American college student. I have spoken to middle-school children so they can see that Muslims are not necessarily menacing bearded men in some distant part of the world. I have given speeches, spoken to administrators, sat on panels, and given interviews to my college newspaper about my experience after 9/11 in the hope that my fears and the fears of my fellow Muslims are understood. During one panel discussion with three other Muslims, I sat before more than two hundred of my Dartmouth peers. At the end of my talk, I summed up in five words the message that I am so eager to convey—"I am not the enemy."

The Islam that has informed much of my twenty-one years has always been spiritually liberating and intellectually stimulating. It has taught me to be accepting of diversity and to have a strong cosmopolitan outlook. Growing up in Canada and attending college in the United States has never been impeded by my faith. I have attended some of the best schools and pursued an eclectic mix of intellectual interests, and I have enjoyed an active social life (albeit sans sex and alcohol) with friends of many religions and ethnicities. I have always been open about my faith, and although people close to me have been very accepting, I was always aware that in many circles, educated and uneducated alike, Islam has been and continues to be derided as some sort of vast institution of backwardness. I never paid any attention to this viewpoint, which I dismissed as mere ignorance. But since 9/11, I have become hesitant to be open about my identity with all people, especially when I sense this sort of ignorance. Even though I have experienced a derisive comment here or a slur there, I am still boldly optimistic that the democratic world's pluralistic ethic will prevail. I am and will remain a full-fledged Muslim citizen of the democratic West.

After graduating from Dartmouth, Aly went on to earn a master's degree from Georgetown. He then served with Canada's Department of Foreign Affairs and is currently a social development specialist at the World Bank. He lives in the Washington, DC, area with his wife and daughter.

This essay was written in the months following September 11, 2001, and was first published in *Balancing Two Worlds: Asian American College Students Tell Their Life Stories*, ed. Andrew Garrod and Robert Kilkenny (Ithaca, NY: Cornell University Press, 2007).

6

Shakir Quraishi   Living Like a Kite

It was a morning like any other. I was sitting in my seventh-grade classroom in Lansing, Michigan, struggling to understand what Mr. Gump was talking about—it had been only an hour or so since we had arrived at school. Then, quite unexpectedly, a couple of men equipped with impressive video cameras entered the room and began to interview the students. I concentrated on their words, trying to get an idea of why this was happening; however, as a recent immigrant, I could not understand a thing. I remember vividly that one of my classmates, a tall African American student, was talking into the lens of the camera as tears streamed down his cheeks. My first thought was that something terrible had happened to his family. Soon after, school was dismissed, and as I happily climbed onto the bus to go home, the image of the African American student haunted me. What had happened to the poor kid? I hoped his family was doing well. It did not take long, however, for my thoughts to shift back to the joy of early dismissal.

Since I knew no English, going to school was a curse. There were no English as a second language (ESL) courses at our school, which meant that I was placed in exactly the same classes as everyone else. I had no idea what was going on about 99 percent of the time—I did not understand English, and obviously my teacher did not speak Dari, the language we spoke in my home country of Afghanistan. Even following such simple directions as "Turn to page 223" was difficult for me, so I would just hunker down in my seat during class and stare at the textbook, looking forward to lunch and recreation time in the gym. During lunch I would sit next to a Bosnian kid, since I could relate to his Muslim background even though I could not speak to him. After the first couple of weeks, I had gotten used to classes, although every moment was a struggle. I would often return home after school and cry for hours because I had so little idea of what was going on in my classroom.

Despite my obvious struggles, I received very little help from anyone in the school. My daily routine was this: I would go to school and sit in a classroom with teachers and students, without understanding a single word any of them uttered. I would anxiously wait for the lunch period, and after lunch I repeated the same routine and waited for the after-school bell. I felt intensely lonely because I had no friends at the time, and I would ignore the students who did approach me, because I viewed myself as an outsider. After all, I was very different from them and one of only three Muslims in the entire school. My language challenges combined with my foreign background and shy nature left me isolated and often hating school, which was ironic since my family had undertaken the arduous journey to the United States precisely to give us better educational opportunities.

Returning to that fateful day, I remember leaving school and thinking of the joy of being out of the classroom. As soon as I opened our front door, I saw my family gathering next to our old wooden-cased television set, which was repeatedly showing pictures of two buildings being hit by airplanes as clouds of smoke lifted into the air. As I gazed at the startling images, I figured out that my classmate had shed tears because of the attacks in New York—an event that, more than any other in the history of the United States, encouraged American Muslims to search for their identity. Overnight, our religion had become an important and very apparent part of the everyday lives of the Muslim community, and many Muslims felt threatened. At the time, I was deeply religious; however, if I had been asked what that meant, I would have been unable to give an answer. My religious beliefs came not from any intellectual questioning of spirituality but from my deep cultural roots in Afghanistan, where religious beliefs and cultural practices are deeply interwoven, and where the latter often override the former.

My grandparents hailed from a village called Kodaman, located north of Kabul, but I had lived in the capital all of my life. Because of the fighting, we fled Kabul for northern Afghanistan when I was six. My family hoped to eventually escape our war-torn country via Russia and to settle in a European country, an all-too-common path for the many Afghans seeking a better life for their children. While I was too young to recall exactly what we had to go through to get onto a northbound plane, I have a vivid memory of the day we set out on our journey. I remember standing in front of our house in the Khair Khana neighborhood of Kabul. The house was separated from the public by high mud walls on all four sides, and the rooms were also made of mud. The roof was supported by tall chinar trees. I remember the feeling of being protected by the tall dead trees that had once stood proudly in Kodaman.

In the house, we had created a little garden and were raising pets. We had a dog, two ducks, a goat, and several chickens. In order to save money on groceries, we grew our own vegetables and used the eggs from the chickens and the milk from the goat. We had created our little haven in the chaotic city of Kabul; this was, however, soon to come to an end.

On a warm summer night in 1993, our house was robbed. At about two o'clock in the morning, several men equipped with AK-47s entered the courtyard and forced our neighbor to come and knock on our door for medicine. When my mother answered the door, the robbers burst in, grabbing my father and tying him with the clothes we had left out to dry. They locked one of my sisters and my brothers with my mother in the bathroom, while I was still asleep in the living room. After demanding cash from my mom, they went through all of our possessions and the storage rooms in search of valuable goods. Luckily none of us was injured, but by pointing guns at my sister and threatening to kill my parents, these men left my family with permanent scars.

Desperate to find a safe environment for their children, my parents felt compelled to move to northern Afghanistan. We were forced to leave most of our belongings behind, including our pets. At the time, there were few commercial flights, so we flew in a huge military plane that was to start its journey late in the evening. All the seats were along the walls, with the cargo in the center. By the time we boarded the plane it was already dark; there was no lighting, so it was hard to see the faces of the other passengers. At only six years of age, I had become very attached to our home in Kabul and to the families who lived there, and I was afraid, nervous, and uncertain about what the future held for us.

As the plane flew over the snow-covered Hindu Kush Mountains, the temperature inside the plane dropped drastically. It was as if we were sitting in a room with the air conditioning on too high. My mother sat with her back to the cold, metal walls, wearing a blue burqa. As the plane became colder, she spread her burqa over my brothers and me to cover us from the increasing chill, "as a hen covers her eggs before they hatch," she would later tell us. We all squeezed together, shaking as if we were in a freezer. My mother protected us, as she did in the years to come, while sacrificing her own warmth and desires.

We eventually reached the town of Hairatan and were taken to stay at a guesthouse. It was primarily used for Russian diplomats visiting Afghanistan and was one of the most luxurious places I have lived in to this day. The concrete walls were covered by beautiful wallpaper decorated with green tree branches climbing the cream-colored background. The house had three bedrooms, and its location was stunning, with the river running through our backyard. Twice a day we were served meals that included fruit, vegetables, and fresh bread—luxuries that were unheard of for many families, whose food usually consisted of rice and several side dishes. Everything we needed was provided at the guesthouse. It was as if we had landed in paradise.

This paradise, however, was soon to become a memory. After living there for a couple of months, our lives took another sudden turn. We were moved to a two-room, dorm-like apartment with no kitchen, and only public bathrooms outside the buildings. The educational opportunities that we had hoped for remained only a dream.

In Hairatan, my father started a kite store. He commuted to Mazar-e-Sharif to buy supplies—kites of different colors, sizes, and designs. From time to time, my brother and I would buy kites from the store to fly ourselves. Nothing was greater fun than flying kites and fighting with others in the sky. We would fly the kites up and down the beautiful skies of Hairatan. Any time the kites would fly up and down, it would make me think of the stark highs and lows of our daily lives. Inevitably, we would lose our kites, and our dreams would crash to the sandy ground, bringing us back to the harsh realities of our life. Life in Hairatan was not promising for various reasons—we did not have a stable financial income, the education system was in shambles, and every aspect of our lives was uncertain.

We were obviously desperate to escape to Europe. In Afghanistan, it is a cultural practice to go to the shrines of revered scholars or your ancestors to ask for help. It was usually women who attended these shrines, where they would tie a *janda*, a piece of cloth, to a tree and pray—sometimes to the dead—for their wish to be granted. Though the ritual is strictly forbidden in Islam, the practice is still very common in most Muslim countries. My mother tied a janda at one of the shrines, but that did not help us reach our goal. After several months of hard work and many sacrifices by my parents, we settled for going to Pakistan, the next best option after Russia and Europe.

While our life improved in Pakistan, there was no guaranteed future or security there, despite the great concentration of Afghans living in

Islamabad. In fact, there were many Afghan restaurants, hotels, bakeries, grocery stores, jewelry shops, and even bookstores. This made raising children easier for my parents because many locals knew our language and culture. However, because of the mixture of Afghan and Pakistani populations, there were many street gangs. One day a huge gang of Pakistanis, mostly college-age students, came to a central meeting place for Afghans called Peshawar Mor with cricket bats and other weapons to crack down on the Afghan shops. They damaged many store signs and display cases and tried to beat up store clerks. While most of the store owners found an escape, some were severely injured. The police showed up thirty minutes later to chase the gang away, but the damage had been done and nobody was held accountable for it. We became acutely aware that any day, any hour, any minute, anything could happen to us. There were no courts to fight for us, no politicians to stand behind us, and no policemen to protect us. Nevertheless, after a couple of years in Pakistan, our new life was beginning to take shape, and although we were all making sacrifices, my family's situation was much better than before. While we were struggling financially, my parents always taught us certain values—in fact, while we lived in Pakistan, my father was known for his honest reputation.

On one occasion, my father cashed a check at a local store, and because of a transactional error, the clerk gave my father 20,000 rupees more than he was supposed to; by comparison, our monthly income was around 15,000 rupees. Without any hesitation and contrary to a friend's suggestion, my father returned the money and informed the clerk of the error. I believe this incident says a lot about my father's personality and character.

My father was also altruistic. I remember how the community once raised money to sacrifice a couple of cows during the Eid al-Adha, a holiday when Muslims sacrifice animals and donate the meat to the poor. Someone had suggested that it would be better to make these sacrifices in Afghanistan, where the money would reach a bigger community. My father took it upon himself to make the exhausting trip to Kabul, and on his own dime. The trip meant that he would be away from his family for the festivities of Eid, a major Muslim holiday. I was fortunate to accompany him on the trip; sadly, that was our last major journey together. My father died soon after that trip, which was a major shock to all of us. The death of my father left my oldest brother, who was only twelve at the time, to become the man of the house.

While my father's death was without question a major setback, it also opened a new door for his family. In Pakistan nothing was guaranteed for us—being threatened by gang members and harassed by the police was a normal part of life. For quite some time, my parents, always in search of better opportunities for their children, had tirelessly tried to escape Pakistan for the West by applying to various programs and talking to different foreign embassies. However, all of our attempts to escape the country seemed hopeless. After the death of *pader jan*, as we called our father, we decided to apply to the United Nations, which was accepting applications from single mothers for emigration to the United States. After an interview, we were lucky enough to be one of the few families accepted. The authorities decided to send us to the state of Michigan, a location that we knew nothing about. All we knew was that we were going to *Amrika* and we knew that it was a good thing. It had been exactly a year since the death of my father when we boarded the plane to come to "Amrika."

After two days of traveling across the globe, from one city to another, we reached the city of Lansing. It was probably ten o'clock at night when we finally landed, exhausted. We were housed in a three-bedroom home, which seemed amazingly large to me. The first floor of the house alone was bigger than most of the places we had lived in. The furniture consisted only of mattresses on the floor and a couple of old couches in the living room. The local refugee office had stored food in the fridge so we could cook for ourselves. One major problem was that the front door did not have a lock. Since we were not sure about the security in Lansing, we piled some furniture behind the door and slept in the living room for the first few days. Being jet-lagged, we would go to bed really early in the evening and wake up very early every morning. Bit by bit, we were learning to adapt to a new culture and a new environment, while we anxiously awaited the beginning of the school year.

As we were adapting to this new culture, we faced many challenges. We did not have money for food, and did not even know where the supermarkets were, how to buy food, or even what types of foods were available to us in this new country. Even such a simple task as lighting the stove was tricky. For weeks we walked half a mile to use a pay phone, only to find out later that there was one right across the street from our house. This is only one example of how difficult even trivial tasks seemed as we were adapting to a new culture. We moved to Virginia two months later because my aunt lived there. In Richmond we experienced even more and greater difficulties.

For three weeks or so, we lived with my aunt. With the help of a local Afghan cosigner, we were then able to move into a three-bedroom apartment, where we would live for the next ten years. Although we got the apartment, we were not sure how we would pay the rent. At that time, my oldest sister, Freba, and my mother took most of the responsibilities into their hands—a unique situation for them, given that we come from a culture where women's responsibilities typically do not extend beyond the household. Freba began working at a 7-Eleven store near our house, while also helping at Bundle of Joy, a day-care center where two of my cousins had previously worked. Richmond's public transportation only serves part of the city, so having a car there is essential; however, we could not afford one at the time. This meant that my sister, who worked from early in the morning to past ten o'clock at night, would have to walk two miles to and from work, regardless of what the weather was like. Though this was not much of a burden during fall and spring, it was a major challenge during the winter, when the days were shorter and the temperature would grow intolerably cold. Freba would walk through the dark, foggy morning wearing slippery sneakers and a light coat donated by the refugee office, not returning home until it was dark once again.

Eventually my sister Adella also started working at the Bundle of Joy day care after school, where she would stay until the center closed each night. To get in a few extra hours, she took on the after-hours cleaning. One evening when we had some guests, my mother sent me to go and walk back with Adella. I remember seeing her through the windows of the dark center, and it was as if I could feel the fear in her heart. While cleaning, she was the only person left at the center, and she would then face the two-mile walk back home—getting home late at night, before she would need to get up for school at eight o'clock the following morning to repeat the cycle. Eventually both Freba and Adella would stay to do the cleaning, and one of the janitors was kind enough to give them a ride home at the end of each day.

My mother made most of the sacrifices for our family. She worked at a local hotel as a housekeeper. After returning from work, she would cook us dinner and, to make some extra cash on the side, she also catered food for Afghan, Pakistani, and Iranian families. It was pretty common for her to stay up until two, three, or even four o'clock in the morning to cook for these families, and then wake up at seven the next morning for work.

These experiences provide just a glimpse of the sacrifices my mom and my sisters have made over the past ten years. Despite their extremely hard work, we were barely making ends meet. Their sacrifices helped motivate and inspire me to work hard in school. How could I not, when the women in my family were enduring so much for my benefit?

My mom, who prayed five times a day, frequently acknowledged the fact that "without God's help, we would not be able to survive in these conditions." For my siblings and me, however, faith was merely a part of our cultural lives. We would fast and pray during Ramadan, but aside from that, religion did not have much significance for us. Our focus was on performing well in school.

In Richmond, school was much better than it had been in Lansing, and I began to grasp the material as my English improved dramatically. I ended up passing the ESL exit test halfway through the eighth grade. Moreover, I was performing really well in my classes—during my second year in the United States, I managed to get almost straight As, except for a B in English. My academic success was a result of numerous sacrifices I was making at the time, including doing without any fun activities. At home, for example, while my family watched television, I locked myself away, spending hours on simple homework assignments. I knew I had to work ten times harder to get the same results as most of my peers. And I did.

By the time I got to Henrico High School, where more than 80 percent of the student body was African American, the social impact 9/11 was having on Muslims was becoming clearer. I occasionally was the butt of jokes for many students, mainly because of my Afghan Muslim background. I remember being in math class the first week of school; the teacher was working on a problem on the board, and I raised my hand to ask a question. She called on me, and as soon as I asked the question, half of the class burst into laughter because of my accent. This was a major shock to my self-esteem, and it discouraged me from participating again in the classroom. Soon, incidents like that became part of my normal routine—a part I was determined to fight. During my freshman year, the students called my siblings and me such names as "Osama" or "Taliban." The insults and name-calling made me question my talents and my abilities and greatly affected my confidence. I did not have the urge to argue with these high-school students, and for that matter, I did not even have the language skills to do so. My response to everything, therefore, was silence. It was perhaps my only option, and I learned to use it as a tool. I would go to class, sit in my chair, and not say anything unless I was directly asked a question. As a result, I got to know only two or three students each semester, and my isolation allowed me to succeed academically, as it kept me away from the trap of "having too much fun" in the first years of high school. Students did approach me in an attempt to get to know me better; this was apparent especially when I was succeeding academically. At the time, silence seemed like a great defense; however, by the start of sophomore year, I began to see its negative consequences.

In tenth grade, I took some of the most challenging courses available. Perhaps the most difficult was comparative government. For that class, we had to write a one-page reflection on an assigned reading, and the teacher asked everyone to share their work. Luckily, I was not the first one called on. However, as my turn was approaching, I became more nervous. When the teacher looked at me, expecting me to go to the front of the class to read my reflection, I said I did not want to read it aloud. I was too nervous—my hands were turning white and I was trembling. After all, most of the kids in the classroom had known each other since sixth grade, whereas I was just an outsider. I had not gotten to know any of them because of my silence and shyness, and it was not possible for me to talk in front of those twenty students. The teacher then asked one of my classmates to read my writing. I learned a lot from this event, most of all that my silence was perhaps no longer a tool but a barrier. Now that my English had improved, I could see that it was time to give up my silence and begin talking to other students, learning from them, feeling comfortable around them—telling them who I was as a Muslim and not running away from my religious and cultural identity.

As I took ever-more challenging courses, the students I interacted with were more aware and appreciative of my background. My fragile self-esteem, however, still prevented me from participating fully in many of the class discussions. While I tried to make friends in high school, my interactions with them were limited to the classroom and lunch table. My mother would not allow us to hang out with friends outside school, as she was protective and did not want us to be exposed to drugs, sex, gangs, or violence. I also could not afford to accompany my friends to the local restaurants. Naturally, and unfortunately, I did not form many close friendships in high school. My life was limited to school, work, and the rooms of our three-bedroom apartment. My siblings and I did not even play with the kids in the neighborhood.

By the time I was a senior, however, I was able to ace my courses and take major leadership positions at the school. I served as president of the student government and was one of the leaders for the countywide student congress, in addition to running a few clubs. These leadership roles allowed me not only to challenge myself but to go beyond my comfort zone. I was also on the varsity soccer team, though I must admit that I was never very good. I usually sat on the bench without a uniform because my school could not afford to provide them for everyone. However, I was very dedicated to the team—I went to every game and was there for every single day of practice. I showed this same dedication to most of the activities I participated in.

From my experiences in high school, I learned that if one works hard, very few things are impossible. Today I am a huge believer in the power of the mind. If we can get in the right mind-set and are willing to make personal sacrifices, we can achieve almost any goal. Neither of my parents had been to college. In fact, my father had dropped out of high school, and my mother, because of her family's circumstances, received no formal schooling. Combined with the fact that my mother spoke no English and knew nothing about U.S. culture, my parents' lack of education put us at a great disadvantage with most of our peers. On the bright side, however, the fact that my mother was uneducated gave her the drive to do whatever it took to give her children the best education possible. Even though I always questioned my chances of succeeding in college, my mother pushed me to work hard and excel academically. Moreover, I have never used the disadvantages caused by my parents' limited education as an excuse for not doing well—I have always held myself to really high standards and worked relentlessly to reach my goals.

When I was eighteen, my sister Adella enrolled at Virginia Commonwealth University and my brother Omaid began attending the University of Richmond. These developments encouraged me to think I had a chance of getting into college too. After graduating from high school, I considered taking a gap year to work full-time in order to support my family, but whenever any of us talked about working or taking a gap year, my mother and sister would say, "No, stay in school," or, "You should finish your studies." It is clear that both of them made great sacrifices so that we younger siblings could get an education.

During the summer before I matriculated at Dartmouth, I was working nearly seven days every week to help support the family. On my days off, I spent time with my family, especially my brothers. We would play chess, read books, and, on rare occasions, fly homemade plastic kites. Kite flying is very common in Afghanistan and a big part of Pakistani culture as well; when we were kids in Pakistan, flying kites was the activity we most enjoyed. In Richmond, one of my brothers made kites from plastic bags and pieces of a wooden broomstick. On one of my days off, we decided to fly the kite since it was a windy day. My three brothers, two cousins, and I all went early in the afternoon to fly the kite. The white, three-story apartment buildings where we lived were arranged in a big circle with a parking lot in the middle, which most of the kids used as a playground.

As we were flying the kite, which by then had reached the top of our three-story apartment building, a van came into the parking lot and a tall African American woman stepped out, followed by her two children. She was wearing a long black skirt and a black shirt with short sleeves. Her two boys were wearing suits. They had just gotten back from church. We were too busy paying attention to the kite as it tugged its way across the sky to notice her. As she came close to us, she said in loud, distinct voice, "*Asalaamu alykum.*" She grabbed our attention, and we were excited and surprised that she knew something about our culture.

"*Walakum as-salaam,*" we replied, with great excitement in our voices. For the first time, someone in our small community had acknowledged our culture and religion.

"Nice kite!" she remarked. We thanked her, even though she didn't sound as if she meant it. "Soon you will learn how to fly a plane." She laughed as she uttered those words and walked away without expecting a reply—she did not even give us the opportunity to confront her. I did not know what to make of the situation, but I learned that many of the churches were rousing people with anti-Muslim rhetoric—an unfortunate reality that gives impetus to the political agenda of the few. At the time, we called her ignorant and continued flying our kite. On further reflection, however, I realized that I had become as ignorant as this woman, for I viewed other religions with a closed-mindedness that was similar to the ideas that had infected her mind. As I reflected on this, I recognized my own lack of understanding and compassion. Up to that point, Islam for me was simply a series of cultural practices, but it was now moving from being a cultural religion to an intellectual faith.

Because of the cultural stigma that surrounded Islam, I had distanced myself from it. Over that summer, however, I began investigating the faith through YouTube lectures, online articles, and intensive reading. By the end of the summer, I was a devout Muslim, praying five times a day, and had become very extreme in my views. I had adopted the extreme views of the scholars I was listening to and had failed to reconcile my faith with the twenty-first-century United States. For example, I was aggressively inviting everyone to join my religion, a lesson preached by several of the scholars I was listening to at the time. During the first semester of college, I would question my classmates' choice of faith and view them as illogical and irrational. "How could they not see the clear and logical message of Islam?" I would often think.

During my first year at Dartmouth, however, these views were transformed through my participation in such programs as the Multi-Faith

Council, where students of different faiths would get together and engage in conversations about our beliefs. Attending these meetings helped me solidify my true faith, even as I came to respect other religions and other interpretations of what is true. As I was forming my own definition of Islam, I was also learning a lot from the beliefs of other participants. In short, one of the biggest gifts I took away from Dartmouth was this transformation of my faith. When I came to Dartmouth, my religious beliefs had little for questions about different interpretations of my religion. By the end of college, I had begun to learn to question various practices and rituals, and to find ways to better reconcile my religious beliefs with life in the United States.

During my time at Dartmouth, I was given an opportunity to pursue my altruistic aspirations, which I saw as expressions of my Muslim faith. My background gave me an urge to give back, to make sure that others did not have to face some of the challenges that I had had to confront. Through working with a service foundation on campus, I was able to participate in tutoring programs and travel to different cities to do service with various groups. These experiences opened my eyes to the educational and economic inequalities that plague the United States today. Moreover, they helped me build leadership and facilitative skills and to develop a strong foundation on which to base my faith.

However, that is not to say that every single moment of my experience at Dartmouth has been great—I have had many challenging moments. I struggled academically, especially my freshman year. I did not have the same preparation as most of my peers, and was shocked to find out that some of my friends attended high schools that cost the same to attend as college. These students had extensive college preparation, and some said that their academic course load was easier at Dartmouth than at their high school. As a first-generation college student from a lower socioeconomic background, I was undoubtedly far behind.

I was also struggling with finances. I took two jobs and worked as many as thirty hours a week throughout college because I had to send money home to my family. I lacked a lot of the material goods many of my fellow students took for granted—I did not have a cell phone until my junior year. Obviously I could not afford the same clothes or luxuries most of my peers could buy, and in fact bought a lot of my clothes from Walmart, which I was ashamed to admit to others. However, while I made a lot of sacrifices during college, I do not regret a single one of them.

One of the greatest challenges I encountered at college was how to reconcile my beliefs and my faith with some of the Dartmouth traditions.

I have never been able to come to terms, for example, with the sexual promiscuity on this campus. In Afghan culture, public sexual encounters are alien and not discussed at any level. Thus I was shocked by the "hookup" scene, the random and meaningless sexual encounters some students engage in. These practices are contrary to the teachings of Islam, and for me it diminishes the dignity of a truly intimate relationship. Even though I do not drink, I joined a fraternity in my sophomore year, but I stayed away from most of the events centered around alcohol. The centrality of alcohol to the Greek scene made me question my presence in the fraternity, and I continuously contemplated leaving the organization. While I ultimately remained part of the house, the "brotherhood" promised by my fraternity was much more evident in Dartmouth's Muslim community, where I found a magical bond forged by our shared Muslim faith. I was extremely satisfied with the Muslim community at Dartmouth, even though I still struggled with those in the Afghan-Muslim community who allowed their cultural beliefs to overtake the teachings of their religion, which has led to violence and the denial of human rights.

A day before my graduation from Dartmouth, I gave a speech at a gathering of students, parents, and family members for one of the student organizations. As I addressed the audience, I said, "No matter how far behind you are in life, you can always catch up while everyone else is having fun." Over time, I have adopted this as my life philosophy. While I cannot be thankful enough for all of the help I received from my family, my mentors, and my teachers, I consider a lot of my accomplishments the result of hard work and sacrifice, both mine and my family's.

I have also had a hard time finding Muslim scholars with whom I agree on most issues. As a result, I have had to take the readings and words of various scholars and develop my own form of Islam to shape my living philosophy, which focuses on maximizing the output of my life. One of the great characteristics of Islam is its adaptability. This has allowed me, through spiritual exploration, to learn what it means for me to be a Muslim. I believe that the range of beliefs within the Muslim community is more varied than in any other religion, which is one of the beauties of Islam. Islam has enabled me to be emotionally stable and has greatly impacted my moral and ethical values. Every major decision I have made has been affected at some level by Islamic teachings. I believe that it is important to live your life for something that will outlast it.

Being a Muslim in the post-9/11 United States, I face people who question my Americanness and have learned that many people form their assumptions based on my "Muslim looks." I realize that the color of my skin has a huge impact on how "American" I appear to others. I sometimes question whether I can be fully American, but when I am thinking more practically, I realize that I am as American as anyone else. I love and cherish the ideals that this country is built on. It is only in the United States that I have had the opportunity to be whatever I aspire to be and have had access to one of the best educations in the world. It is only in the United States that I can have friends from many backgrounds—be it spiritual, ethnic, or racial.

So I am strongly both Muslim and American. This is far from a paradox, as both stand for ideals like freedom and liberty. In fact, I believe the United States is the best place to practice Islam. It is only in the United States that you can enter a mosque filled with African Americans, Arabs, Pakistanis, Indians, East Asians, Afghans, Turks, white converts, Europeans, and Hispanics. The unity and the brotherhood formed in these Muslim communities are unmatched anywhere else in the world, including the so-called Muslim world. Hence, I think it is in the United States that the best and most inclusive form of Islam is practiced. I am a Muslim and an American, and I am proud of both identities.

Throughout my life experiences, I have learned to live like a kite. When a kite is in the sky, it is accepting of everything around it. It cherishes the changes, accepting and adapting to the ups and downs, the blows the wind brings, while altering its path based on the breeze. Similarly, I have learned to take each step of my journey with the same flexibility and adaptability.

After graduating from Dartmouth College, Shakir worked with the U.S. military, helping with cultural and linguistic training for the troops. He subsequently taught eighth-grade social studies through Teach For America, and is now pursuing a master's of science in education. Shakir continues to cherish his close ties with his family and hopes to pursue a career that will revolve around helping others through education.

PART III

STRUGGLES WITH SEXUALITY AND RELATIONSHIPS

7

Abdel Jamali   The Burden

The first year of my parents' marriage went well. They lived in Islamabad, Pakistan, and were both career professionals, my mother a doctor and my father an engineer. I was born a year after they married. My father was pleased to have a firstborn son, but he soon had qualms about my mother working after my birth and demanded that she work less. He started sleeping in a different room, which he kept locked, and would beat her for what he claimed was her negligence toward me. Finally she left him, and took me to live with her parents. My grandmother insisted that my mother go back home before people started talking, but, realizing that she needed a respite, my grandfather was more sympathetic.

After a year, my father called my mother and apologized. She moved back to his house and they constructed a peaceful rhythm of life, with me at the center of it. I had just turned three when my sister was born. Only days after her birth, my father went back to his abusive ways. It was my sister's misfortune that she was born a girl, which my father saw as a burden to the family. His paranoid nature also started to resurface; for example, he placed locks on the fridge because he thought we were wasting money on food. This decision forced my baby sister to go a couple of days without her formula, but he showed little concern for her.

One day, my mother arrived home to find she couldn't open the locks of our house. On hearing the jingle of the keys, my father peeked out the window and said, "Go home. I have divorced you." He had told the neighbors that my mother was sleeping with her colleagues, perhaps the worst insult to a chaste Muslim woman. She used my grandfather's connections to gain access back into our home, and had just prepared some baby formula to feed my sister, when a mob of my father's family members attacked her. They slapped her, but she fought back, throwing at them whatever was close at hand. I still have the images of this burned in my mind. I recall a plate smashing into my father's head, and I remember my mother on the floor, being punched and kicked. I remember my sister crying and me running to help my mom.

My grandfather came in and broke up the brawl, then took us to his home. The courts eventually finalized my parents' divorce, and my mother was able to bribe officials to gain custody of my sister and me. My father was ordered to pay child support but never complied.

My mother worked three jobs, trying to save up as much as she could to realize the dreams she had for us. It's strange how love can make individuals live not for themselves but for others—I think my mother probably would have died were it not for us. Many of her friends, accomplished women living in a patriarchal society, had committed suicide after their divorces or failed attempts at love. My father had tried to control my mother and suffocated her every attempt to be herself. He disrespected all that she did and didn't value her attempts to make a home for her two kids. What she wanted was in fact quite simple: to have a house where her kids would grow up, prepare for college, eventually marry, and then take care of her when she got old. She still holds on to some of this, but her life has been full of surprise twists and turns. I, unfortunately, am one of them.

As I grew up, I sometimes took on aspects of my father's nature. My mother tells me that I once ridiculed a doctor while he was giving me an injection, calling him derogatory names I had heard my father call my mother. I also abused my sister, hitting her for making the tiniest mistakes. I was quite an unstable child, and pieces of my past still haunt me. I sometimes hit our housemaids and I even had the audacity to raise my hand to my grandmother. Of course my mother reprimanded me, but she didn't do it as strongly as I wish she had. I think she pitied me for having never really known my father. She saw the difficulties I would face in my life, and because of that she held back on my punishment and became determined to do everything she could to make my life better.

When it came to education, I wasn't keen on completing my homework or doing anything school-related. During our homework hours, I would ask to go to the bathroom and lock myself in there, where I played with water. I remember her chasing me as I ran away from my schoolwork, threatening to hit me with sandals, hangers, and broken lamp wires. I was a fast runner, but she still got me with those wires and they stung. She now says I had ADD, but she refused to put me on medicine, as she felt my behavior was the result of a child's normal curiosity and sought to control me through harsh discipline instead.

At the age of six I lost my grandfather, just two years after losing my father. This time I felt the loss deeply, knowing that my grandfather was irreplaceable. He died from food poisoning after being tantalized by the smell of the *pani-puri* sold in the local market, even though we had told him not to eat street food. Despite being a doctor herself, my mother couldn't save him. I remember her coming home from the hospital and fainting in the living room. I can still hear the thud of her fall and remember crying over her motionless body.

My grandfather's death was a turning point in our lives, because my mother came to the realization that she was incapable of living in Pakistan without a male figure to protect her. My grandfather had applied for a U.S. visa for her, but she hadn't been keen on using it. With his death, the possibility of going to the United States became more real. My mother went to perform the hajj before going to the States, leaving my sister and me in the care of my aunts. I was at the age where boys don't cry in public, but the tears I shed privately didn't go unnoticed. I became protective of my sister in my mother's absence and began to take care of her rather than hitting her. I encouraged her to go to school, which my aunts allowed her to skip. Although I had difficulty learning, my mother's strong belief in education had filtered down to me, and I insisted that my uncles take me to school every day. When I cleaned my mother's room, I looked through her jewelry, clothes, shoes, and makeup, lifting everything and placing it back again. I remember sniffing her saris that hung in the closet, hoping to capture her scent. When I sensed that everyone was busy elsewhere, I would take her picture behind the living-room curtain and cry. My uncle once caught me when he noticed a bump in the curtain, but he didn't say anything until my mother returned.

We eventually left for the United States with my uncle. Between the four of us we had seven suitcases—the full extent of the possessions that would help us begin our life in the New World. Even when my grandfather died I didn't see my mother cry, but she cried for the first time in my memory on our first day in the States. She sat on the porch alone, silently crying—and for good reason. She had left everything behind to start all over again in the United States with two little kids. A well-established surgeon in Pakistan, in the United States my mother wasn't even allowed to practice. She got a job teaching MCAT classes while studying to pass her medical licensing exam. During that time my sister and I were raised by my uncle's wife, who took care of us like we were her own children, her kindness and generosity unsurpassed. She raised us side by side with our cousins, giving us what seemed like a normal childhood.

After coming to the States, my family fell to the lowest level socio-economically, and my mother soon had to give up her dream of studying and becoming certified. She felt she had failed in marriage, and now had to struggle on her own to get a green card so she could work legally in the United States. She thought she also had failed as a mother because so much of her time was devoted to making a living. She spent the little free time she did have helping me with my homework, but she was too busy to know about many things happening in my life—such as my being called gay at school.

The incident that profoundly affected my conception of myself and of the world—and something I continue to struggle with—occurred during the summer of my junior year in high school: I developed my first crush on another boy. Something about his look captivated me. At the time, he was synonymous with my definition of beauty. Although we had only a few interactions, I couldn't stop thinking about him. He had created a storm within me and it swept me away. It was the first time this had happened to me and I couldn't think of anything else. After this crush, I was never the same.

It is easy to make fun of me, as I am flamboyant and my hips bounce when I walk. My voice has dramatic ups and downs, my hand gestures choreograph my conversations, and my face dances to the words I speak. At school, everything I did was sort of a gay joke, and I soon lost patience with being scrutinized in this way, although most of my friends never made me feel different. But one day, when a friend said to me in jest, "Shut up, faggot," it was like being hit with a rock. Although I laughed to defray the tension, I gave him the cold shoulder after that and stopped talking to him.

Sometimes I wonder why God created me as a gay male. If He meant to make life hard for me, well, He did that well enough in other areas already without having to also make me gay. I especially hated the effect my sexual orientation had on my mother: Was she being punished for her unknown sins by having a gay son? They say that God is merciful and compassionate and never tests a person more than they can handle, but did He forget my mother in this instance?

I tried so hard to change myself, but I failed. Life had become dark and dreary for me, as I felt imprisoned by stifling rules that took the joy out of life. Each morning I wanted to continue sleeping to escape the pain of my daily reality, but I couldn't escape the pain of what I was. During my sophomore summer in college, I was at my lowest point ever. I have tried to erase the memory, but I remember the tastelessness of life. I was so lonely, surrounded by thoughts of my inflicted depravity, of my otherness, of my deviant nature—each day I felt I died a little bit. There was a song that consoled me, about a girl who had epilepsy. She sang that she had joy for her dreams as they were filled with love stories that she couldn't attain in life. That was me. I felt that love had stopped in my life but it occupied my dreams.

My life revolved around my hated "disease." I was drowning in questions of why this happened to me. At one point I resolved to stop thinking about men and to think about girls instead. Each night, instead of lulling myself to sleep in the arms of an imaginary husband, I imagined myself holding girls I thought were pretty. I did this somewhat success- fully for two months, but each time I saw an attractive man, my resolve was tested. If someone looked back at me, my imagination kicked into high gear, but I had to stop myself, convinced that being gay was against God's way. I tried so hard to change, but there were moments of weakness. For two months I succumbed to Internet porn, searching for romantic scenes; throughout this time, I wasn't motivated by lust, but romance.

In the summer of my sophomore year, along came David. I had met him in the spring, when I was attempting to "make" myself straight, but he had known I was gay and sensed the repressed impulses I was holding in. David was the "pretty boy" who revealed his sexuality with exaggerated eye rolls. I was envious of his looks, and little did I know that he found me attractive. Then one summer night a friend invited both of us over for dinner, with me unaware of her plan to bring us together. As David and I got better acquainted, I became interested in his work with a nonprofit. We ended up taking our conversation to a student cafeteria that stayed open until three o'clock in the morning, but we didn't stay on the subject of nonprofits. David eventually broke the ice, saying he knew that, like him, I was gay. At first I was a bit shocked at his audacity, but it also was wonderful to talk to someone about it after having spent a whole year try- ing to avoid it.

I remember smiling as the voice I had known inside me returned. My cheeks turned copper and my eyes flashed as I gazed at David. I asked what he knew about my being gay, and the floodgates opened. Out came the stories I had wanted to talk about, the incidents I wanted to analyze and reflect on. I told him about my crushes and attending gay parties and other gay events. I told him of my religion and of the tests and trials

God puts us through, and how my life is a testimony to God's grace and kindness. I ended our conversation by saying that even though I knew I was gay, I was going to lead a straight life because God deems it must be so. I said I couldn't change what I am biologically, but I could die trying to change my personality. I said good-bye to David with a long embrace. He had become a close friend within the span of three hours. Our shared sexuality brought me closer to him than to anyone else in terms of both mutual attraction and friendship.

That was the first time, after many interminable sleepless nights, that I slept soundly and calmly. I remember dreaming about happiness: I woke up at one point feeling great happiness and wanting it to last, so I went back to sleep. I was woken up at ten a.m. by a phone call from my mother telling me my grandmother had died. I cried with the phone clutched to my ear. I thought briefly that maybe she had died because of my sin of indulging my homosexual feelings, but the thought quickly passed. It was simply her time. I reminisced about the time she had come to visit us in the States. She didn't touch or hug much, but her presence was warm and maternal. She gave me a sense of safety that helped me trust and rely on my faith and gave me a respite from my restlessness.

Coming to college made me realize just how different I am. For one thing, my family was far less wealthy than most of those around me, but more than that was how I was automatically identified as a person of color. This feeling of difference made it even more difficult to be comfortable with who I was, but it was also through my experience at college that I realized my Muslim identity. It had never before occurred to me just how integral my faith is to my life. But this realization came to me only after an exercise in stupidity. I decided one day to leave my religion in rebellion against God. I didn't pray, and I went out of my way to just do what I felt like doing with total disregard for my religiously guided judgment. I wanted to be seen living life to the fullest. But at the end of each day, I returned to empty introspection. I soon discovered that there had to be more to life than self-centeredness and satisfying only myself. These actions revealed to me that I was lost and confused.

I wouldn't say that I found God again because I never truly lost Him; however, I did gradually come to realize His importance in my life as a source of the consistency and stability I badly needed. My life was changing so rapidly that I sometimes didn't know what to hold on to, and I feared I could even lose my family when they learned the truth about my sexuality. I felt God was the only one who wouldn't abandon me, and I consoled myself during those days by reading from the Quran about the Prophet's life at a time when he thought God had left him because he wasn't being sent any revelations. God told the Prophet, "God does not hate you. Did I not care for you while you were an orphan?" These words comforted me again and again and they spoke to me of my own situation. Was I not a fatherless child? Was my life not filled with impossibilities that became realities? It showed me the existence of a kind and merciful God who did not forget the tired and weary and through whom hope was possible.

I thought many times that my sexuality was a test. I remembered the example of Abraham, who distinguished himself through total subordination to God's command. When God ordered him to slaughter his son Ishmael, he blindly obeyed. Because of his blind obedience, God instead asked for the sacrifice of a ram, which Abraham slaughtered in place of his son. I have often thought that my sexuality was a test from God, but whether or not it is, I fear I may not be able to live through it because my life involves deceit and injustice since I cannot openly present myself as I am, and in Islam, justice triumphs over all other considerations.

Through my self-imposed loneliness and isolation at college, the struggle to find my true self began. I don't think that many college students realize that life isn't only for the now. Although we are in an isolated bubble while at college, we still have homes to return to, and the ailing lives we left behind are very much alive. I came to realize that college wasn't going to last forever, that it was ephemeral and I would have to return to my family and to the responsibilities I was expected to carry. It was this knowledge that limited my tendency to explore. I knew I couldn't just major in anything I wanted, that there had to be some practicality in my choice of what to study because of the family that was waiting for and depending on me. I knew I had to limit my trips to other countries more than other students because of the financial burden on my family. I also knew that my self-expression had to be limited because I wasn't brought up with the luxury of doing what I wanted for myself alone. I had others to hold up along with myself.

I think again and again about the appropriate time to come out to my mother and whether it's even necessary. I am sometimes so unsure and scared. Should I marry a girl? What if I marry a girl and then end up cheating on her or not loving her the way she deserves to be loved? Will that be a greater injustice than not marrying at all? God may forgive, but humans don't, and we will be held accountable for any injustice we create in this world. I may come out to my mother if I have a compelling reason to do so. That would ideally be when I have a Muslim partner whom I want to marry and build a life with. My current strategy is to avoid the question of marriage for as long as possible, but I know I can't handle loneliness for too much longer.

My consciousness of injustice guides the major decisions I make in my life. I feel I can't tell my mother about my being gay because she has been wronged by the cruel world too much already, and telling her about myself will shatter the dreams she's built and the life she's imagined for herself. This is the dilemma that always confounds me—I don't know what to be anymore and I have a hard time living this double life, this two-faced existence. I am alone and split and realize there are few ways to reach a compromise.

We are told not to get angry at God, but many times I am. Why me? Why am I continually put through these tests and tribulations? When will it end? I would be happy if there could be just one week when I didn't have to think about my dilemma, but the cloud of conflict always hovers nearby, sometimes infusing every moment of my existence. I wish I weren't so different, and I wish I could have the "normal" aspirations of finding a job, getting married, having kids, of loving someone and growing old with them. I don't know if I will ever be fortunate enough to enjoy these things.

Sometimes I just want to escape, and so I think of death—of hurling my body against a speeding truck, leaving all the burdens I carry shattered into pieces, annihilated. That would enable me to escape from this mind that refuses to live freely and instead chooses to tie everything into knots. I would escape the religion that makes me aware of signs all around me. I want to be normal. I want to be like my cousins. I want to talk about girls and feel the way my cousins do about them. I wish I weren't so feminine. I wish I weren't troubled with the past, the present, and the future. I want a savior to come and rescue me. I am tired of trying to do it on my own, without anyone understanding or helping me carry the burden I bear as a gay Muslim, a burden of generations past, present, and future. My burden is made heavier by the dreams of my parents and all those who have made me who I am. And it is the burden of a misunderstood religion. This never-ending pain is too much to take—I just want out.

My cousin recently told me that sometimes when we successfully pass a test, God gives us a harder test to see how strongly we hold on to Him. I know that I haven't yet passed this second part of the test and I know I have to do it on my own, yet I am eager to find someone to help me through it. In the strength I need to face my difficulties, I find my masculinity, because it's not the flailing of wrists, the bounce in my hips, or the tone of my voice that defines how masculine I am—it is my ability to carry on through difficult circumstances without inflicting my own pain on others. I just hope I have the strength to continue doing so because I know my life will be full of challenges.

My aunt tells me that God tests those whom He wants closest to Him, and that it is such tests that keep us mindful of God. Being gay is a test for my life, and the way to get through it is to stay true to my core values of justice, kindness, and submission, which have helped me travel through life thus far.

After graduating from Dartmouth, Abdel moved to Chicago to be closer to his family. He accepted a managerial position at a Fortune 500 company and helped his family build their first house in the United States. Abdel plans to have a career that is closely entwined with the development sector in Pakistan. He has started his own outsourcing venture targeting poor women in his home country. Abdel envisions helping women like his mother, whose example helped him find his own voice and space.

8

Sabeen Hassanali   My Permanent Home

When I called home to Houston to see how my family was doing, it was relatively late, but everyone there seemed wide awake. My mother's best friend, Rosie, was visiting from San Antonio for the first time in several years, so they were having a sleepover. She had brought along her oldest son, Kamran. As children, my younger sister and I played house with Kamran and his younger brother. My outlook on life then was very simple: Kamran and I would grow up together and, when we were older, get married. It made perfect sense.

Fifteen years had gone by, and we have seen very little of Aunty Rosie's family in the interim, so it was nice to hear that they were visiting. My mom sounded unusually happy as she said, "We were just talking about you." There were giggles in the background. I heard the word "marriage."

When Aunty Rosie got on the phone, she pleaded, "Sabeen, dear, you have to promise me that you'll do as I say when you see me." Something began to gnaw at the back of my mind, but I readily gave her my word since she is not just a close family friend but also my godmother, and I have always had a special place for her in my heart. Yet I was hesitant. When I talked to my sister, things began to make sense. She mentioned Kamran as well. "Sabeen, he's really cute. And he's nice, too. You should definitely check him out. He's perfect for you. He and Aunty will visit in December, so you can meet him then." I felt a slow and uneasy churning in my stomach as I tried to ignore what I thought might be happening. These comments from my mother, Rosie, and my sister had a subtle undertone that came in loud and clear on my end of the phone. In December, they're planning to come down so I can get to know him better. And were they discussing a marriage proposal? *My* marriage proposal? No!

And yet I had seen it happen often enough to other girls to recognize that that's what it was.

After I hung up the phone, I thought to myself, "This is incomprehensible. How could this be happening to me? I'm a college student, an undergraduate. I've never even been in a relationship. How do they think I'm ready for marriage?" Yet I *knew* this had been coming. These subtle "jokes" about marriage had begun before I finished high school, even though my family knew how much I despised even the casual mention of it. I was eventually able to ignore or dismiss whatever came my way, and I had assumed I would always be able to. But this time, with family friends and heightened expectations involved—I had certainly not expected my godmother to be arranging things—it was not so easy to dismiss the idea as a harmless joke. I also had not expected I would have to face this reality so *soon*. Maybe I shouldn't have been too surprised, however. After all, my mom was my age when she got married. All of her seven sisters (she has no brothers) also grew up modestly in Karachi, Pakistan, and married fairly young, all arranged marriages.

The custom of arranged marriages is one of a number of values that my parents and I disagree on. For me, growing up as a Pakistani American with traditional parents has meant constantly dealing with fundamentally divergent attitudes, including those toward education, love, and "home." Reconciling these differences means that I have had to assert my independence and make choices that my parents do not agree with—in a way, I suppose, I have had to be an "American." Still, in this struggle, I have made a conscious effort to remain a "Pakistani," grounding myself in my faith and culture while asserting my autonomy. I understand that my parents may not agree with the choices I have made—I would not expect them to—but over the years they have also come to see that I have not abandoned them, and that I will continue to remain both Pakistani and American.

My father's family lived in poverty in a community of mud houses in urban Karachi. His family of nine shared a 160-square-foot living space that had no electricity. The only bathrooms within walking distance were communal government bathrooms, which were rarely cleaned. While he was growing up, food was scarce and there were many mouths to feed. After completing tenth grade, my dad began working at a local bank, and his family moved to a one-bedroom apartment. The eldest brother of seven children, he had decided to take on a job to help support his younger siblings and ensure that his brothers could continue their high-school and university studies. His brothers, like all respectable Pakistani men, were expected to provide for their future families, and hence had to take advantage of educational opportunities. His four sisters, on the other hand—like most other poor women in their community—completed only elementary school, and were expected to be ripe for marriage soon after. They did not need further schooling.

A few years later my dad was working at a bank in Qatar. Prompted by his mother—my paternal grandmother, or *Dadima* in Urdu—he decided to take a month off work to return to Karachi and find his future wife. "Shopping around" for wives consisted of going to families' homes, seeing the girls briefly, and conversing with their parents. An informal network of older ladies in the community kept tabs on the single males and females who were of age to be married and how respectable their families were. They were the personals—personified.

While my father and Dadima were looking in a neighboring town, they came across a lady named Jena Bhai. At the time, my mother was twenty-one and teaching, having recently graduated with a BA from a local university; but she often tailored clothes for Jena Bhai, who was quite fond of her. Jena Bhai suggested that my father and Dadima check my mother out, since she lived nearby. They heeded Jena Bhai's advice and visited my mom's home, asking to see her. As it happened, when my dad and Dadima visited, my mom was just getting ready to go to Jamat-khana, the place of worship; my mom's parents told her to serve the guests drinks on her way out. In the tight, humid room, small talk between the elders wafted through the thick air. My petite, five-foot-tall mother hurried into the room, her *dupata*, a long scarf, flying behind her. She did not think to ask who the guests were. She quietly served the glasses of Coca-Cola to the now silent bodies around her, careful to touch only the base of the glass as she passed each one. (I would be trained on this exact glass-passing technique ten years later.) She left the room without ever looking up to see any of their faces. She had no idea what serving those Cokes had implied.

The next day, Jena Bhai informed my maternal grandparents that the young man had liked my mother and decided he wanted to marry her. My grandmother informed my mom of the proposal. And that was that.

I can't help but wonder what my mother's feelings must have been. Wasn't she surprised? Wasn't she scared? Was this what she wanted? How could she know if he could be right for her? *She never even saw his face!* The engagement date was set for the following day, October 1, and because of my dad's work schedule, the wedding itself would have to occur within the next ten days. That week, my mom and dad went out a couple of times for dinner, their only "dates" together before they married. On October 11, with full faith in first impressions, their parents' decisions, and an unquestioned destiny, my parents were joined in marriage. A week later my dad left for work, and two months later, when her visa arrived, my mom left alone for Qatar, boarding her first flight wearing a new, light-pink sari.

My mom and dad got along well in Qatar, and were soon blessed with children: first me, and two years later, my sister, Nadya. My memories of living in Qatar are happy ones. It now seems like a dream—a quiet, happy life where my dad worked a nine-to-five bank job and my mom stayed at home. I cheerfully attended the local private school, and would wake my parents up even on Fridays (the day schools and offices are closed in Qatar), because I loved school so much and wanted to go every day. I remember evenings at home when Nadya played with my dolls while I learned the multiplication tables with my mom at the dinner table. Sometimes my dad would be watching an American movie and would say something like, "Sabeen, come here. Look, that's snow. They have snow in America. It gets very cold there." Snow looked stunning and beautiful. My dad would often talk of how wonderful America was. I believed him completely—these were dreams and pictures of a land far away from what our simple world held.

When I was six, my mom became pregnant with our younger brother, Faisal. Around this time, my dad's bank began laying off many employees, and eventually my dad's number was up. Fortunately, they offered him a visa to either Pakistan or the United States in exchange for the layoff. After quickly discussing the matter, my parents decided to take advantage of the rare opportunity. My dad's younger brother was already in the States, working as a successful businessman in New York, and having some family there meant we wouldn't be completely alone in an alien land. Soon after my brother was born, when I was seven, our family of five left the only home we knew and headed for a new life in the United States.

In New York, my dad took a day job at a donut shop and an evening job as a taxi driver, which worked out well because he loved seeing the sights of New York and he loved to drive. My mother would babysit neighbors' children while taking care of my baby brother. We lived on the fourth floor of a five-story building in New York, not quite downtown, but en route to the outlying suburbs. The main room of the apartment was the living room, brightly lit with two economical, white tube lights. With its borrowed sofas, wooden wall unit, and doily-covered glass coffee table, our apartment personified the "fresh off the boat" image. Family pictures in dollar-store frames and plastic flowers in large vases colored the room, which permanently reeked of Indian curry, though we rarely noticed. The five of us shared a bedroom: my sister and I had bunk beds, my mom and baby brother slept on another bed, and my dad slept on the floor. Driving around in a cab all evening, he found sleeping on the carpeted floor to be better for his back.

As was my nature, I was excited to start school in the United States. My third-grade class was full of people with different colors of hair, skin, and eyes, something I had never encountered before. My teacher, Mrs. Jackson, had light-yellow hair and blue-green eyes that fascinated me. Her eyes would change color every day. I yearned for a doll with yellow hair and desperately wished I had "colored" eyes. My black hair and dark brown eyes, I concluded, did not count as legitimate. I was sad that I could never really be "American" because I looked so unlike one. Compared to these doll-like faces around me, I concluded that I was and would always be too plain. Instead of worrying excessively about my appearance, however, I decided to focus on things that I could control, such as the work we did in class. In my three years at Woodson Elementary School, I truly loved the experience of learning, especially when it meant a teacher, an actual "American" teacher, cared. Mrs. Jackson gave me the confidence and motivation to work hard in everything I did thereafter. Even now, after fourteen years, I stay in touch with Mrs. Jackson, who is still a teacher in a New York public school.

I was in fourth grade when my family suddenly decided to move to Houston, where one of my mother's sisters lived. Leaving New York was painful because I was once again leaving behind everything I knew—and because I had only vague images of Houston as a town full of cowboys and horses. I wasn't even sure if they would have cars over there. We drove down to Houston in my dad's cab, which he had bought at a discounted price and painted light gray. As we approached the Houston skyline (insignificant compared to New York's), I felt nothing but angry uncertainty. I had been told that I needed glasses, but my family could not afford them yet, so everything looked hazy—especially Houston and my future in it.

Eventually, my family adjusted to Houston and worked to make it our permanent home. Since my parents would leave for work at six a.m. and not return until six p.m., I looked after my siblings and the house after coming home from school. The increased responsibility made me mature early, particularly as I began my adolescence. At the same time, my academic motivation continued to increase and became a way for me to develop an identity and to make friends in the different schools I attended.

Because our family switched apartments often, however, my friendships tended to develop less in school and more from my relatively stable religious community. The sense of permanency this community provided also helped build a strong sense of identity within me. Our community of Shia Ismaili Muslims consists of 10 million people spread out across the world, most being of Central or South Asian descent. One key distinction of our faith is that we have a living spiritual leader, an Imam, to guide us. The Aga Khan, who resides in France and was appointed Imam while completing his senior year at Harvard, is a direct descendant of the Prophet Muhammad, number forty-nine in a line of Imams who descended from the Prophet's time. Going to Jamatkhana to pray regularly, and being involved with its social organizations, such as Girl Scouts, kept me very active within our *jamat*—our community. Service and excellence also fit in perfectly with the teachings of our Imam, who emphasizes living an ethical and balanced life. Islam has always been a part of my worldview, and I cannot perceive myself as separate from it. As such, I have always been a very spiritual person, consciously meditating since I was ten (following in my parents' footsteps). I feel the comforting presence of God with me, through good times and bad. As the turbulent waves of adolescence entered and took over my life, my faith became the anchor that grounded everything else—family, school, traditions, and friends— and helped me realize my potential.

As a sophomore in high school, I found myself confronting several new stumbling blocks: I discovered that elections were popularity contests that I could not win. Classes were becoming significantly difficult and I struggled to keep up. It seemed impossible to get into a competitive college in the Northeast. My friends all had boyfriends while I remained unattached. I found myself not fitting into a particular clique, failing to identify with one strong circle of friends. Reflecting on these troubles plunged me into a spiral of depression in which I no longer felt a connection with my school, my friends, my family, and even life in general. I longed for this connection, but did not expect it and did not experience it. Instead, I shut myself off from everyone, hiding behind a casually pleasant smile and dedicating myself to academics, looking for the hint of appreciation in an "A" at a time when I needed nurture and love.

Interesting opportunities for service in jamat and school would present themselves, and I would always decline. I heard about a weeklong youth camp, and although I declined initially, I was persuaded by organizers and grudgingly applied to be a counselor. During the first day of training, I noticed a bouncy, twenty-five-year-old South Asian American in a ponytail named Azim, who looked like a carefree surfer. He began the training session by having us all sing and dance in a circle, and the session soon continued along the same unpredictable, unorthodox vein. The other counselors-in-training all had quizzical looks on their faces—this was not what we were expecting our "training" to be. Yet, confusing as it initially was, this concept of surprising people, and keeping them on edge in order to teach them, strangely thrilled me, and the intensity of my emotions baffled me. Being so accustomed to not feeling anything, I breathed in this rush of excitement with all my might. Throughout the training session, I avidly participated in discussions, raised issues concerning youth, made analogies, and probed the minds of my fellow adolescents, who, before this, I had believed were doomed to hopelessness. Growing up, we craft such amazing dreams and fantasies for ourselves. Why do we let others over time allow us to give these up as childish or idealistic? At one point I thought of my secret image of Aladdin. After seventh grade I stopped telling people that *Aladdin*, with its rags-to-riches story, was my favorite movie because it seemed too childish. Reality, I had learned, was not full of hope. I wondered: If kids heard affirmations that their hopes were real and legitimate, how much better could the world be? How many more young Muslims, or youth in general, would grow up feeling comfortable in their own skin?

"Can anyone guess what my favorite movie is?" Azim asked, suddenly jolting me out of the maze of a hundred different ideas and hopes that were whirling through my mind. "*Aladdin*. This is our chance to show these participants a whole new world." I stopped breathing. Suddenly, everything else around me faded as I looked into Azim and saw the vision I had been thirsting for. In this "surfer boy" with a ponytail, I felt my potential, my *full human* potential, for the very first time. Throughout the camp, an invincible spark ignited me. I rarely slept that week because of an urge to instill hope in my campers, an urge so strong that it inevitably became a reality.

More than the camp itself, my relationship with Azim gave me a reason to live and care once again. Azim saw the same potential in me that I saw actualized in him. He and I stayed in touch and worked together on a number of different youth-leadership programs within our community. This renewed spirit also showed up in my classes and relationships with friends. During the spring of my junior year, when my family moved to South Houston, I quickly befriended some of the top students in my new school and gained leadership positions by working extremely hard. What could have been a horrible experience of once again starting anew actually pushed me to succeed even further, mostly because of a renewed faith in myself.

All year long there is a stifling heat in Texas that consumes you and makes you boil inside out. During the summer, people stay indoors in nicely air-conditioned homes and malls, shunning the outdoors, where one is fried alive. Growing up, however, my version of this heat existed not outside, but indoors, at home: the scalding melting pot in which the traditional and the modern, the old and the young, the Pakistani and the American collided, and my sister and I yearned to escape this crucible. In our first-generation immigrant family, the home became a battleground between the idealistic, assimilated American teenagers (Nadya and me) and our self-sacrificing, old-school parents. On the front lines—our dinner table—Nadya and I fired off staple English phrases like "You never understand" from our side, while ceaseless lectures in Urdu hit or missed our ears from the other side. The battles we fought (and still fight) revolved around going to parties, wearing shorts, highlighting our hair, or talking loudly. To my parents, who came home tired from twelve-hour workdays, these childish desires to be more American seemed like imposing threats from a distant culture. It was understandable that they could not relate well to the Americans they served at work. However, facing the same foreign culture and language in their own home must have been a much more alienating experience. Meanwhile, my sister and I detested our parents' dogmatic rules. For example, I never understood the American concept of grounding children while I was growing up because the only permissible way to leave my home—regardless of my recent behavior—was to go to school, to an extracurricular activity, or to our place of worship. To my sister and me, my parents' concerns seemed irrational, devoid of any faith in us, and replete with fear of a corrupt, alien society.

Eventually, Nadya and I found two ways to avoid the bitter arguments: to live with the oppression or to defy it with lies. I chose the former and dedicated myself to community activities, while my sister chose the latter and lived a "full" teenage experience. The arguments with our parents eventually became less frequent, but the sense of feeling isolated grew. For my sister, acknowledging her identity as the difficult child of the family meant that she could get away with going to parties and piercing her belly button, whereas I was thought to be above these childish whims. I would usually relent in the short term because I knew that if I worked hard in school, my time to escape would arrive on graduation. In the meantime, with a renewed faith and the experience of making a positive difference in other youths' lives, I threw myself into community service and leadership positions, both in school and in my religious community. Part of my rationale for being so involved in extracurricular activities—rather than, for example, challenging my parents' restrictions—was that colleges valued them in addition to grades. Because my faith emphasizes meritocracy in school and hard work, my parents could not argue. I became the model child that all the parents wanted their children to emulate.

At home, however, my accolades and ego melted under the crucible of culture. My mother's endless tirades to shift my focus to cooking and cleaning stabbed at my heart. During my sophomore year in high school, I received a national honor in recognition of my academic achievement. My mother's way of congratulating me on this award was to say, in Urdu, "Now that you've proved that you're smart, you should concentrate on learning to cook." Then, adding in English, "Ee-school ees not ev-ary-theeng." During high school, I became so involved with community programs that I dedicated whole weekends, and eventually entire summers, to working away from home. My mother said, "You serve all the world, but not your own parents." And it was true. I put the whole world before my own parents. I never cooked dinner for them. I didn't make it a daily habit to put in a few hours at the grocery store they owned. I made them drive me to and from meetings and activities at odd hours. And I never massaged their feet after they came home tired from working all day. I would sometimes see my friends doing this—massaging their parents' tired feet—and I would think, "Wow, how can they do that? They must really love them." I could never massage my parents' feet. It was too close for comfort. After years of listening to lectures about being too social and too involved in outside activities, the physical closeness of soothing another's feet was a sign of intimacy that I could not handle.

An emotional divide formed within me as I found solace in helping others outside my home. I cannot remember the last time I kissed my parents. It would not occur to me to do this. Even now, three years after entering college, I still have trouble saying "I love you" to them. They must miss that, and certainly would like to hear it, but I can only slip it in casually or playfully, rarely with emotion. Maybe because of a lack of strong bonds with significant others, maybe because of the fear of being seen as weak, and maybe because of my naturally introspective personality, I held my emotions inside. Although I loved my parents, by the end of my high-school career my bottled-up emotions and my dwindling patience in dealing with their traditional impositions and endless criticisms made home a pressure pit where I was afraid of feeling, for fear of exploding. My only escape, and my culminating goal, became to leave home to attend a school far away.

My leaving for college was much more difficult for my mother than it was for me. I counted the days until I could escape the heat and breathe easily, on my own. I longed to have friendships and schedules on my own terms, without my family judging me for it. My mom and dad wanted me to live at home through college. Although they knew that I was going to a prestigious school in the Northeast, they refused to accept it. Every time we drove past our local community college, they would say, "Sabeen, wouldn't it be great if you went to school at Sweetwater? You could just live at home. It would be so much less expensive, and we hear it's a good school." I grew up hearing, "Family is everything. Friends and acquaintances are nothing, because when you're in trouble, you can only count on your family to be there." My act of attending college far away meant that I defied this expectation. I left my family, even when they needed me.

My dad and I pulled my bags from our rental car and searched each door in the hallway for my room. A girl wearing nothing but a towel passed us and smiled. I came to the end of the hallway, reached the room she had just stepped out of, and realized that this would be my first-year roommate. She realized the same and turned around. It was an awkward moment for all of us—she in her towel, me with my luggage, and my dad standing next to me, looking down at his feet. "Ashleigh?" I said, while she asked, "Sabeen?" At the moment, all I knew was that this redheaded, tanned Caucasian girl was a field hockey and squash player from Greenwich, Connecticut. I did not know what squash was, or that being from Greenwich put one in a very select and privileged group of people in society. It would take over a year for me to really understand the differences between Greenwich and South Houston. Ashleigh could take her dirty laundry home and I could not. Her younger siblings were bound for the Ivies and mine were not. Her parents often visited her and mine still have not. On the phone, she could jokingly curse out her mother and laughingly describe what a "blowjob shot" (an alcoholic drink) was, while I spoke quietly to my mother in Urdu about the upcoming college bill, wondering if we could afford to pay it off, even after all the subsidies we'd been granted.

Still, Ashleigh and I found more common ground than the 180 square feet of our room. We were both the oldest of three children. Our younger siblings were the same ages. We both talked in our sleep. We both cleaned in order to think straight. We both listened to Sarah McLachlan to calm ourselves down during finals. We both ended up with the same major. And when our parents would call us, they often could not distinguish our voices. As we got to know each other better, our polar backgrounds remained in the background, while our similar personalities brought us closer. I have often said to people that I could not have wished for a better first-year roommate. During the day we had very different friends and schedules. At night, we would fall asleep talking to each other, sharing the quiet thoughts of two sisters and their new experiences away from home.

Every three months, while spending breaks at home with my family, I became accustomed to a conversation that occurred more and more frequently. My parents and I would sit at the dinner table, discussing my future after college. One evening, I mentioned that I wanted to get some experience before heading back to graduate school in a few years. I got an interesting response: "Sabeen, why you don't finish all of the school now? You must think about your future." I *was* thinking about my future—just not the future they wanted me to think about.

"I told you," began my standard response, "I'm not going to get married for another ten years. You'll just have to wait and accept it."

"*Aisa nahi bol.* Don't talk that way. You have to think about future. Two years maximum. Then you have to settle down. What will people say?" My mother's words poked at my patience, causing me to shake my head, cringe, and roll my eyes all at once. What followed was a list of girls' names, girls with whom I had grown up, who were now either engaged, married, or married with children. After that, they would mention some guy or another, a computer scientist or a businessman, very wealthy, from a good family…By that time I had not only tuned out, but also left the room.

Eventually I came to a realization. Somehow, there was an underlying foundation in our home, something so subtle that I only became aware of it on visiting Azim and seeing how differently his family functioned. In my family, "home" was a temporary dwelling that you had to leave sooner or later. *Home was an interim situation before I was married and settled into my "permanent" home.* This sudden truth shocked me simply because it made so much sense. Being with Azim's family demonstrated the contrast in our situations: his home seemed permanent; even I felt at home there. My home, however, seemed to have a looming expiration date stamped on it. Maybe this is why leaving Houston for school or activities was never difficult for me. Maybe my parents had prepared me well for leaving for my "permanent" home. Regardless, a silent sadness remains in my heart, knowing that my parents brought my sister and me up with the intention of having us leave.

As I prepare to go home for winter break, I'm not quite sure how to react to this potential marriage proposal with Kamran. I consider this idea of an arranged marriage to be a thing of the past, a thing of the uneducated masses, a thing that living in the United States has permanently dispelled for me. At our weddings, the bride has to sit quietly, look pretty, and rarely raise her eyes to the crowd. I feel uncomfortable as I imagine myself in that bride's shoes. Every parent and aunt and cousin I know has been through an arranged marriage. Even though it is a sign of respect for elders and a tradition in my family, for me it means the official stamp that I was unworthy and unable to find love on my own.

Azim is keeping my faith in love alive. He and I have built a strong relationship that, at first, was difficult for me to put in perspective. Azim, eight years my senior, would ask me to travel with him and work on various projects. I felt subordinate to him at first and doubted my abilities. However, as the years have progressed, I have learned that we make a dynamic and empowering team. I have also opened myself up to his friendship, realizing that he needs me just as much as I need him. The closest parallel I can give is that he is my older brother. There are times when I can feel our souls talking with each other. I can sense when something is going wrong in his life even without having contact with him. He knew what college I had chosen even before I had a chance to tell him.

Sometimes I feel my relationship with Azim is strong enough to carry me through without the need for a significant other in my life. At other times I feel our relationship has deterred me from having boyfriends, because the care and love he has shown me sets a high expectation for others. In either case, the fact remains that through junior high, high school, and college, I have never been in a romantic relationship. About two years ago, I began feeling that my spiritual, intellectual, and emotional growth was being stunted by this empty space in my life; dealing with this space meant acknowledging a need for acceptance. Some nights, my walls and pillows soak up soul-filled cries and tears as I slowly surrender to faith and sleep. I want to care about someone who also cares for me. However, I cannot get past the wall of finding a decent candidate.

Throughout adolescence I was always more concerned with the emotional benefits of relationships, partly because I knew that physical experiences would be limited for me. I knew I would not have premarital sex, and thus I was not really concerned with that aspect of intimacy. Recently, though, I have come to understand the power of relationships to threaten people's deep-seated morals while promising to satisfy intense physical needs. In a way, this experience humanized me.

During my junior year, I met someone in Chicago and was shocked at how attracted I was to him—and how attracted he was to me. Sam was a Pakistani American who shared my religious faith and was one year my senior. He was handsome, and he seemed sure of what he wanted in life. My attraction to him was shocking and new for me—I had never felt such an innate *physical* drive to be with someone. Yet parts of him morally repelled me—Sam was a mysterious, immoral, flirtatious rebel who lived life by taking risks. And yet again, this opposition of character seemed to fuel the attraction even more. After our initial meeting, we talked on the phone often, though "just as friends." Sam had a longtime girlfriend at the moment. However, whether we were together or not, my body lost all control when thinking about him. I felt like a teenage boy with raging hormones on his first date, eager to sexually devour his unsuspecting companion. Maybe these urges are normal feelings that all adolescents experience, but they were new to me, and as a twenty-one-year-old without any prior experience, I felt lost at my lack of self-control. The three months during which we interacted were like one continuous, intense state of arousal. However, as we became open to learning more about each other (as people and not solely as sexual beings), I realized that he did not care for me enough to tell his girlfriend about us. I became scared at the prospect of meeting again. Long-distance conversations were fine because they were just talk; if we were to meet up again, though, I knew it would be a test for my morals. Before this experience, I had never really understood the power of sexual attraction in a relationship. Sam seemed too great a threat to me at the time, both physically and emotionally, and although I knew I was forsaking a potential relationship, I concluded that it was not founded on a strong basis of mutual love and concern. At my request, we stopped talking after three months and never met again.

Azim and I often discussed my relationship with Sam, and he was always quick to remind me that I deserved someone better, someone who genuinely cared about me. Azim has shown me how much another person can care for me, and although our relationship has never been romantic, I would value the type of intimacy we share in my future relationships. In considering potential boyfriends, I do not necessarily limit myself to dating only other Ismaili Muslims or South Asians, or any specific minority. However, when I get married, it will be to an Ismaili Muslim. It is a given that my family expects me to marry another Ismaili. Still, the decision to marry an Ismaili is a strongly held belief of mine, not one that my parents or Pakistani culture forces on me. I see the bond of marriage as transcending the two individuals, to include the union of two families and a shared sense of faith that ties this new, larger family together. As a Pakistani American and an Ismaili Muslim, I hope to instill this sense of faith in my children and in my children's children. For me, this faith lies in my religion and community.

The faith I speak of is an intimate connection with God that guides me in my daily interactions. One of the reasons I chose to come to Dartmouth was to share this complex faith and culture with others. Coming to Dartmouth also challenged my faith because I did not have a religious community around me. The closest Jamatkhana is two hours away from campus. Class meetings and work often interfere with prayer times. Yet my faith has persevered and has even become stronger than it was when I lived at home. I pray every night and morning. I try to live an ethical life. Most important, I have made a concerted effort to remain in touch with the Ismaili community through service, which has been a defining factor in my life.

Another defining factor invaded and shaped my life when, on September 11, 2001, the two World Trade Center buildings and a side of the Pentagon collapsed after being hit by hijacked planes. In the first days after the attack, my body and mind throbbed at night from the pain I felt for those who had lost loved ones. As the days wore on, however, talk about terrorists and Muslims sparked another emotion within me: fear. Flags sprouted everywhere, including in my parents' corner store. My mother religiously wore her red, white, and blue ribbons, encouraging us to do the same. I went to the grocery store to pick up some bread, and was even more than usually aware that I was wearing a traditional Pakistani garment, a *shalwar kameez*. "Please let me get back into my car safely," I remember thinking.

All the South Asians I knew became experts on the latest incidents of backlash. We got a glimpse of what to expect on September 12, when, instead of continued World Trade Center coverage, the local news reported that three mosques in neighboring suburbs had been shot at that morning. Islamic schools were shut down in fear of being attacked. My worst fears were heightened when a Sikh owner of a gas station in Arizona was shot and killed a few days later. Sikhs are South Asians who wear turbans to cover their hair, which they do not cut, out of respect for God's creation. Sikhs are not terrorists—and are not even Muslim—but by virtue of being brown, they became a ready target for the ignorant and scared masses in the United States. These incidents of stabbings, shootings, and murders of South Asians pierced my heart. Every morning at 6:45, my dad (a Pakistani immigrant and a U.S. citizen) opens our corner store in a small suburb in Houston. The town's burgeoning population is mostly Caucasian, many of whom have come to know and respect my parents as decent people. My parents work in our grocery store all day long; I hate the fact that they are so vulnerable to the ignorant lunatic driving by with a gun, and that there is little more they can do than to put up our flag and wear our ribbons, both in support and for protection. Everyone feels sorrow for those who lost their lives and their loved ones. Everyone feels anger and helplessness at those who could conceive of such atrocities. However, those of us with darker skin and hair must now also fear being the next victim. I shudder, knowing that my mom and dad in their store or my brother or sister in school could so easily become the next target. This fall was one of the few times I felt uncomfortable leaving my family as I headed back to school in late September; I felt even more helpless about ensuring their safety while at college. In light of the attacks on September 11, my family has become a high priority in my life. I call home often, just to make sure they are safe. The tragedy has brought me closer to my family and given me an outlet for beginning to express the emotions that I have had such a difficult time sharing with my family.

As a senior in college, at a time when I should be excited about the possibilities of graduating, getting a job, living on my own, and becoming an adult, I find myself apprehensive about what the future may bring. I know that I must face certain pressures from my parents while living up to the expectations I have set for myself. I know that my parents have sacrificed their youth and adulthood to ensure that their children will realize the American Dream, and I feel a sense of duty and honor in returning the favor. I know they want me to return home to Houston after graduation. Yet having physical distance from my parents during college has actually helped bring me closer to them. I would like to continue to strengthen this tie, something I cannot do in Houston. I know they want me to get married soon so that they can be happy, seeing me settled in my "permanent home." Yet I refuse to give in to the pressures of arranged marriage, fighting for the chance to find mutual love on my own terms. At the same time, I am no longer that restless eighteen-year-old desperate to escape home. I find myself caring more about the well-being of my parents and wanting to look out for their future. In a sense, these four years away from them have made me able to be my whole self, my Pakistani American Ismaili Muslim self. Regardless of the challenge or opportunity, I always end up relying on my faith to carry me through. In the end, this *faith* is my permanent home. It continues to define my values, my practices, my culture, and my identity. It guides me and follows me wherever I go.

After graduating in 2002, Sabeen pursued a career in international education and development issues, and she continues to work actively on matters of youth development in her professional and volunteer capacities. In 2008, she met her husband, a fellow Ismaili Muslim, through a mutual friend, and they married in 2011. She and her husband share their deep sense of faith and enjoy spending time with their families in Texas, while always looking for opportunities to travel abroad.

This essay was written in 2002 and was first published in *Balancing Two Worlds: Asian American College Students Tell Their Life Stories*, ed. Andrew Garrod and Robert Kilkenny (Ithaca, NY: Cornell University Press, 2007).

PART IV

STRUGGLES WITH PIETY

9

Arif Khan   On the Outside

One of the greatest teachings of our religion is encompassed in the saying
"kun haythu aqaamka allah"—be where Allah has placed you. Allah has placed
us here, in this moment, for a reason, and may He open our eyes each day to
the wisdom in His plan.

A shaykh once said, "The way of the believer is optimism, because he knows
that there is no defeating Allah." So too must this be our attitude.

—David Coolidge

There are times when I am covetous. It is often a feeling inspired by
the mundane: the crispness of a new shirt, the sleek form of a perfectly
weighted pen, the sinuous curves of a fast car. It is as if the very atoms
themselves conspire to reach for some base desire tucked away in all of
us. With proper training, we can reason past ourselves; if all else fails,
walk away. Perhaps there are some desires, however, that we cannot shake.
They bury themselves deep inside of us. Perhaps they even grow out from
us. Mine is one I cannot walk away from, for it follows me. In the face of
worldly comfort, family, and friends, I cannot escape an inner yearning for
a place of true belonging.

I knew early on that something about me—about my family—was different. I reach back into my memory and find strange bits: a clinging sense
of want, despite the fulfillment of my basic needs; simple joys of birthdays
and celebrations but with a bittersweet film; a chronic disengagement and
a closed-off self caused by the fear of failure or the tainting of virginal
perfection. I'm not quite sure when or why it began. I don't trust my
memories of the past to not be tinged by hindsight. Even I don't know
how much of my current state I project onto these intangible wisps born
of wrinkled, pulsating gray matter. I think, though, that from an early age

I internalized a sense of otherness and a fear of reaching out to anyone (or anything) lest they crumble underneath my touch.

My father arrived in the United States as a graduate student, and my mother and I followed soon afterward. They uprooted their entire lives in search of a better future for themselves, but mostly for their children. They struggled through layers of uncertainty, their entire futures hanging on my father's ability to earn an assistantship to pay for his education. His part-time jobs paid for our costs of living. My mother eventually found a niche bonding (and commiserating) with wives of other international students. The small Bangladeshi community was far better than nothing but likely not nearly enough to offset the memories of what they had left behind and the realities of what lay ahead. She worked small jobs babysitting and sewing to pay for the rare luxuries that graced our bare-bones existence in those early years. As a four-year-old, I luckily did not fully realize how close to the breaking point we came. The threat of losing (or leaving) it all never came to be, and my father's employment after graduation provided the financial stability and legal course for permanent citizenship.

If from nothing else but this very sacrifice, I know my family loved me dearly. In a sense, their hopes for the future rested with me and my brother. I was the elder, and I am not the first immigrant child to have borne the weight and responsibility for their family's assimilation. Early on, my parents—fresh from the trauma of having left behind loved ones and familiar places—sought to re-create the world they left behind. In doing so, they inadvertently fractured mine.

Through life's complicated calculus, the sum of these early experiences left me with a firmly held sense of unease. The hardships of starting a new life beat down on my parents' relationship and strained their arranged bond. Sometimes their arguments erupted out of nowhere. They were never violent, but they were sometimes harrowing. They clashed over issues of money, family, and individual demeanor. My mother was not frugal enough for my father, while my father was too miserly for my mother. My father's family meddled closely and maddeningly according to my mother; in my father's opinion, they were to be held dear. My father hoped my mother would be more religious so that his children would be, too; my mother distrusted religious institutions and those who preached from them, but her spirituality was strong and clear, if closely held. I came to understand both of my parents as I grew older, just as they came to understand each other. My parents mellowed with age, and they either came to accept their new lives or simply became resigned to them. Thus, our home life eventually became more stable—though only after I had become solidly askew.

During the tumultuous years, it did not help matters that so much in our household went unsaid. It was clear that my studies were to be my one and only priority. I was to be calm and quiet—excitability was generally frowned on. Drugs, sex, and alcohol were not only forbidden dangers, but unfortunately forbidden topics for conversation as well. When I was a child, scenes on television of a couple kissing or teenagers talking about their relationships merited a quick channel change. The reality that humans are sexual beings was never acknowledged. My parents strove to impart the skills and knowledge necessary to survive in a society hostile to their values. It was a responsible move, though complete with the flaws in execution that only hindsight can detect.

I spoke Bengali at home and English at school. This was a source of pride for my parents—a shared, familial embrace of our culture. Unfortunately, my emotional depth and lexical range in Bengali failed to keep pace with the complexities of life that maturation brings. My means of expression contracted just when I most needed to express and understand; I often had no idea what my parents *really* wanted, just what I thought they wanted.

My brother almost avoided this linguistic fiasco entirely. As a child, he abandoned Bengali. Had I followed his lead, perhaps my parents would not have forced him to pick it back up—this time off-key and with a staccato rhythm. I might have been his counterpart rather than a quasi-parent, picking at his Bengali and pushing it further underground.

I picked my brother's name, Asif. And though our parents challenge us with their chronic juggling and muddling of our names, we are not to be confused. He is leaner than I, his slimmer features providing the illusion of greater height. He was also once happier than I, his childhood innocence blinding him to the strains of the immigrant experience that I constantly saw tugging at the fabric of our existence. On the surface, his childhood was more stable than mine. While I transferred elementary schools almost every two years as my parents probed the public-school system, he enjoyed the results of our experiment, learning in the same school and growing with the same friends from kindergarten through sixth grade. By the time he was old enough to remember, we could afford the small luxuries—brand-name snacks, McDonald's, candy from the checkout counter—that our once-precarious situation had forced me to go without. Still, throughout our lives he has seen me as the privileged one, and I have seen him as the insolent one.

Asif was born in Mississippi and—as my mother would sometimes refer to him—is "our little American." I don't know how much the little things we say and do add up to who we are, but I can't help but sometimes feel that my parents' references to his blue passport gave him more leeway. As a five-year-old, my brother had simply to go to school. When I was five, I went to school and returned home every day to more arithmetic practice and Bengali lessons. I was positioned to be the flag bearer of our Bengali culture and Muslim identity in this foreign place; my brother was simply a child.

I did not understand then that my brother was younger, and that his cheerfulness hid a more sensitive side that he expressed in tantrums more often than words. I did not understand that he was not like me, and that his experience would not be like mine. When he wouldn't eat the food at home, we got to go to McDonald's. When I wouldn't eat, I just had "to understand" that I must. When he hated school lunches and tired of Lunchables, my mother delivered fast food to him in his lunchbox. And she could, for by this time our family could afford two cars, and she had her license. I quietly dealt with being picked up in the carpool lane in my dad's humble red car with the chipped paint and cracked windshield. I could not understand why it was acceptable for my brother to request that my father go home from work to pick up the newer car—the one that made a better impression at the ritzy private school we both attended after our elementary graduations—before showing up at the school to pick him up. I would have been too embarrassed to ask this of our father, but Asif insisted.

To say there was constant tension between us would be to mischaracterize our relationship. I remember running around the house, miniature pink feather duster in hand, pretending to be a reporter chasing down my brother for an exclusive interview. I was the gate agent and Asif the passenger when we cordoned off the bedroom hallway, converting it into a boarding gate fully equipped with my toy computer and boarding passes from bygone trips. I was the teacher and my brother the pupil in my mock classroom; Asif seemed to enjoy watching the red ink spill from my father's grading pens as much as I enjoyed enacting deliverance with impunity on his "cursive."

Truth be told, there was no conspiracy, no conscious decision to hand the baton to me. We are simply a product of our different times. I was passed the responsibility when I was young and my parents were huddled under the weight of their decision to emigrate. No one looked back to tell me I could let go of it in favor of my own banner. Perhaps it was because I never told anyone that I still held on.

I moved from school to school as my parents navigated school districting and homeownership in a town where the legacy of segregation still floated very near the surface. It was not until fourth grade that I spent more than two years in any one school or any one home.

I became accustomed to being the new kid, and bowed deeply to the authority of my teachers. It took much time for me to open up to my friends, and I was at times deeply embarrassed if my teachers or parents saw me engaging in the norms that define childhood play, relationships, and mistakes. I wanted to be older, a model student, and perfect. These desires trumped my hope to make close friends and be seen as something more than a novelty. Even after my most social moments, I still felt like an outsider. I knew I did not look the same, and that my parents did not sound the same or know the same things as our neighbors. I knew that I would not dare break the rules with the same ease that my classmates might, and that my schoolwork would always come first. I knew that I carried with me religious beliefs that kept pork off my plate and my nose out of the Bible. My understanding of my religion and culture—born more from an idiosyncratic, unspoken family doctrine than from any ancient text—kept me from approaching girls or attending dances. And when I began to realize that I was the only one really holding myself accountable, I again turned to my culture and religion as a solid excuse to escape the awkwardness of these adolescent rites of passage.

Again, it was the unsaid. I held on to the subliminally imparted values: if an action feels bad, it is; even an atom's worth of good is worth doing; without Allah, there is nothing, and with Him, there is everything. I did not have the knowledge to understand the subtleties of the religion or the complexities of its jurisprudence. At times, I felt myself aping the moves of the rituals. My beliefs were simple and reflexive. They left no room for those extreme viewpoints that grow from culture, intolerance, and frustration—not the body of the Faith. From my limited experiences, I built a mold of how individuals in my position—immigrant, Muslim—act and believe. In doing so, I placed my sense of self on unsteady ground.

Through the tumult, I found in my grandfather—my Nana—a sage guide and powerful constant. It's been years since his gentle eyes followed the rolling, kudzu-covered hills as they flattened out into the Mississippi Delta, my home. I imagine him sitting erect in the front seat, only his paralyzed index finger able to resist the nervous jitters of his anxious energy. My father drives him from the airport, my grandmother guarding the wares of their travels. The ride must have been familiar to them, if not exactly old hat. Their occasional visits mapped well onto the slow change in my Southern hometown: frequent enough for them to witness the crawling evolution of life there, though not frequent enough for any of us.

Nana always had his finger on our pulse and the wisdom to interpret what he saw of our lives. He was the one to give voice to the unsaid. He—rightly—did not feel that everything would simply fall into place for us.

My brother and I were likely not the only children to have looked forward to visiting with grandparents, but the fact that mine had to travel halfway around the world to see us made their visits all the more meaningful. My grandparents helped me create a world apart from the daily strains of being the elder child in a first-generation-immigrant household. I still have cassette tapes of my grandfather telling the tales of Ali Baba and the Forty Thieves and Naseeruddin Hodja with his gentle, brilliantly powerful voice.

As I grew older, my grandfather's stories grew in complexity. Anticipating his arrival, my mother used her free book-club selections to order books for Nana to read during his stay. (Money was tight as my father grew into his teaching career at the nearby university, but books and encyclopedias were luxuries we allowed ourselves.) I was amazed at the speed with which my grandfather inhaled the giant tomes recounting the histories of Europe, Arabia, and the medieval Muslim world. I listened in wonderment as Nana retold those tales, complete with information injected from his past research and experience making the hajj in Saudi Arabia.

For my grandfather, these histories wove into his conception of the Islamic faith. Nana certainly ascribed to the tenet of the oneness of Allah proclaimed in the Sharia, and his five daily prayers were five more than my mother performed. But his sense of religious wonderment struck me as more pragmatic than spiritual. As far as I could tell, it was not based in a cathartic rush, but rather a careful assessment of the wonders Muslims had achieved under the benefaction of our Lord. The voluminous library at Cordoba, the gleaming white of the Taj Mahal, and groundbreaking discoveries in algebra, medicine, and science were products of earthly toil with divine inspiration. As seen by my grandfather, the Quran was a guide to daily life, and chief among its teachings was the near-holiness of scholarship.

Nana took great pride in retelling and reshaping these stories. They served as a pressure release for his ever-churning mind. Our small-town home gave him the opportunity to see us grow, but took away the responsibilities—grocery shopping, building maintenance, charity work—that he could savor in Bangladesh.

Visiting my grandparents' home in Dhaka for the first time when I was in the fourth grade, I witnessed this history in the aged engineering books, ledgers, and personal diaries, and the volumes and volumes of classical Bengali poetry and literature that lined the delicately maintained shelves. There, in his natural environs, I understood for the first time my grandfather's resourcefulness. And, thinking back now, I understand his kindness then with a new clarity. Traveling by rickshaw at a time when Dhaka was not yet choked by a claustrophobic jostling (cars, people, high-rise after high-rise), Nana took me to stores so I could find creature comforts to make me feel at home during what then seemed like an endless summer stay (imported Pringles and Tang did the trick). He would crisscross the city to bring me fresh-baked yeast rolls and Western-style fried chicken from the finest hotels. He and my grandmother took us to New Market, where he bought me (pirated) Mariah Carey tapes and textbooks written in Bengali so I could continue to practice reading and writing in my native tongue. And, when my brother and I tired of all of this and impetuously claimed boredom, Nana sent us on an adventure around the house collecting melted candle wax to recast and reuse. When we wanted a new sketchbook, my grandfather sat down on his cold terrazzo floor and made us one, complete with hand-stitched binding. In his hands, the shells from the coconut he picked for dessert became our newest toys.

For my seventeenth birthday, Nana gave me two books: a taxonomy of modern Islam and a guide to following Islam in the modern world. Though the physical distance between us was often vast, Nana seemed to understand the nature of the struggles I faced. His example was powerful, and his teachings were crucial as I moved forward.

To claim that I had no friends because of my many moves would be both inaccurate and self-pitying. In elementary school, I was certainly respected and appreciated, and perhaps even liked. I bonded closely with Mark, an immigrant from the Philippines, in the third grade. Until he and I moved to different schools, we shared a love for Power Rangers and the manner in which neither of our families had completely assimilated. In sixth grade, I became close to a small group of my peers. I related particularly well to one friend, Stephen. I have made few male friends in my lifetime, for I have never been adept at the posturing that defines male relationships. Stephen and I found common ground, and we—along with our female friends—formed a close-knit group. Still, for reasons not completely clear to me, our friendship did not extend far beyond school hours. Perhaps it was only my paranoid perception, but it was as if my connection was slightly more superficial than everyone else's. The division between life at school and life at home was sharp.

As fate would have it, our small Southern town eventually became home to six Bangladeshi families. I was loath to admit it to myself then, but among this group I made some of my closest friends. We laughed at our parents' accents and strange interpretations of the world around them. We understood the pressures that we all faced to excel and justify our parents' tremendous sacrifices. And we understood what it meant to believe in a faith whose practices and tenets seemed so at odds with the values of our non-Muslim peers.

Our families came together on alternating weekends for what we called "Arabic class." It was as much a time for the children to learn to read (but of course not understand) Quranic Arabic as it was an opportunity to socialize. For us children, the Arabic class was merely something that had to be gotten through. The real delight was our time spent together.

In retrospect, those relationships could have been much more, had I allowed myself to connect deeper. For whatever reason, I enjoyed the company of adults almost more than that of children my age, and I sometimes eschewed computer games for politics. As we grew older and our secrets grew edgier, the degrees of separation between friend and friend's parent were sometimes too few for comfort. I never considered myself popular, but by middle school I considered myself better adjusted than some of my Bangladeshi peers. Thinking back, this was somewhat of an outrageous sentiment to hold, based on the shifting nonsense of adolescent social hierarchy. I may have been tolerated in multiple social groups, but even then I knew it was questionable as to whether I was really wanted. Until I found close friends in band my sophomore year, my life remained clearly demarcated into the two cultural spheres of school and home.

Sophomore year of high school marked a turning point, the beginning of a new phase of self-discovery. The preceding summer and that school year, friendships that I had made matured. I found myself connected to others on a level of understanding that I had not reached before. My social activities were well within the context of my personal limits, with a midnight curfew intact and parties and dances not up for discussion. I did not consider myself deprived or constrained by these boundaries. Rather, I found in these friendships hope for a sense of place.

For my junior and senior years, I left home and attended a public residential high school for gifted students. My school drew students from across the state and put me on a college campus two hours away from home. Here I could be free of the odd embarrassment of being caught in social interaction by my parents.

Though I still found myself anxious and socially risk averse, I made powerful new friendships during these two years. From almost the beginning, I connected with Mike and Kelly. Both white and from well-regarded families in their respective hometowns, Mike and Kelly found themselves just a shade different from their expected norms. I felt safe with them, free from being judged. Like me, they did not feel the urge to sneak off campus and drink. We found our joy in conversation and silliness and forged a bond through common experience. I also found other Muslims and other friends from Bangladesh. Unbeknownst to them, their life experiences held up a mirror to my own. Though they were the result of the same immigrant-plus-Muslim-in-America formula, they embodied a different final product. Many of them were much more uninhibited in their interactions with others. My roommate, Nayeef, fasted for all of Ramadan—even during school—while I never had before. I was inspired to follow his example. Living with him, I discovered that his practice of Islam was piecemeal in a manner that approximated my own.

Just as meaningful as my friendship with Nayeef had been was my sense of betrayal by him. My invocation of the word "betrayal" overstates the change in our relationship (there truly was none) but captures the depth of my feeling and confusion at the time. It was my personal choice to abstain from alcohol; Nayeef felt comfortable with the alternative choice. In Nayeef and my other Muslim friends, I grasped for a model to follow. I wanted a simple way to reconcile my values with my desire to engage in fulfilling human relationships within the context of Western teenage society. I assumed that I could find in Nayeef the cohort of Western Muslims I was searching for, and was disappointed to find that I was again alone in my views. And while Mike and Kelly shared in my teetotalism for the time being, I found myself on the outside of each of two worlds.

I don't pray five times a day. I don't fast through all of Ramadan, and I have not yet made the hajj. I do, however, avoid pork and abstain from drinking alcohol and engaging in sex. Islam is by definition wholesale; taking the religion à la carte is not an option. But I pick and choose and—despite my best efforts—I judge. I feel spiritually grounded and mindful of Allah. I tell myself that this sense of faith, along with ethical conduct, gives me wiggle room. It should be all or none, but some is still better than nothing, I tell myself. Assessments of my stance range from the cut-and-dried logical pronouncement of "hypocrisy" to shades of gray that are more forgiving. I'll reach for my own ideal and leave it to Him to decide.

I do wonder why my aversion to alcohol runs so deep. Perhaps it is part cultural, as my immediate family and most respected relatives do not drink. It is certainly part biological, as my habits with food and spending have shown me that I cannot always help myself; it is best not to risk alcoholism. And maybe abstaining from alcohol is something that keeps me from the edge of some greater moral, ethical, and spiritual abyss. Despite all of my transgressions, at least here I am holding fast to something in the face of powerful challenges. If I slip further down the slope, who knows where it will lead?

I dwell on my relationship to alcohol because it is now—in the adult world—an ever-present fixture. And, in a bizarre manner, alcohol defined my experience in my transition to adulthood in college. A common refrain, and one that I have repeated with surprisingly great gusto, is that you don't have to drink to have fun at Dartmouth. This might be true, but I never completely saw this experiment through. For the first half of my collegiate experience, I was trapped in the rules and inhibitions of my past. In a time when my peers were using the presence of one thousand other equally clueless and awkward first-years on campus as an immediate (if only superficial) transformative experience, I held up religion as both an excuse and a reason to avoid those situations that made me uncomfortable. I adored my first-year floor and our adventures, but overall I felt disconnected. It was a repeat of the school-versus-home dichotomy I had grown up with. I did not spend time with my class friends outside of class, and my floormates constituted my home sphere.

Of course, even the "home" at Dartmouth was a very rough approximation, and I did develop some close friendships. I became an undergraduate assistant in part to create floor communities that provided alternative social spaces for those who chose not to drink. Through my UGA experience, I became more comfortable being in the presence of alcohol and connecting to a broader swath of individuals. As my range of friends evolved, social habits and norms shifted. As with my friendship with Nayeef, it would be dishonest of me to say I took the changes completely in stride. While the strength and nature of my friendships remained unchanged, I held inside the sadness of having lost a plank in our platform of solidarity.

My time at Dartmouth also—more than any other experience—forced me to question my relationship with Islam. While the Muslim community at Dartmouth and in the Upper Valley is small, it was far more robust than anything I had experienced prior. I acutely felt the inadequacy of my technical knowledge of the religion. The self-doubt stemming from that realization was compounded by the array of Muslim experiences on campus. I found myself in the middle of the spectrum between practice and belief. I again was faced with the tenuous nature of my à-la-carte position. I was also confronted by the idiosyncratic nature of my self-constructed identity. Dancing, dating, drinking—these were all things that other well-adjusted, Muslim, South Asian immigrant students did. What exactly was I holding on to? Had I built my identity on a lie that I had myself fabricated? In interpreting the unspoken expectations of my family and adhering to them unquestioningly, had I actually even incorporated any broader truths? As a senior, I sometimes felt that I had clung to something for naught, that I had missed my opportunity to tailor the fabrics of my identity into a more modern, better-fitting form.

In recent years, I have been suspended between the grip of the past and anxiety about the future. Through reflection, experience, and mostly the passage of time, I now feel ready to more fully engage the present. Old habits are difficult to shake, but I find myself more willing to take positive risks. Perhaps I am just now (and still very cautiously) living the life of a teenager. After all, some is better than none.

As I stridently questioned my interpretation of Islam while at Dartmouth, I attended prayer for Eid al-Fitr, one of the most important holidays in the Muslim calendar. Through what one might call serendipity—what I might call His hand—the chaplain, David Coolidge, delivered a sermon focusing on communities and the sense of place. Of all the esoteric scripture that I—holding only a rudimentary technical knowledge—might have been confronted with, Dave held those glorious words to the light. I do not know where they come from, whether from the Quran or the Hadith. I do know the power of those words and the tears they still bring to my eyes. *Be where Allah has placed you.* My not having a place is of itself a place. *The way of the believer is optimism.* There is hope for moving forward.

Arif is currently pursuing a career in medicine. This undertaking has blessed him with friends and an outlook that has brought more peace, and also a sense of place, to his life.

10

Adam W.   Being Muslim at Dartmouth

The more I think about it, the more convinced I become that I have been a Muslim my whole life—it just took eighteen years for me to realize it. Many English speakers who come to Islam prefer to label the process as one of "reversion" instead of "conversion." This is based on a saying of the Prophet Muhammad (peace be upon him) that every child is born in the state of knowing God and wanting to observe His commandments (i.e., wanting to be Muslim), but the child's parents and culture convert him or her to other ideologies, such as Christianity and Judaism (and to this may be added systems such as consumerism, capitalism, and scientism in our modern context). I feel this in my own life, not just because I have always had faith in God and a desire to submit to His will, but because for as long as I have been able to contemplate religious devotion, my conclusions have fit most closely with the Islamic view of obligations, rites, and practices. I never questioned God, but I can remember always asking myself how to proceed with a knowledge of the Divine.

Early Faith, and No Reason to Question

I lived for the first seven years of my life in southwestern England, spending weekdays with my American mother and most weekends with my British father. I attended a private school where I suppose we had some kind of religious education, but I have no recollection of it. I do remember a few elements of our weekly chapel service: the deputy headmaster would take out a lightbulb and tell us that God could make us illuminate the world, which sounded fine to me. Church visits came once or twice a year; all I remember of that is sitting with my mother for a long time in some vast, Gothic, stone sanctuary, surrounded by a sea of pastel-colored hats. It must have been Easter.

When my mother remarried and we moved to Minnesota, I had my heart set on becoming a member of a church. My mother tells me I was eager to get baptized. I'm not sure why, but perhaps it had something to do with my desire to belong. I remember the loneliness of second and third grade, when I was an oddity to most and a friend to few—a boy who spoke strangely and wore trousers that reached only to his ankles. One classmate called me "Accent Boy." I can imagine I wanted a community to which I felt I could belong, a community whose rites of passage were a little easier and more tangible than developing a new wardrobe and cleansing my voice of British sounds and terminology. My mother and I found a nearby church where the choir sang Purcell and Vaughan Williams reasonably well and the sermons were intelligible. In less than two years, we had both made it through new-member classes, and I had had water sprinkled on my head in front of the congregation. It was a Presbyterian church, but the only person who cared what denomination we belonged to was my Norwegian grandmother, who despaired that her daughter and grandson had strayed from the upright Lutheran path.

Maybe I'm not giving myself enough credit. Maybe it really was religious conviction, not just a desire to feel welcome, that led me to join that church in the first place. It certainly looked a lot like religious conviction after a while, as I would often talk to the pastors about spiritual issues, and even gave the sermon one Sunday during my senior year of high school. Most of the congregation knew and respected me, as I was in the children's choir, went through confirmation class, joined missions trips to New Mexico and the Czech Republic, and played the piano as a prelude to church services at least once a year. The whole congregation treated me well, and I had no reason to complain, no reason to question the practices or the dogma.

During this time I attended a private Christian school. Spending most of my time in this environment, I was never given a choice not to believe in Christianity. The atheists there were also the ones who misbehaved and later started drinking, so I wasn't about to look to them for examples of how to live my life or how to think. There was only one non-Christian on the list of people whom I cared about and respected, and that was my father. He and I had never been close; after I moved to the United States, I saw him a mere seven weeks each year, and we never talked about anything significant. My mother and I talked every night, discussing how we were feeling and what was going on in our lives, but Dad said little and didn't understand me when I wanted to talk. I can't blame him; we never had enough time to get used to interacting with each other, so our relationship remained more superficial. I knew little about his ideas on spirituality, and the little I did know, I didn't quite comprehend. Fat little Buddhas sat in the bookcases and on the windowsills of every room in his house, but I never tried too hard to understand why. I asked him what it was like to meditate every day, and he gave me only cryptic responses such as, "It's about letting yourself be an observer of your own life." The religion I followed was much simpler and more sensible: God came down as Jesus, Jesus died to cleanse us of our sins, and in order to get into heaven we all need to acknowledge that He did this—there was none of that sitting alone, cross-legged stuff that I often saw my father do.

I do remember worrying about my father's soul. I went to my pastor once while in middle school to ask what I could do to get my father to accept Jesus, because I did not want him to go to hell. My pastor, who also liked to speak cryptically, told me that many people come to Jesus (peace be upon him) through Buddha, and hearing this frustrated me further. Why couldn't my Christian pastor share my enthusiasm to bring a lost soul into the fold?

Seeds of Doubt

Until about age fifteen, I tried to understand my father as best I could: he was simply delusional, and someone needed to give him the right pair of glasses so he could finally see how important God and Christ should be in his life. However, for my fifteenth birthday he bought me one of his favorite books, and my respect for him grew. It was *The Way of Chuang Tzu*, a collection of Taoist sayings edited by the Catholic writer Thomas Merton, and as I read it, all of my ideas on religious thought and writing started to change. I would read a few pages each night and spend the next day contemplating the wisdom I found in them. At first I felt guilty because I had read the Bible and never felt this way about my own holy book: the Bible was a collection of laws and dubious historical stories, followed by conflicting accounts of Jesus' life (peace be upon him) and a few boring letters about belief and practice. It was so long! *The Way of Chuang Tzu*, on the other hand, was a collection of terse allegorical tales, most no more than two pages, each one leading me to think about essential questions of conduct and the nature of life.

> If a man is crossing a river and an empty boat collides with his own skiff, even though he be a bad-tempered man he will not become very angry. But if he sees a man in the boat, he will shout at him to steer clear. If the shout is not heard, he will shout again, and yet again, and begin cursing. And all because there is somebody in the boat....If you can empty your own boat crossing the river of the world, no one will oppose you, no one will seek you harm.

I felt that this new book was teaching me how to think, whereas the Bible had been commanding me what to think. I never imagined that foundational religious literature could be enjoyable to read. Like going to church, reading the Bible was a chore that made me feel better about myself once I'd done it.

I credit this gift from my father with the beginning of my journey to Islam. It made me ask myself how so much truth and wisdom about the world could come from a tradition that did not emphasize the divinity of Jesus the Messiah (peace be upon him). Was it possible that Christianity was not the ultimate truth? If acceptance of Jesus (peace be upon him) is the key to heaven, why would God try to trick His people by placing joy and wisdom within religions that did not acknowledge this?

Having been exposed to the wisdom of another spiritual tradition, I started thinking critically about my own and allowed myself to wonder what was lacking. For example, if it were true that God created the world, gave me life, and blessed me with everything I have, then shouldn't I have a duty to express my thanks for all that He has done for me through some constant obligation or devotion? The idea of regular prayer appealed to me, but I never quite understood what form it should take. I wanted a set ritual that showed me the best way to worship God and the best words to use. I tried praying every night before bed, but the prayer soon became little more than a long list of things I wanted and people I wanted God to help. When I prefaced this with a review of my day, thanking God for everything beneficial that had happened, I still felt I was doing so merely to justify going through my personal spiritual wish list afterward.

I also began to realize the many things that bothered me about the devotional practices of my Christian environment. The "praise songs" from chapel services at school—with a rock band onstage and an audience swaying with hands raised—seemed more of a show than a sign of sincere devotion, and I disliked the speakers' insistence that Jesus (peace be upon him) was their supreme Lord and Savior, all the while speaking of him as if He were their buddy. Such rhetoric didn't strike me as befitting a divine reality. As for church services, I hardly ever enjoyed them. Heaven forbid that I would ever admit that, even to myself, but as soon as the services started, I wanted them to end. Going to church was an ordeal that brought me rewards once over, such as seeing friends or getting compliments on my tie. In other words, it was a means—I had to earn my place within the community, and sitting through church proved I was worthy to be a part of it—but rarely an end in itself. I acknowledge that others might be satisfied by this, but I needed something else.

A Call to Islam

I looked for a spiritual community when I arrived at Dartmouth, but nothing I found satisfied me. I went to Catholic student gatherings, attended several services at the local Episcopal church, and spent time at the Episcopal student center on campus. Looking back, I admit that I did not try too hard. The church services were long and drawn out, and, after discovering that the choir and organist were not as good as those at my church back home, I gave up on them. I heard of some other good congregations in the area, but I didn't spend any time investigating them. I concluded that religion could wait, as I was having too much fun discovering what it was like to be a college student in a beautiful town with a good number of friends. Something was lacking in my spirituality, but just having a sense of God's presence in my life felt like enough for me during that time, and I didn't think I needed anything more.

I knew what I wanted to study at least a year before entering college. Being a detective or FBI agent had always been my dream job, so I had called up a family friend, a homicide detective, and asked him what college major the FBI would like to see. He said they were in dire need of speakers of Middle Eastern languages. I'd always enjoyed languages and learning a new alphabet sounded interesting, so I decided to study Arabic.

I aimed high when applying to colleges and was accepted at Dartmouth College and the University of Edinburgh. I chose the former because the head of Oriental Studies at the latter was a Dartmouth graduate who advised me to go to his alma mater. Once I got to Dartmouth, selecting my classes and major was easy since I'd already decided on what to study, and during the winter term of my freshman year, I found myself in a class on Arab culture. It covered the key beliefs and texts of Islam, most of which I had heard before, with one exception. The professor showed the class a documentary on the spread of Islam, which used the call to prayer as a transition between topics. The voice of one man repeating the simple Arabic phrases—"God is Most Great, I testify that there is no deity but God and that Muhammad is His Prophet, come to prayer, come to your good"—reached something deep inside me and took hold. I felt like God Himself was calling just to me, that His creation was calling out, begging me to follow wherever He would lead me. At first I didn't know what to do, but one night when I couldn't get to sleep, I sent an e-mail to the Muslim Student Association at Dartmouth, asking to speak with some of their members. Within a week, I'd had several dinners with two of the Muslim students, who took me to see the Muslim prayer room on campus and showed me how they prayed. In the prayer room I met two women, Sara and Mariam, who agreed to have dinner with me and answer my questions, though they later told me that I seemed to already know the answers to the questions I asked.

Some people, especially my family members, have told me they believe I converted to Islam rather naively, without giving it much thought. Although I wouldn't call it naive, I do admit that the process was not complex. I didn't do a comparative study of doctrine and theology between the Bible and the Quran, nor did I assess the problems that Islam might have in a modern context, such as encouraging violence or withholding rights from women. Quite simply, I heard the call to prayer, and everything else felt inevitable. Everywhere I went, the haunting words of the call to prayer looped through my head, making me feel peaceful inside. It seemed to echo from the snowy landscape I walked through each day. The way the branches on the bare trees stood stable under a heavy layer of snow said to me, "*Ash-hadu allaa ilaha illa Allah.*" The pure black of the clear night sky said, "*Allahu akbar.*" I have an image of walking out of the library and taking in the empty landscape, the snow covering everything with desolate blankets of white, absorbing all sound, the bitingly cold air, and people off in the distance wrapped up in their many layers. I looked out and all of this said to me, "*Ash-hadu anna Muhammadar-rasul Allah.*" The world was calling me to true life, life in Islam, and I had a sense that I was sitting on a raft that had been set out for me to journey down a river, and all I had to do to get to the luscious garden at the end was stay seated and ride it out.

I'm trying to describe here what for so long has eluded description. I used to tell people about the process: how I heard the call to prayer, started reading about Islam, and had some discussions over dinner with Muslim students, and after two months or so decided to convert. But the truth is, it wasn't a process at all—more like two leaps and a splash as I landed in the most soothing, pleasurable lake in the world.

Hearing the call to prayer was the first leap. The second was the first time I attended Friday congregational prayer. I left it feeling that this was how a worship service should go, that this was the kind of devotion I imagined God would be pleased with—nothing unnecessary, just a short sermon, a short prayer together, and it was done. There was no performance; although one person stood to give the sermon, he talked more about beliefs and practices than about knowledge he had gained through his own experience, the latter being what I was accustomed to hearing in church. When this man led the prayer, he stood in front of the congregation and recited the Quran with a beautiful voice, but did so while facing the wall, turning away from everyone gathered as if to assert that he would not have recited any differently had he been standing alone. Unlike the "statements of faith" we all had had to repeat at church, we weren't indoctrinated through collective speech; the only thing we all said together was "Amen" when the Imam finished reciting the first chapter of the Quran.

The space had a much different feel from any church I had been in. There were no hard wooden pews to squirm in, no giant figures in the windows, no stern statues at the front, and no vast ceilings soaring overhead to intimidate me. All of us sat on the carpet with our shoes off, some leaning against walls or cushions during the sermon. It felt like an intimate gathering and, despite being a newcomer, I felt comfortable. In church I had never felt I could be my true self; the religious art, wrought-iron lamp holders, seats of dark wood, cold stone arches, and high vaulted ceilings of the sanctuary called me to put on an austere and composed demeanor along with my suit and tie whenever I entered. But in the Muslim prayer room I didn't have to wear another face. The personality I presented to God in that sacred space could be the same one I took with me throughout the day, and the work I did to develop my character in either place would affect my identity in the other.

When that first congregational prayer ended, a few people noticed I was new and introduced me to the community, which included graduate students, undergraduates, Dartmouth staff, community members from around New Hampshire, African Americans, Arabs, white American converts, and South Asians. This was one of the most diverse groups I had ever met, but it struck me that one thing was the same about all of them: every person there was pleasant, welcoming, and genuinely happy to be there. After a life of attending church as a means to gain access to fellowship and other opportunities, I had never imagined that a worship service could be an end in itself for so many people. I saw the light emanating from everyone there, and I desperately wanted to have all of them as friends.

That was my second leap toward Islam. It amazed me how content I was after attending congregational prayer, and the peace and light I received from the service stayed with me for the rest of the day and much of the following week. For perhaps the first time, I found myself looking forward to the next service I could attend.

In the meantime, small positive things had been happening. Every time I tried a new Muslim practice, something in my day went very well. The first time I prayed on my own in the Muslim fashion, the whole day somehow just felt right. The first time I got up in the early morning to pray the dawn prayer, I slept less but finished a paper that day in record time. These were small things, but they happened too predictably to be coincidences.

The greatest benefit, however, was that every time I asked for something in prayer, I received it within a day. This phenomenon has stayed with me: every time I ask for strength or resolve, or for the answer to a specific question or issue I'm dealing with, God grants it to me. I remember how, during my first week in the Middle East, a month after I had converted to Islam, I felt alone and out of place everywhere. Within my U.S. program, I was the only male Muslim, and at the mosque, I was the only non-Arab. I decided to pray one afternoon, and during the prayer I asked for an answer as to why I had ever converted in the first place, why I had left my original faith, and why I needed to pray so many times every single day. That night, I went to the mosque feeling sorry for myself; I left an hour later with a huge smile on my face. One of the brothers at the mosque had noticed me; he introduced me to his group of friends and they all took me out for the best dessert in the city, later insisting that I would have to eat every lunch and dinner for the next two months in their homes. That was the answer to my prayer. God was giving me a taste of the joy and other good things that I could receive as part of a Muslim community.

To put it simply, I was bribed. The call to prayer struck something inside me and caught my attention enough to get me thinking about this new faith. Congregational prayer showed me the possibility of enjoying religious services. Little positive things that happened to me after I started performing some Muslim practices enticed me to go further. Had I been drawn to Islam intellectually, I'm not sure that would have been enough to bring me into the fold; although the beliefs of Islam make more sense to me than any of my Christian beliefs ever did, the simple argument that I am not supposed to understand a God who is beyond the limits of my comprehension was sufficient for me as a Christian. My emotions needed to be drawn into it for me to believe fully. And so, after two or three months, I came to realize that Islam was giving me an offer I couldn't refuse. One Friday, after congregational prayer had ended, I approached the Imam and told him I wanted to convert. The half-dozen students who were hanging around after prayer were witnesses as I professed the short statement of faith: *Ash-hadu alla ilaaha illa Allah. Wa ash-hadu anna Muhammadar-rasul Allah.* I testify that there is no god but Allah. And I testify that Muhammad is His Prophet and Messenger.

A Deeper Faith, a Richer Life

Sometimes people who should know me better see me as a Muslim first and Adam second. I got into a fight with my stepmother a few months ago. We regularly get in fights (usually just a product of my being stupid), but this one was particularly nasty. I had been rude to her on several occasions, expecting her to cater to my every desire. Considering that she was in the midst of training to be a teacher and looking after two young children, it was a disrespectful assumption for me to make. She had every right to be angry, but I wasn't expecting all of what she said:

> I know you're sorry, Adam, but you keep doing the same thing to me and it's getting harder and harder for me to take your word for it. Plus, you know what? You know what I was thinking? A while ago, I told my friend that you converted to Islam, and she said to me, "Oh dear, you know how they treat their women…" And I know that that's not all true, and it can't be completely true of you now, but I just can't help thinking: look what you're doing to me! You, a Muslim, treating me like this. Look, I know that's a bit unfair, but I just wonder if you'll learn to treat women right.

I had a similar experience when I was in Egypt on a study-abroad program to learn Arabic. I fell for another American student there, and we had been in love for at least a month when one day she turned to me and said, "I'm terrified, Adam. I'm absolutely terrified that you're going to want me to wear the hijab. I see how limited the women are here in Egypt, and I know you haven't come up with a definite position on the hijab—I'm terrified of what's going to happen when you do."

That was the only argument we ever had. I had spent a month prior to this telling her sweetly, and quite sincerely, that I loved her for who she was and not for who I wanted her to be. I had told her many times that she was the only girl I knew whom I would be happy either to follow or to lead, someone whose life could truly complement mine. Yet she still felt the need to express her fear that, as a Muslim, I would eventually want to limit her as a woman. I thought she trusted me when I told her I loved and valued her as she was. For this, among other reasons, we separated two months later.

For a while, I was insecure about my choice to convert and constantly tried to prove myself to others, rattling on to them about why they should convert too and why I deserved special treatment as a Muslim. But now I'm more comfortable with my faith, and it has started to produce genuine change in me. The largest change is that I feel more in tune with the world around me. When I traveled to Jordan on another study-abroad program, I made more friends than my U.S. colleagues did, as I met average Jordanians through the nearby mosque I attended. Back home in Minnesota, the prayer rooms are filled mostly with African Americans and immigrants, many of whom live on the other side of the shopping district in my neighborhood, drive taxis, or work service jobs. If it weren't for congregational prayer, I would never have a chance to interact with them. Being involved in Islam gives me a better connection with life around me, something I could not have said when I was a Christian. Going to church meant putting myself more firmly into my social niche, interacting with white people from the upper-middle class with lots of money to donate, whereas every congregational prayer in my experience of Islam has brought me into a community much more diverse than the groups with which I spend the rest of my time. Even at a privileged, selective school like Dartmouth, the Muslim community is the most diverse group on campus.

When I was a Christian, I often heard people talk of the global Christian community as a "brotherhood of believers," but I never felt that brotherhood then as I have in Islam. Before I converted, I had done service work through my church in my community, in the Czech Republic, and in New Mexico—these were the experiences I had with people from other communities and other socioeconomic levels, but I never felt brotherly love between us. It was almost always a relationship based on us giving and them taking, a dependent interaction in which I gave my time and money to help those in need. This was my experience with other communities within the Christian faith, and I rarely felt a sense of brotherhood with them—it felt like nothing more than a "service opportunity" for me. But when I do service work with other Muslim communities, such as a local prison we go to every Friday, I feel more on the same plane with those I'm helping—we can all discuss the same theological concepts, and we pray together in one line.

I feel more secure now that my religion is part of my whole life. No longer do I feel as if the person I am on Sundays at church is different from who I am the rest of the time, because my daily life has been infused with prayer and remembrance of God. I start everything by saying, "*Bism illah*" (in the name of God), and the same Arabic phrases I use in prayer come into my head when I'm grateful, fearful, or unsure of anything. Guidelines from Islam inform most of my daily etiquette, from how I wash my hands to what topics I avoid discussing with my friends.

Islam has also brought me a greater desire to deepen my relationships with everyone in my life, from family members to friends to anyone else in the world around me. Respect for and care of family members are essential obligations in Islam, regardless of whether or not they are Muslim. In the Quran, taking care of parents is mentioned along with major religious duties such as fearing God and doing good works. Several sayings of the Prophet Muhammad (peace be upon him) emphasize the importance of respecting one's mother, since she is the one who gave so much of herself in raising her children. I couldn't think of a better way for my mother to have raised me, but through the years I have felt a lot of indignation toward her: I hated the fact that she never let me play video games and often told me to practice piano. I saw other parents being more lenient with their children, and I wanted to be treated similarly. I remember my mother saying I'd thank her when I got older, and even then I felt deep down a strong inkling that she was right. Now that I am older, I'm certain she was, and exhortations and writings in Islam constantly remind me that I need to rethink my relationship with my mother and finally give her the respect she deserves. Islam is not just for Muslims—the Quran addresses non-Muslims in several places and calls Muhammad (peace be upon him) a "mercy for the worlds." I live by the belief that if my Islam doesn't make me at least try to be a better person to those closest to me, what does it give me?

For years, my idea of happiness had been tied up in my search for a soul mate, and no matter what Islam gave me, there was no way I would concede any points that had to do with my pursuit of an amazing romantic relationship. Islam discourages physical contact between the sexes outside of marriage, and I pretended I didn't hear that. I have always been committed to abstaining from sex before marriage lest I take away the value of sex with my final life partner, but anything besides intercourse was acceptable to me, for it gave me that feeling of deep connection I longed for. When I read in Islamic texts that it is potentially dangerous for a man and a woman to be alone together, I dismissed it as hyperbole, because otherwise I would have had to curtail my constant scheming with girls. I could see the value in regular prayer, fasting, polite speech, and everything else Islam called for, except the suppression of romantic engagements before marriage.

A few months ago, I was absolutely convinced I had found my soul mate, and the painful end of that relationship shattered the last major barrier I had toward full acceptance of Islam. I thank God that I was pulled out of my self-deception. I can now admit that although a physical or emotional union with a girl brings me to incomparable heights of joy, it's fleeting, and it brings unease into every other aspect of my life. Studying Islam, on the other hand, can sometimes be difficult, and the joy it brings is not as intense, but it enriches every single element of my life. Before, I cared for my garden by shooting spurts of water onto the surface of the plants—it made them glisten for a while, but all it took was a gust of wind to brush all the water off, and if there was no wind, the water soon evaporated under the scorching sun. Now I water the garden with care and let the drops seep into the earth—new life is brought forth, and my plants grow up strong, fed by a constant sustenance that wells up from depths below, no matter what the conditions on the surface are.

As for friendships, much has changed for me there as well. I used to feel more worth in life when I seemed to have more friends. But we sustained our friendships by sitting together in front of the television for hours or by going to dance parties that reeked of alcohol and blasted music. In many instances, what we in fact shared was a few experiences of being distracted. However, I feel completely different about my friends now. My friendships with fellow Muslims are nurtured through praying together and debating ideas from the Quran. With my non-Muslim friends, I have a stronger desire to have meaningful conversations with them rather than living vicariously through the action and adventure of Arnold Schwarzenegger. I used to feel uneasy and frustrated about the time I spent doing nothing with my friends, but the time I spend with my current companions is replete with growth, meaning, and depth. Remembering the time I have spent with them brings tears to my eyes, and there are few things I look forward to more than being reunited with them in the Garden of the next life, God willing.

For a while after I converted, I felt I had figured life out and needed to show everyone else how right I was, so I tried to convince others to accept Islam. But this was simply a product of my own insecurity. The deeper I get in my faith, the less I need to explain myself to others and the more I respect others' beliefs. The Quran tells me never to assume that someone else is not a Muslim, and never to tell someone else where he or she has erred in faith. Even if others want to attack my beliefs, the Quran gives me two options: either to explain to them what I believe myself, or to walk away and have patience.

Two years ago, I feared, as did several others around me, that my decision to accept Islam would create divisions between me and everyone else in my life. But in fact it has brought me closer to the people whom I should value. There are whole groups of people I have met and interacted with because of Islam. I also feel a great need to have deeper relationships with all members of my family. The acquaintances and infatuations that don't matter have fallen away to make room for the friendships that do. Given all of this, I would find it difficult to contend that the richer life I now experience is not the result of the decision I made two years ago to become a Muslim.

Leader of a Community

Eight months after I joined the Muslim community at Dartmouth, I found myself leading it. I converted in May of my freshman year, and when I returned to campus in the fall, I became quite involved in the Muslim Student Association, coordinating a week of events to raise awareness about Islam. Other members noticed my efforts, so I was elected to the board for the winter term. Then it became apparent that I was the only one of the four board members willing to take on the role of president.

One moment I'm a WASP with aspirations of working for the government, and eight months later I'm the main person responsible for Muslim life within a sixty-mile radius of our campus—ours is the only Muslim prayer room in the area. As strange as it seemed at times, I understand how I came to lead the Muslim community here. As a convert, I put a great deal of work and effort into the religion because I had so much invested in it. If Islam turned out not to be right for me, I would have to confront the idea that I had made a mistake, and that all the constant praying, the awkward times I went through explaining my conversion to my family, and the hours I had spent reading about the faith would have been a waste of time. Since I had spent so much effort thinking about whether I agreed with each aspect of the faith, it would not have been easy to retreat and forget the conclusions I had come to.

For the other Muslims in the community, almost all of whom were born into the faith, it was harder to get so excited about Islam. They had lived with it for all of their lives; it had probably been a form of limitation and parental control during their teenage years, and they had experienced both the good and bad moments of life in the United States as Muslims. To me, however, there was always something new to learn about; Islam gave me a sense of freedom from the confines of my culture and upbringing, and I was still riding on the spiritual high that came with choosing a new way of life and being exposed to unique religious and cultural experiences. Islam had brought me nothing but good things, so I was one of the few people within the Dartmouth Muslim community with enough enthusiasm to oversee it.

I'm still enthusiastic about Islam, but I understand why many others are not. As one of my friends put it, when your experience with the dawn prayer is ten straight years of your parents making you wake up at four o'clock in the morning, it's hard to get rid of the bitter taste that prayer has brought for so long. Whereas I had chosen to confine my life with the aim of submitting to God, others' submission had been forced on them for as long as they could remember. I also had a better view of the whole situation because I had been on the other side of the river where the pastures aren't as green and there isn't much shade, and therefore I knew how much I should value what I had found in Islam. I know many people who call themselves Muslim and don't pray or follow Islamic regulations regularly, but they're also not prepared to try anything else or to abandon the fundamental beliefs of their religion. This is both a blessing and a curse: although they never lose their general faith in a just and merciful God, they don't know what it's like living in another spiritual tradition, and thus it is very hard for them to appreciate Islam fully.

Another reason why I have a better time with my religion than those who grew up Muslim is that wherever Islam became the dominant religion, it got mixed up in the culture of a people. Once that happens, it's hard to determine from within what is part of Islam and what is simply cultural tradition. I am fortunate to have had the chance to look at every aspect of modern Islam and to research whether or not that was part of the original faith as proclaimed by the Prophet Muhammad (peace be upon him). Those who grow up with Islam as part of their culture rarely spend time questioning whether the way their family approaches women's issues, the way they pray, or the way they speak to others has a sound basis in the Quranic and Islamic tradition, and they usually have to reject some of the practices of their family and community if they want to follow the original message of Islam more closely.

Daring to Question

Granted, I had to wade through my own swamp of mixed culture and lofty ideals of freedom and justice. When I decided to convert, I still hadn't completely reconciled myself to Islamic ideals in certain areas, such as the role of women in society and the proper use of violence. I had grown up with the beliefs that women in Western societies had been fully liberated and that peaceful means were the only way to accomplish anything effective in this world. I assumed that the Islamic way of looking at these two points was slightly flawed, and I didn't want to think too much about it. But I did ruminate on it occasionally, and the more I did, the more it struck me that I had looked at my own culture with selective vision. In the West, where a woman has more freedom and is allowed to work wherever and wear whatever she pleases, her life is much better than it would be were she to live by Islamic ideals, having to stay at home to look after the house and children, covering up completely when she did need to go outside, and deferring to her husband in all matters. Or so I thought. But to assume, like so many of us do, that the West has all the best ideals and answers to society's problems is dangerous. In the West, is it not true that many women feel pressure to wear revealing clothing to draw attention from the men around them? And that they often have to take on as much responsibility at work as men do despite also being expected to look after their children?

It seems that sometimes we're so focused on providing equality for all that we forget to ask ourselves if that's really what we should be striving for. If everyone did the same jobs for the same amount of time, we wouldn't have a chance to specialize, to carve out a role and a realm for ourselves over which we can exert authority. In the Islamic tradition, women are not forced to give up their rights in a marriage—rather, they are given more rights with more options: the right to stay home and devote time to child rearing, the right to dress in a way that hinders men from seeing them as objects, and the right to be free of broader financial responsibilities. In Islam, the wife has authority over and responsibility for the home, while the husband has authority over the family as a whole and a responsibility to ensure that all the needs within it are provided for. Unfortunately, in many contemporary Muslim societies, these points are forgotten and men demand that women dress appropriately, stay at home, and obey their husbands. This is a perversion; it's like forcing the bright student in a community college in the Midwest to transfer to an Ivy League university simply because he has the right to a good education and the government is willing to support his studies—his desire to stay close to home and enjoy his community college's opportunities is not taken into account. Similarly, many Muslim societies are twisting ideals intended to give women more respect into methods of oppression while rejecting other Islamic rights such as education for all, and this is blatantly wrong. Forcing a woman to wear a veil and stay at home is wrong, but so is not allowing her to wear a veil (as in French state institutions) or making her feel she has to go back to work once her maternity leave runs out. It may seem it's not my place to argue that it's better for women to stay indoors and dress more conservatively, but had I not heard women express the ideas above, I would not write about them. It is a fact that, in the West, more women are converting to Islam than men. Can that many people be fooled by misogynistic propaganda, or do they perhaps see in Islamic values something that Western culture lacks?

Violence is another issue that I found troublesome initially. I was taught that nonviolence alone solves problems, whereas some parts of the Quran call for violence. Once again, we must look at how some Western ideals fit into reality. Our nation is involved in two large-scale wars, in Iraq and Afghanistan, and all our police forces are trained in the use of deadly force. I've always wanted to go into law enforcement, and it has struck me that I had never tried to reconcile my Christian upbringing, which called me to complete nonviolence, with the idea that my future profession could involve carrying a loaded gun at my hip and knowing how and when to use it. Personally, I appreciate the Islamic view that violence is necessary in some cases—if it can prevent more violence or stop oppression—but there are many regulations and rules to keep in mind if one must resort to violence. This seems like a more sensible view than the idea that we should proclaim complete nonviolence until we're put in a tricky situation, and then feel guilty for the rest of our lives about choosing to use violence for noble ends.

Violence and the position of women are only two of the many realms in which we in the West often take issue with Islam. There is much more I could address about these two topics, let alone others, but more educated and qualified people have done it better in lectures readily available on YouTube or in articles in various publications and online. The Californian convert Shaykh Hamza Yusuf and the British convert Shaykh Abdal Hakim Murad have helped immensely with my understanding of difficult verses of the Quran and elements within the Islamic tradition.

To put it all simply, Islam is a tool that has enabled me to work through all the cultural and experiential baggage I've amassed. The more I look into the Islamic view on issues such as the position of women in society, the more I realize how wrong I had been never to question how fairly my own culture seems to treat those topics. My new faith has brought me experiences I could not have had before and given me access to different perspectives on a number of issues. I don't know how I otherwise could have had the opportunity to pray from eight at night to three in the morning with dozens of people from all areas of society, as I did during several nights in a mosque in Alexandria, Egypt, and how else I could have had the chance to dine in the home of Chechen refugees as an honored guest.

I will admit that my view on the Israeli-Palestinian conflict, globalization, and other world issues is different from the average U.S. citizen's, but I haven't blindly switched sides either. There are Muslim leaders who talk constantly of the chaos and injustice that the Jews are spreading throughout the world, mainly in Palestine and in the U.S. government. Such blatant antisemitism frustrates me, and I view it as running contrary to Quranic injunctions on respectful dialogue. On the other hand, is being fanatically critical of a state any worse than being blindly supportive of it, as so many of us are toward Israel or our own government?

Maturity, Not Rejection

I'd like to think of my conversion narrative not as a jump from a bad place to a better one, from a misguided culture or religion to a smarter one, but more as a slow process of guided self-discovery. And it is a process. When we pray, the one supplication we have to make several times in each prayer comes from the first chapter of the Quran. We say, "Guide us to the straight path"—not "Keep us on the straight path." This reminds us that no matter how much good we have done recently or how far we've come in the faith, there is always more distance to cover. In the preceding pages, I have written much in the form of "my life was like x, but now that I'm a Muslim, my life is suddenly like y," which makes it sound as if my whole life consists of two points separated by a religious conversion. In truth, I am hiking up a mountain of wisdom and knowledge, and when I look down to where I was before, it seems like such a huge difference in altitude that I feel compelled to describe it in black-and-white terms. But I know I've been hiking up the mountain since I was born, for eighteen years before I converted, and that in my life Islam is simply a more direct path with fewer avalanches and slippery spots. I know I'll never reach the summit, and I don't know how long this path will remain quick, easy, and direct, but as long as I have the strength to keep following it, I will.

Through Islam, I am slowly coming to know what it means to respect everything and everyone around me, to respect myself, and to be my true self, to be human. This doesn't mean I'm rejecting my previous life as unproductive and immoral, but Islam is a fulfillment of the framework I was using before, in which I continue to improve and question the assumptions that my society and my experiences try to force on me. Shaykh Hamza Yusuf was once asked if he thought Islam was compatible with modernity. "In some ways," he replied, "I don't think our souls are compatible with modernity."

In the words of the man whom the Prophet Jesus (peace be upon him) cured of blindness, "Whereas I was blind, now I see."

W'allahu alam. And God knows best.

Adam graduated as valedictorian of his class at Dartmouth and went on to study Arabic in Damascus, Syria. He subsequently moved to Berkeley, California, to teach and study at Zaytuna College, the first Muslim liberal arts college in the United States. He works closely there with some of the scholars who inspired him in his early years as a Muslim, such as Shaykh Hamza Yusuf and Imam Zaid Shakir. He reconnected with Sara L., one of the first Muslims he talked to before converting at Dartmouth, and married her a year after graduating.

11

Sarah Chaudhry Shadowlands

Perhaps my parents' immigrant story is one that we rarely hear because it does not fit into the established view of what is and is not a good reason to flee your homeland for a foreign place. Their journey to the United States was not undertaken because of material struggles but as the only viable way to escape from my father's nuclear family. My parents were married in an era when only arranged marriages were proper. My mother was too beautiful and too wealthy to be trusted by my father's family, particularly my great-aunt. Although they increased their prestige by his "marrying up," they were wary of this city girl now living in their midst in a small village in the heart of the Punjab region.

My parents had no honeymoon period. On their wedding night, my great-aunt let her displeasure about the marriage be known and demanded that my father spend most of the night with her and his mother. This set the tone for what was to be six years of constraint and tiptoed steps while they lived in my great-aunt's presence. My parents speak little of how their relationship developed in an atmosphere designed to stifle it and keep them apart. Their relationship was so concealed that they, too, only remember it in stolen snatches of memories. What I do know is that they wove their love in the torpid air of summer nights, speaking softly lest my great-aunt object to their burgeoning relationship. My great-aunt treated everyone in the family, especially the women, as though they were nothing but interlopers in her world.

My parents, unable to carve out a life for themselves and their family in such an oppressive atmosphere, opted to leave the land of their ancestors and come to the United States. For years, this decision was not discussed in our home, and my siblings and I grew up thinking that we too were the poor, oppressed peoples of the earth who came to the States seeking refuge. My father, son of a hardworking but far-from-prosperous farmer, worked his way up the social ladder by obtaining a master's degree in economics. He had a rather lucrative job as an insurance agent, and we likely could have been a part of the comfortable class in Pakistan had we stayed there. But regardless of how wealthy my family could have become in Pakistan, we would have lived with my father's family, as is customary in Pakistan and among Pakistani Americans. Despite my mother's less-than-ideal experience with my father's family, she laments the lack of love in our modern world and attributes much of it to the breakdown of the extended family.

As a child, what I knew of being Pakistani and Muslim was defined by mainstream society. Being Pakistani in my suburban Long Island neighborhood meant being strange and misunderstood. In second grade, I went to school with *mehndi* decorating my hands, and I was excited to show it off to my classmates. When one boy proclaimed, "That looks like shit," some girls came to my defense by saying, "It is weird, but Sarah didn't do it—her mom did." They had all seen my mom come to school wearing *shalwar-kameez*, with a diaphanous scarf loosely wrapped around her head. Some students had already assured me that I was not quite like my mother because I was as light as their parents or relatives. I was young, but not too young to know that the other children's parents did not speak to my mother when we had class day. I was hurt that they were blaming my mother for my strangeness, and I became combative. I told the whole class that I was special because I had a secret language and secret traditions that they could not share in. My defiance of their second-grade authority was short-lived, however, as my teacher looked at my hands and exclaimed, "What is that!?" She sent me to the school nurse because she feared that the unfamiliar marks all over my hands were a sign of a contagious disease. I was ashamed for being singled out and sent away while the rest of the class giggled, glad that they did not share in secret traditions that sent them to the school nurse.

It was not the first time I was singled out for my difference, but it was a pivotal experience; the joy I took in gathering with the women of my family to put *mehndi* on our hands was tainted by the realization that others thought it was ugly and looked suspicious. My mother was outraged, but she also thought the teacher's reaction was hysterical. Her laughter showed me that I did not have to resort to anger in the face of others' ignorance. I saw the joy in laughing at my teacher, who we could forgive for not knowing what *mehndi* was, but who we could not forgive for not listening to my explanation that *mehndi* was used to celebrate Eid.

I dealt with ignorant comments about my family by convincing my-self that we had had no other choice but to come to the United States. Although this may be true in some sense, I did not know the full truth of why we came until the seventh grade. My siblings and I shrouded ourselves in the traditional immigrant story, and I spent years rewriting my family history by telling my teachers and friends that we came to the States for greater material opportunities. I did not feel betrayed when I discovered the truth, but I did feel as though I did not know myself. The world that I came from was blanketed in darkness, and I had been fixated on trying to make myself palatable to our nearly all-white suburban community. I felt unmoored, and I wanted to know who we were, rather than casting aside my history as an unfortunate circumstance that we had overcome by moving to the United States.

My mother began telling me more stories about her life in Pakistan once I entered middle school. As I listened to her stories, I came to understand how her departure from Pakistan was just one in a family history characterized by displacement. My distant relatives became people to me once I learned their stories, desires, and fears; before they were just the vestiges of our abandoned past, people I did not often wonder about. I particularly dismissed the history of my grandparents' generation. I learned of the 1947 partition of India, out of which a new nation, Pakistan was born, through my mother's stories about our relatives that were forced to flee from India to the new nation of Pakistan. It was the "Land of the Pure," but my mother's aunts did not forget India and spoke of their longing for their *Wataan*—their homeland, their village, their life as they remembered it. As a child, my mother was unwilling to hear that her elders loved and missed India because the Pakistani "national project" was already in place. It was designed to make people forget India as they remembered it and instead regard it as a place where Muslims were made to suffer and feel permanently displaced. The songs of longing her mother and aunts sang—about a place where countless generations of their ancestors had walked and waked in the dust—did not belong in a nation committed to forgetting its own ancestry. My mother is a part of that legacy of forgetting, and although she does not have the same sense of Wataan that her elders had, she has started to understand that her longing and their longing are connected. Her memories of her elders, as she recounted them to her children, reopened doors she had not looked through in decades. Together we perused the contents of a forgotten and displaced people. Today when I speak of who I am, I cannot do so without speaking of those I have come from.

Imagined and actual histories are what have created my generation of Pakistani Americans. The very way we practice Islam is intimately tied to partition. My grandparents' generation was forced out of India because the leaders of the day could not agree on how to address the "Muslim Problem." India was gearing up to structure itself after the great Western democracies, all of which had strong centralized governments. Muslims could not be given the seats in Congress they were demanding, as it would weaken the centralized nation. The political leaders' refusal to imagine a strong nation-state led to the call for partition; no one could foresee the violent upheaval that would signal the appearance of two new nations that were birthed in blood. When my ancestors left everything they knew, often under violent and humiliating circumstances, they needed to embrace the reason that made them flee. Pakistanis became Muslims first, and everything else second. Islam took the forefront of Pakistan's national identity, whereas it previously had been but one component of a complex culture.

My father's family does not recall many instances of human kindness in the midst of partition. My father's grandmother was burned alive in a mosque, along with three hundred other women. Even the sacredness of the mosque had not been enough to protect them. Those unwritten rules of respect and decency were violated again and again—no one was spared by the crazed mobs that were bent on destruction and driven by the sense of purpose that war and murder often give to those fighting and killing.

I know far less about my father's family than I do about my mother's. My father was a stoic figure in my life, but we became closer in the middle of my high-school years. Although he was always a stern disciplinarian who did not verbally communicate his love or feelings, he became, and continues to be, my friend. It surprises me how similar we are and how well my father knows me, considering that we did not speak for much of my youth. My father does not often discuss his family history, and much of what I know of it comes through my mother. My father's family is far more religious than my mother's, which is partly rooted in their disparate partition experiences. Tragedy tore them apart, and Islam helped piece them together again.

My mother's aunts and all the women of that older, pre-partition generation sang, danced, wore bright colors to weddings, and understood what it meant to be joyous. That is a thread of history that I hold on to and try to trace back to the larger fabric of what was, before we were told that being Pakistani meant following some odd manifestation of Islam. The fact that my ancestors danced and reveled does not seem like a big revelation, but it is when you are raised in a community of people who believe that Islam forbids music, dancing, and the mingling of men and women at weddings and other gatherings. These people were struggling to form an identity that set them apart from others, particularly Hindus, Sikhs, and people from the West. Music and general revelry became and remain easy targets because people often regrettably equate joy with decadence and worldliness. But it was not enough to forbid dancing and music; it also became necessary to deny that our ancestors ever sang and danced, or else to state that the only reason they did so was because they were too close to Hindus and Sikhs. One of the first questions I learned to ask my mother about weddings was "Is it separated?" If she said yes, I often refused to go. For a few years, my siblings and I were forbidden to listen to music and were told that music, unless it was for Allah, was the Devil's song and dance. I once told a kindergarten classmate that she should consider Islam, and when she asked me what it was about, I told her that Islam meant no singing, no dancing, and praying five times a day. She twirled around in a circle a few times and respectfully declined, because she liked singing and dancing.

Nowadays, I am often embarrassed at gatherings where people expect me to know traditional Punjabi songs and dances. But stronger than embarrassment is the sense of sadness I feel at knowing that our traditional songs have been lost, that the songs my ancestors sang will never leave my lips to link our voices across the ages. My parents now jokingly claim temporary insanity as their excuse for the years they spent believing and teaching us that we should prefer to mingle with Muslims over others, and that singing and dancing were strictly forbidden.

My parents did not do away with rules entirely, but their understanding of Islam was more holistic than that of many other people in our community. I felt both cursed and blessed to have my parents; they were more strict than any of my American friends' parents, but less strict than many of the Pakistani parents. Saying that my parents were strict seems like an understatement, but I struggle to find a term that does not demonize them. My siblings and I were forbidden to go to our friends' houses, attend parties, or hang out with anyone outside the house. Much of this strictness was rooted in their fear that we would be subsumed by mainstream culture and no longer be Pakistani, leaving them alone in an already strange and hostile land. Whenever we pushed to go out with friends, our parents would firmly state that we were not like our friends, and if we acted just like them, then what would show us that we were different? I was exasperated because I was reminded of my difference every day, when I just wanted to wear tank tops and shorts. My sullen young self often listened to stories about how my people bled and died because of their faith, and here I was, privileged, spoiled, out of harm's way, and willing to abandon my faith because of the whimsy of fashion. My parents spent a lot of time watching me roll my eyes and exclaiming, "Oh my God!" every time they tried to prevent me from walking down the forbidden path of Western fashion. My parents did not expect to face such opposition from me once I reached middle school because I had been, by all accounts, a pious young girl prior to adolescence. In fourth grade I started wearing a hijab to school and even approached the vice principal to set up a space where I could pray during recess. My mother was proud that I was praying in school, but worried that I was starting to wear the headscarf too early in my life.

It was a strange turn of events that led me to wearing the headscarf and becoming more religious. This transformation occurred when the spirit world loudly interjected itself into my family's lives and we were all changed. Fear of the unknown spirits turned us toward Allah—another unknown being, but one that protected us and was our defense against this palpable, but hidden, other world. Even before spirits entered our lives in a hostile manner, I grew up listening to stories of *jinn*, omens, and dead relatives who appeared in dreams to impart some wisdom or offer consolation. I learned that the spirit world was not completely separate from our world and oftentimes spirits and humans interacted with one another. There was a litany of rules to follow so that one could live in harmony with the world of the jinn. It was strictly forbidden to go outdoors during Maghrib, since that was when the worlds were in flux and the jinn were emerging for the night. As children, my siblings and I would try to keep playing outside during Maghrib, but my mother would always appear and usher us indoors, only to let us out again after dusk had fallen and the time of transition had passed.

My mother, who has always felt a deep connection with the spirit world, was the first one to sense that something was amiss in our house. We began to glimpse figures, sometimes shadowy and sometimes translucent, and my mother heard whispered words of warning. I began to dread going home, and we all turned to Islam as a way of dealing with our fears. I stopped rushing through my prayers and talks with Allah and felt, for the first time, prayer emanating from a place so vulnerable that it sometimes seemed as though Allah were close at hand. He heard my whispered words, as well as those words I thought, but dared not say aloud. Allah used to be terrifying in His omniscience, but now Allah was a personal friend whom I wanted to show affection to and respect for in return. I could not just take and ask without doing my part by obeying His commands and showing Him that He was a daily consideration.

To the skeptical outsider, it may seem that my family suffered from some collective delusions, but I continue to hold that it is foolish to believe that all you can see is all that is there. It was during this haunted period that I found the courage, born of fear, to wear a headscarf and to pray in school. The self-consciousness I felt about wearing the headscarf did not quite dissipate, but it became mingled with a sense of defiance and posturing pride. More than ever, I had to defend myself and my strangeness, or else become a student who was ostracized and constantly bullied.

The instances where I have faced discrimination or had to listen to the ignorant words of classmates, store clerks, and teachers, particularly after the 9/11 attacks, are so numerous as to nearly blend into a feeling of simultaneous superiority and inferiority relative to my hometown that has not ever left me. When it became clear that a terrorist attack had occurred, I remember hoping that Muslims were not behind it. My horror at the attack was quickly followed by wondering what life would be like afterward for Muslims in the United States. I was somewhat prepared for a backlash because life in my hometown had always been a bit uneasy and often required me to defend myself and others like me.

I developed a particularly unforgiving attitude toward many of my classmates because of a traumatic incident that occurred in seventh grade. More than forty students were sitting in the stadium-style study-hall classroom, doing or pretending to do our work. Our study-hall teacher was known for her strictness about speaking during class. That day, three boys who sat near me decided to speak to me. One of them began by saying, "Hey Sarah, will you go out with me? I mean, will you be my girlfriend?"

The other two boys snickered, and one of them followed up with, "Will you suck my dick? I mean, do you know what a blow job is?"

At that point, I was confused about why I was being targeted and why there was such harshness in their voices. I feel a sense of humiliation recounting this story even now. As I responded by telling them to "fuck off," they revealed why they had picked me for this attack. One of them asked, "So, do you help your brothers build bombs?" I have repressed most of the conversation between myself and these boys and can barely remember what I said back to them. What I do recall is that I did not cry and held my own. I also remember swallowing back tears and looking around the room to see that many people whom I expected to say something were instead sitting silently; one guy was even repressing a smile. Our "conversation" lasted for the entire study-hall period, our voices echoing through the quiet room, and not a single person stepped in, including our silence-obsessed study-room teacher. After class, my "I don't give a fuck" attitude quickly crumbled in the bathroom, as I sobbed and told a friend what had happened. She was sympathetic, but I do not think she understood the enormity of the incident for me, other than that "some guys are jerks." I remember telling the vice principal, who gave the boys a day of detention. That was the extent of their punishment. The boys were not pushed to analyze their racist and sexist beliefs, nor were they required to apologize to me.

This encounter made it easier for me to dismiss the feelings of classmates I deemed to be racist, sexist, or classist. I began to view some of them as incorrigible and had no desire to consider their frames of reference. The battle lines were drawn, and we were on opposing sides. I often found myself alone on my side, with the only words of support coming from a sympathetic teacher. Some classmates concurred with my statements after class, but never during. My ability to place myself in opposition to many of my classmates cannot be traced to one source alone, but much of my courage to risk ostracism came from that day in study hall and from wearing a headscarf in my younger years. I learned at an early age that integrity stems from committing and adhering to the beliefs and practices one holds to be true, regardless of the public discomfort and repercussions that come from such viewpoints.

Shannon, my best friend in high school, was instrumental in teaching me how to retain my integrity while placing myself in situations that I normally would have shied away from. We went to parties together and interacted with people who sometimes were terribly ignorant, but we supported each other and learned how to confront people in a way that was more about dialoguing and less about winning an argument. Before I met Shannon, I was satisfied with having friends whom I could enjoy spending time with, while never talking about my family life or inner feelings. It is my fault that I did not get close to people in high school, and I cannot blame them for having misunderstood me. It was easier to hide my feelings and project an image of a smart, outspoken young woman.

For many years I dismissed my childhood observance of Islam. I now understand that although fear may have been the initial force behind my embrace of Islam, my childhood understanding of Islam transcended the fear and became the true emotional basis for my lifelong desire to understand and deepen my faith. I have not forgotten that Allah was once my intimate friend, and although I have neglected my faith and questioned my beliefs during many periods of my life, I have always returned to seek the guidance and strength of Allah.

I spent so many years defending Islam and correcting people's misconceptions about Muslims that I did not spend enough time reflecting on my own private thoughts and desires. Teachers would often assume that my mother was a subservient, cowed woman because she wore a headscarf and did not speak much, if at all, during parent-teacher conferences. Her behavior fit the stereotype of a Muslim woman, and they half expected my mother to walk two steps behind my father. When teachers would express their surprise at the fact that I was strong willed, I was sure to tell them that I learned this trait from my mother. I remember explaining to a teacher that my mother was quiet during conferences not because, as a Muslim woman, she did not feel entitled to speak, but because her discomfort with English often made her hesitant to do so.

I do, however, remember feeling stifled by my parents' strictness, and vowing that I would do whatever I wanted once I was in college, even if that meant disobeying Islam. When I got to college, I immersed myself in the "work hard, party hard" culture and took risks, including a number that were not the smartest or best use of my time, but what mattered was that I was setting my own boundaries. I had inadvertently grown accustomed to my parents defining the parameters of my life, and though I did not always walk within those parameters, I rarely veered too far from them when I was living at home. College was not only a place where I found people who reflected my own beliefs, but also where I found people who pushed me to expand my narrow boundaries and abandon some of the bitterness I had developed in my earlier years. For the first time in my life, I felt I had more than one friend who understood and wanted to know who I was. It was freeing and exhilarating not to be the only one aware of and bothered by racism or any of the other myriad forms of discrimination. I met two of my best friends, Amber and Manida, during my freshman year at college. Manida, who is Thai American, and I often discussed the tension between mainstream U.S. culture and our own cultures. We were raised in similar ways, and we both wanted to honor our cultures, while still allowing ourselves room to try things our parents may not have fully approved of. What was and continues to be so refreshing about our friendship is that we do not have to explain our frames of reference to each other; we both understand how vital sacrifice, familial honor, and integrity are to our sense of self.

Meanwhile, Amber and I bonded over our shared experience of feeling like outsiders, both in our mostly white neighborhoods and within our own communities, because of our status as highly educated women. Amber is black and from Texas, and she has experienced a different form of racism than I have. She felt like an outsider while growing up, but also felt distanced from the black community at our college because most of the black students there came from solidly upper-middle-class backgrounds, whereas Amber's family had struggled with financial insecurity. We learned to ask each other questions when we did not understand each other's frames of reference, and to listen to one another before passing judgment. With both Manida and Amber, I was able to stop shielding my emotions because I felt that they understood what it meant to straddle different worlds and struggle to preserve aspects of yourself that seem to be in conflict with who you are slowly becoming.

The friends I made at college continue to be my closest friends. Although they transgressed many of the laws of Islam, I was not bothered by their behavior, but I was bothered by the behavior of my friends back home. At home, I refused to drink or assimilate too much because I felt that doing so would in some way be a betrayal of my heritage. I resented my parents' strictness, but I also resented friends who urged me to drink and go to certain parties with them. It sometimes seemed they did not want me to go to parties for my company, but so that I would break my parents' rules. With my college friends, I did not feel I was betraying myself in any way because they respected my culture and faith and did not care what substances I tried or did not try.

Nonetheless, it was during these early college years that I began to distance myself from Islam, and I was not even aware that I had done so until the World Cup in 2006. France was one of the final teams in the tournament, and one of their star players was Zinedine Zidane, a French player whose family had immigrated to France from Algeria. Zidane had been careful to describe himself as a "nonpracticing Muslim," and I had started to do so as well by saying, "I'm not really religious." It was only after a conversation with my sister-in-law about Zidane that I began to realize that his statement may have been a self-hating attempt to disassociate himself from his heritage. People of other faiths do not often comment on whether they are practicing or nonpracticing, yet I notice increasingly that Muslims are quick to offer up that they are nonpracticing, perhaps in an attempt to show that they are not at all like those "crazies" shown on the news. I assume that my desire to tell people that I did not really practice was rooted in the same need to be normal and accepted. But there was something else—the sense of shame I felt declaring that I was a Muslim when I was clearly doing things that were forbidden, such as going out to frats and dating. I did not feel worthy of associating myself with Islam because I did not outwardly practice the faith.

After years of believing that Islam played only a peripheral role in my life, I made a close friend during my senior year of college who changed my understanding of my faith. Layla, a Muslim American interested in spirituality, helped me understand that my faith was not defined by how closely I followed dogma. We would make tea, read Rumi, and discuss how faith informed our understandings of ourselves and the world. Layla was and remains my only Muslim friend that I have actually spoken to about Islam. Rumi's writings, though embraced by cultures across the globe as the words of a universalized spiritual man, are still firmly rooted in Islam. His poems clearly transcend religious dogma and address human sentiments and characteristics regardless of religion, but many of his metaphors and stories find their sources in Islam. By reading Hāfez and Rumi with Layla, I began to understand and discuss the beliefs that had been passed down to me. I was unaware that some of the Islamic stories I had been told were part of a larger history of storytelling. It was empowering and affirming to see in print many tales that my mother had told me when I was a child, especially because when Islam was discussed at school in my younger years, it was usually treated as though it were some bizarre artifact.

Many of the parables that my mother raised us on as children were centered on withholding judgment on others and not assessing a person's worth based on their social status. We learned more about Muslim men and women who were moral people than we did about the particulars of Islam. Our heroes were flawed men and women who strove to be better, not by following rigid rules but by engaging with the world and reflecting on their beliefs and actions. I was enthralled by two women: Rabia Basri, a famous Sufi and *vali* (enlightened scholar), and Khola Bin Waleed, a fearless woman warrior. I wanted to be self-sufficient and strong like these women. Hazrat Aisha, one of the Prophet Muhammad's wives, was another woman I respected and admired. She was a scholar in her own right, as well as a teacher. Many of the most famous and revered women in Islam are lauded for their fierce wit, intellect, and courage. These are the women who have helped me value integrity, and it is their stories that have inspired me to be ambitious. I do not aim simply to become wealthy or powerful, but to struggle against myself and stay devoted to a life of learning while using my skills to better our world.

So much of my understanding of culture and faith is rooted in Islamic rituals that I would like to share with my children and have them pass down to their descendants. While I was in high school and college, I often told people that religion was a personal choice and it did not matter to me if I married a Muslim. But now I believe that religion is not just a personal choice and that it is often necessary to be supported by a community in order to feel a part of something bigger than oneself. I always enjoyed fasting when I was in middle school and high school, but while at college I often missed many days of fasting because there were not a lot of other people with whom to share this ritual. Growing up, we would always wake before dawn to eat as a family in order to prepare for the day of fasting ahead, and it would be difficult to continue this tradition if I were not married to someone who also believes in Islam.

One of my great aspirations is to experience Ramadan in a Muslim country, preferably Pakistan. I want to know what it feels like to have the whole rhythm of a community shift because everyone is engaged in a common observance. Much of my extended family remains in Pakistan, and I would like to be able to stay there for a prolonged period of time in order to establish more significant ties to my relatives. I fear that my generation will lose ties with Pakistan and our children will see it as little more than their "background," that banal term that connotes no connection to a place or people. When we do visit Pakistan, it is difficult to have meaningful interactions with many of our family members because we go from house to house in an attempt to see everyone we have not seen in years. It is my deep hope that Pakistan will not become radicalized and will instead seek to intertwine faith and culture in a holistic fashion, but the current political climate in Pakistan is creating growing discontent. Pakistanis are increasingly angered by U.S. meddling in their affairs, which is causing certain segments of the population to turn to radical factions that they see as offering them a way to retain some semblance of power and dignity. But the cost of this dignity may very well be the soul of the nation, and I worry about Pakistan's uncertain future.

While fasting is one of the aspects of Islam I will continue to practice in my life, I am willing to abandon some of the ways in which my parents defined their faith. We were always told that showing bare legs or arms was a sin because such behavior was immodest, but I have come to realize that although the Quran urges modesty, there are many different interpretations of what modesty means. Nevertheless, I also have discovered that I am more conservative than I had thought in terms of dressing, and that I feel rather uncomfortable when exposing skin. Dating, too, was strictly forbidden in my parents' generation, and as children we were told that dating is a sin for Muslims, but the ban on dating is more of a cultural practice than a tenet of Islam. Many of the Muslim kids I knew grew up to find their own spouses, and such behavior is no longer considered shameful. I am not opposed to my parents introducing me to someone and getting to know them through the arranged marriage system because I trust my parents' judgment and know they would never pressure me into a relationship that I did not feel comfortable with. Casual dating also does not appeal to me, and it is important that the person I marry be able to respect and integrate themselves into my family.

My mother knows I have dated, and have not always worn clothes that completely covered my body. In my younger years, these were the behaviors I was taught to avoid because they would result in a lack of identity and condemn my soul to an eternity of hellfire. Throughout college, I never spoke to my mother about my social life and always pretended that I was still exactly who I was when I left home. It has only been since graduating and disclosing some of this information to her that I've been able to see how my parents' beliefs have also evolved over time. They no longer fear assimilation as much as they once did because they have seen that assimilation does not necessarily negate one's identity. My mother and I have grown even closer than we already were, and she is a confidante who gently guides without being overbearing. I never tell people anymore that I am someone who does not "practice" Islam. It is true that I do not pray five times a day, but I do believe in Islam, and when I pray, I pray to Allah.

After spending a few years living in (and loving) Brooklyn, Sarah went on to study law at Columbia Law School. She graduated in the spring of 2013 and is trying to make time to continue writing.

12

Sara L. The Headscarf

When the Soviets invaded Afghanistan in 1979, my grandfather resigned his position as Afghan ambassador to Germany and then moved his family to Saudi Arabia to keep them safe from the political turmoil at home. However, my father stayed in Europe to continue his education, as he had just started college with plans of studying to become a doctor. A few months after his family left for Saudi Arabia, Dad bought a plane ticket to visit them. When he arrived there, he learned that his father had died of a heart attack. The shock of my grandfather's death still reverberates in my family today. My dad rarely speaks about this moment when, as the eldest son, at age nineteen, he quit school and took on the responsibility of supporting his mother and four siblings in a country whose language he did not speak.

My mother met my father while attending the same school in Europe. She soon left Europe to settle in Colorado, where her father was stationed with the U.S. military, after having been stationed several years in Europe. She continued working on her undergraduate degree at the University of Colorado in Boulder. She and my father kept in touch, writing letters to each other every day. Years ago, my dad found a cassette that my mom had made for him; she was singing while her brother, Uncle Danny, accompanied her on the guitar. During this period and in the following year, when she was an optometry student at Indiana University in Bloomington, my mother began to study Islam. After this extended period of correspondence, my parents, ages twenty and twenty-one, got married in Colorado. My father flew back to Saudi Arabia shortly after the wedding, while my mom remained in Bloomington. She quit college after a year and moved to Saudi Arabia to live with her husband. It was not long before my eldest sister was born; three more daughters followed, each a year apart, with me being the last.

I have always marveled at my mother's family for their easy acceptance of her rather radical decisions. To convert to Islam, to get married so young, to wed a foreign man, to quit school, to move to Saudi Arabia, to have so many children so quickly—my grandparents must have had infinite trust in their daughter. My mother still values her Catholic upbringing and often refers to her conversion to Islam as "switching lanes on a highway"—both faiths are heading in the direction of God.

The six of us lived in an apartment with my grandmother and her four children, my father's siblings. My parents describe the seven years in Saudi Arabia as some of the best of their lives. Their family was blossoming. They had become close friends with families in the area who had children our age, with whom we are still in touch. We would picnic on the beach, drive in the desert, and make small pilgrimages to Mecca, called 'umrah.

However, this period could by no means be described as easy. My grandmother (Bibi Jaan) and my mostly adolescent aunts and uncles suffered with the passing of our paternal patriarch (Baba Kalaan), and they struggled to come to terms with the shift in their circumstances: from spacious courtyards to cramped apartment quarters, from mother tongue to a foreign one, from stability to utter uncertainty. And yet, even they look back to Saudi Arabia with warmth. We circulate stories of my grandfather's life, about his early academic brilliance, the prominent government positions he held, his rigorously upright character, his wishes for his children, and the hard times in the years leading up to his end. His absence is filled with our stories of him, stories that, in a way, motivate each of us, and bind us together.

When I was three years old, my dad's family having all immigrated to Germany, we moved to Colorado to be near my mom's family. My father's first job in the United States was as a newspaper deliveryman. He tells us about the rhythm he developed while delivering the papers, how all the motions and walkways and flicks of the wrist became so familiar to him. Thinking back on this time brings me a sting of sadness. My father wanted to be a doctor. The rich stories about his youth in Afghanistan stand in stark contrast to my dad's humble beginnings in the United States. But he quickly rose above his adverse circumstances, providing security and care for his family all the while.

When I was five years old, my father began experiencing chest pains. He had inherited the heart disease that killed my grandfather. Though he recovered well, my mom soon after decided to go to dental school—this was her way, I believe, of ensuring that we children would be well taken care of, were my father to pass away. This turned out to be an incredibly wise move; while my father's health bounced back and he was promoted every few years in his company, my mother earned a degree that guaranteed future financial stability.

When my mom graduated from dental school, my two eldest sisters were fifteen and fourteen and had begun hanging out with kids that my parents disapproved of. When Mom and Dad speak of that time now, the fear they had for their daughters is palpable. In many ways, the changes in my sisters were the typical teenage spectacle: secretive phone calls from boys, skipping school, talking back, etc. The shock of these behaviors was exacerbated by circumstances in the neighborhood where we lived: friends were getting pregnant, gangs and drugs were rampant. My father says it was as if he woke up one day and found that his daughters were strangers to him. One sister in particular was bursting at the seams. The urgency she felt for release from my parents still rings loudly in my memories. Any friction between my sister and my parents ended in an outburst. In those moments of fury, I coped by sitting near the combatants, silently crying; I felt that if I remained apart from them it would mean it was *all* falling apart. It was during one such argument that I experienced my first wholly personal expression of faith. I began reading the Quran, drawn to it for tranquillity.

At this time, my dad got an offer from his company to spend two years in the Middle East to bolster their dealer channels in the region. My parents viewed this as a chance to pluck their daughters out of that space and time, and so they jumped at the opportunity. The summer after seventh grade, we moved to Abu Dhabi, the capital of the United Arab Emirates. Although it was difficult for us to adjust, in retrospect this move represented a critical turning point in our lives. While back in Aurora, Colorado, my elder sisters didn't speak about college as a real possibility, here it became their number-one priority. We all flourished academically, socially, and athletically. It was here that I discovered my leadership skills on soccer and basketball teams, and in founding my school's yearbook. The family fights that had occurred so often back in Colorado petered out in Abu Dhabi; we were all in a new place, and family became our island of familiarity.

After a few weeks, my mother and sisters, who had all started wearing the abaya and scarf, decided to stop wearing it. Their expectation that Abu Dhabi would have public dress standards similar to Saudi Arabia's was quickly dispelled, and they felt unmotivated by any religious or other reasons to continue wearing the garments. In the Emirates, black abayas are worn almost exclusively by Emirate nationals, a sort of signifier of indigenousness. I had not joined my sisters in wearing the abaya during those first few weeks. It was years later, in unlikely Hanover, New Hampshire, that I first chose to don a headscarf.

In Abu Dhabi, with mosques broadcasting the call to prayer five times a day, Islam felt like something residual and unthinking. It seems that, without a need to swim against the tide of Colorado's majority Christian society, I simply fell in line as a passive Muslim. While in Colorado, I often spoke of my half-Afghan heritage, my birthplace in Saudi Arabia, and my Muslim faith; in Abu Dhabi I identified strongly as an American and a Coloradan. I owned those aspects of me that made me unique, depending on the context. While I was at the time aware of this identity shift, I never really confronted myself with the admission that if *this* was as deep as my faith went, I might be missing something.

Today, as a woman who announces her religion to the world, I confront myself with this internal legacy. Do I publicly identify as a Muslim because it is unique in my context? Or is my faith unmoved by my circumstances? *Place* can shape everything, even faith, especially in the early formative years of life. If I had stayed in Abu Dhabi beyond those brief two years, would Islam still occupy a backseat in my life? Would Islam be wholly different to me if I had remained in Saudi Arabia, or if my parents had decided to settle in Afghanistan instead of the United States? There is no way to know. And yet—now—my faith is *rooted* in me, as an adult who has chosen a way of life for herself, as a heart that is created and yearns to know her Creator.

We moved back to Colorado in June 2001, a few months before I was to begin tenth grade. My eldest sister prepared for her freshman year at the University of Colorado in Boulder. I was still too young to get a job, so while my sisters worked at a local grocery store, I spent my time mentally preparing for a quintessentially "American" high-school experience: sitting on porch swings and going to sports matches, homecoming, and barbecues. During my two years abroad, I had constructed "Americanness" in a very particular mold, forgetting that I, a child of mixed ethnicity and a Muslim family, had always been American, with or without those features that I imagined to be essentially "American." I could not have predicted the tragedy that was to ignite simultaneously my growing Muslim consciousness and a more nuanced identification as American.

The attacks of September 11, 2001, happened two weeks into my sophomore year of high school. A student walked into my morning physical-education class and said with bewilderment, almost as if she were asking a question, "We're under attack." I considered myself one of the bewildered "we" until the televisions that blared in all classrooms announced the suspected perpetrators: Muslims. Most of my classmates already knew I was a Muslim by the time 9/11 happened, and I felt defensive, urgently needing to disown the attackers' actions. Not long after, therefore, a friend and I cofounded the Muslim Student Association at my high school. We had two goals: to provide a space for discussion and spiritual reflection for Muslim students, and to educate our high-school community about Islam in order to counter the negative perceptions that surrounded it. There were over a dozen Muslims at my high school, and we met weekly for discussions and to plan events, such as an Islam 101 panel. The panels typically consisted of five Muslim college students who would present basic information about Islam and then answer questions from the audience. These events filled auditoriums.

A few days after 9/11, two FBI agents came to our home to ask my father some questions. We suspect they got his name off a list of members of our mosque. Or perhaps my father's Afghan origins and decade in Saudi Arabia were a suspicious combination. Somehow the intrusive case of profiling didn't feel so violating then as it does to me in memory now. I remember my dad saying afterward that, sure, they profiled him based on ethnicity and religion, but they didn't take him away for good, which is more than you can expect from some other countries, including some so-called Muslim countries. Of course, my father has a U.S. passport; if he did not, I wonder whether the government would have felt at liberty to be a bit more illiberal.

In retrospect, I see that 9/11 was the beginning of my struggle to make sense of what it means to be a *public* Muslim, to be connected with a community beyond my local mosque. What is the *ummah* (global Muslim community) exactly? What connects us? What duties do we have to each other? Could I correctly say, "Bin Laden is not a Muslim," as I so often felt the urge to assert? These questions puzzled me at the time, but it was not long before I was presented with a way of viewing my identity that was both intuitive and satisfying for me.

In April 2002, Tariq Ramadan, the world-renowned Muslim scholar and public intellectual, who until very recently was unjustly unable to get a visa to enter the United States, spoke in Denver on "Purifying the Heart, Nourishing the Mind." Up to that point, Islam had been all the things I had learned in Sunday school. It was deep inside of me, but in an automatic way, as something that came naturally and instinctually. Ramadan's talk opened up the possibility of Islam as a process, as something beautifying and meaningful that engaged the *heart*.

I began to read Ramadan's writings, in which he spoke about identity, about the fact that being an American and being a Muslim are not mutually exclusive identities. Cannot one be, for instance, both a vegetarian and a poet at the same time? To believe that there is an intrinsic conflict is to ignore the layers that make us human. None of us has just one identity, but a bundle of overlapping and connected ones. Furthermore, although humans inhabit social identities, these should not be reified into rigid tribal affinities. Being a Muslim does not mean just to carry a title that binds me with others who carry that title, but to struggle to live up to certain values.

Ramadan gave words to both internal and external conceptual challenges I had rolled around in since 9/11 but could never step out of and understand with clarity. Most important, after the lecture I began to read the Quran in earnest, lining the margins with sticky notes on which I had written exclamation points, question marks, and references to related verses.

Soon thereafter, a group of Denver families came together to form an organization that did community service, brought in well-known speakers for public events, and hosted a variety of interfaith dialogues and speaking engagements. It was through this group that I met a young man who had recently converted to Islam. We were both sixteen years old and became close friends, talking daily on the phone. The relationship, though, felt inappropriate to me; Islam values behavioral modesty between genders, though where each Muslim draws that line may differ in significant ways. I felt that I had crossed my own line. This is one of the reasons that the headscarf, which I began wearing several years later, is so important for me personally; it protects me from *myself*, from easy infatuations, from becoming involved with someone with whom a long-term commitment is just a possibility and not a goal. It also publicly signals that I am unavailable to lascivious eyes or brief intentions. I seek to hold myself up with the dignity of a woman who honors herself, her body, and her heart, and for me the headscarf eases that struggle.

I gained a reputation in high school as a liberal activist. For several months after the outbreak of the Iraq War, I wore an embroidered banner across my chest that read "Pro-Peace." I reactivated a dormant chapter of Amnesty International and attended meetings on everything from immigration rights to antiwar rallies. In the classroom, I was exploring issues that animated my activism. I took a two-year art course in which students developed a theme to explore in-depth through visual means. My topic was "boundaries"—I sought to show the absurdity of barriers between humans, both physical (the Berlin Wall, the Mexico–United States border fence, the wall being constructed along the Israel-Gaza border) and nonphysical (racism, hatred, xenophobia). My final piece was a large canvas that revealed the identical musculature below the skins of two apparent opponents. As part of the International Baccalaureate program, I wrote a culminating essay titled "Is Tolerance Part of the Islamic Theological Construct?" In retrospect, I see that I have come full circle; my earliest intellectual explorations are echoed today in my current academic focus, which I will describe later.

Although I was considered a leader of my high school, I was also basically a loner. I was at my best chairing meetings, but at my worst in a social setting with a group of peers, almost crawling out my skin with awkwardness and urgently wanting to get away. It was during the summer after high school that I found close friends in a group of very dynamic and intelligent people—none of them Muslim. That summer was about thoughtful adventures. We hiked and read poetry at the summit. We lay on a lakeshore in perfect silence to watch the stars. We read books together and had political and religious discussions deep into the night. We lit a fire in the pit in my backyard and roasted marshmallows or apples. The summer was idyllic, free, exciting, and everything that could have made me yearn to stay home in Colorado indefinitely.

When I look back at my freshman year at Dartmouth, I remember a lot of movement but not a lot of thought. This was entropy—nondeliberate motion for the sake of motion. My world was incredibly small—I thought only of the people and things immediately around me. At the same time that I was able to muster the discipline to complete my academic work, jog daily, and socialize, I lost my dedication to the five daily prayers. By the end of spring, I was praying only rarely, though by that term I was, hypocritically, copresident of the Muslim Student Association. I was deep inside this unreflective mode, oblivious to the toll it was taking on my internal state.

A turning point came for me when I incorrectly accused a friend of gossiping about me behind my back. I had landed in, I suppose, the typical nineteen-year-old's gossipy drama spectacle and felt shocked at the person I had become. I saw how profoundly I lacked wisdom. It wasn't that I felt guilt or that I hated myself; but in being confronted with what I conspicuously lacked, I sensed that I could become someone excellent, a woman who has dignity and, through her way of being, honors herself and the people around her. Thus it was the very triteness of my freshman year that motivated me to seek the ennobled, tranquil, and sturdy woman that I had the potential to become. This sense that I wasn't living in the best way is almost certainly the result of the Islamic values with which I was raised. The idea of engaging in petty drama was so off the mark in my household. I was taught, following the example of the Prophet Muhammad, peace be upon Him, to furnish eighty excuses for the unexplained or confusing behavior of another, rather than to be suspicious.

Thus it was natural for me, as I underwent this critical introspection, to turn to the teachings of Islam and the prophetic example. It was clear to me that nothing in this life ought to shift my center. Just how to define that center and how to go about finding it was what I sought on my return home in the summer after my freshman year. Despite my spiritual low, I had arranged to intern with a Muslim nonprofit social-services organization and became very active in the Muslim community, especially in helping to plan a retreat in New Mexico. The planning committee consisted of men and women, all Muslims in their early to mid twenties, whose behavior I quickly saw as a model of how I wanted to be.

That summer was the beginning of my attempt at *tarbiya*—the process of improving oneself systematically through reflection and personal challenges. I began to write in a journal, critically reflecting on my behaviors and thoughts. I sought to be deliberate in all my actions, to make the best decision available to me at each locus of choice. I longed to pray, not as an item to mark off on my to-do list, but as a moment to connect with Reality (one of the names of God in the Islamic tradition)—to slow down in prayer, to allow each bone to become settled in each position, to recite the words of supplication slowly. I attempted to build a relationship with the Quran and to learn the precise rules of Quranic recitation. I yearned to be only a positive moral force in the lives of others. The mantra I had adopted in high school gained new meaning during this time. In *Walden*, Henry David Thoreau writes, "I went to the woods because I wished to live *deliberately*, to front only the essential facts of life, and see if I could not learn what it had to teach, and not, when I came to die, discover that I had not lived."

Formative for me were the online lectures of well-known English-speaking Muslim scholars to which I listened. They addressed the heart, and I became deeply aware of a life in which the heart is engaged, in which one is anchored to meaning. The quality that my Muslim friends and role models embodied was their sincerity in seeking to emulate the Prophet Muhammad, peace be upon Him. Nothing could take them away from this center. I would look at them and understand—they had something *else* motivating them, something deeper and more natural than any exclusively worldly project. This gave them an aura of serenity, even while each had a buoyant personality.

There's a narration in the Hadith literature that says that there are three ways of conceptualizing connection. The first is *islam*, which literally means to internalize peace. It is submitting to God in one's external actions. Islam is constituted around five pillars: declaration of faith, prayer, fasting during Ramadan, charity, and pilgrimage to Mecca. The second way spirituality is conceived is *iman*, literally, to internalize belief or trust. This is a yearning for God; it is the source of motivation for the external actions. Iman is the passionate or emotional realm of surrender. The third way is *ihsan*, which literally means to internalize beauty. It is to worship God as if you see Him, and if you cannot see Him, to know that He sees you. It is to take in the magnitude of being enveloped by *all of this*, to internalize, deeply, that God understands us intimately, that God is the eyes by which you see, the ears by which you hear. Ihsan is the most complete expression of a belief in the oneness of God (*tawheed*). This is the center of the path of Islam, this idea of God in *all of this*. Petty ordeals just deflate when one seeks to live in the ihsanic way. Ihsan gives one firmness and tranquillity, strength and an unfailing awareness. A person who lives with ihsan just emanates God-consciousness (*taqwa*), and you can't pull them away from thinking of God in *all of this*. This is the project of *life:* to live up to that honor that God has given us to worship Him, to ennoble oneself as a creation of God, to illuminate the dignity of all the creation of God.

The month of Ramadan, in which Muslims fast from food, drink, and sexual intercourse during the daylight hours, began a few weeks into the fall term of my sophomore year. This was the first time I tried to use each moment of that blessed month for worship and self-improvement. Every evening I attended a nonrequired evening prayer, at which communities gather to recite one-thirtieth of the Quran in prayer, so that by the end of the month, the entire Quran has been read. It was a few days into Ramadan when, instead of taking my scarf off after the prayer, I began walking back to my room still wearing it. The darkness ensured that few would recognize my face, thus quelling my fear that friends and professors, on seeing me, would be utterly confused and not know how to react—or else would completely ignore me, not recognizing me because of my headscarf.

This was an anxiety I had experienced two years before when, on the first day of my senior year of high school, I came to the kitchen wearing a headscarf. My stomach was in knots. In the car ride to school, I laid the scarf on my shoulders; I simply was not ready. Though neither my mother nor my sisters did so, for me the vision of wearing a headscarf was always dangling somewhere in my future. I assumed I would choose a landmark day to begin: the first day of college, for example. But it didn't happen that way. It happened slowly, on night walks back to my room across the center of campus. One day during the second week of Ramadan, I looked in the mirror and said, "Today is the day." The anxiety that had prevented me from wearing a scarf in the past evaporated, and I left my dorm confidently. If people do not recognize me, I told myself, I will say hello first. Most people were unfazed by my new appearance—some made ice-breaking comments like, "Whoops, almost didn't recognize you!" Others never mentioned the scarf, but signaled their acceptance by extending an extra-friendly greeting. My professors did a double take, but for the most part not much changed. After most people had seen me with it on, the headscarf became part of me, and I knew I'd always wear it.

Soon, I sensed a pressure descending on me, as though all my actions represented all Muslims. In addition, I felt some people assumed the external change signaled a frightening internal one, that perhaps I had become intolerant of other religious paths, or that I was more serious in general. I felt that my identity was preconceived, and I felt unable to represent *myself* fully. At the time I wrote, "Questions peel away the soft tissue that is *me*. I become nothing more than my identity."

This outward change drew me inward. I felt I was seeing myself in the raw for the first time. I became overwhelmed by the bigness of *all of this* and at the same time potently aware of my shortcomings. I yearned for solitude and isolation. I felt I was my worst around other people, that with others I was taken away from my center, while alone, I felt anchored—living with roommates was almost unmanageable for me. I wanted to be better than I was. I cried often. In retrospect, I see that I was not sure how to improve myself without erasing my personality. I wanted to wholly change, become someone different from who I was instead of (as my father often says) "tweaking" my attitudes and actions throughout my lifetime. I was on quicksand—every change I made shifted the entire landscape of *me*.

I finally experienced the isolation I had desired at college during the winter of my sophomore year, while in Berlin on a language study-abroad program. Every afternoon, I took the *U-Bahn* (subway) to a different stop and strolled around. Finally I had the chance to be *inside* of myself, rather than to be *perceived*. I felt anonymous and independent and located myself within.

The following fall, during my junior year, I went to Scotland for a philosophy foreign-study program. My first afternoon in Edinburgh, I walked along the cobbled road outside my apartment building and found, just five minutes away, the central mosque. I walked inside what would become my home for the next three months: here, I would sit on the emerald-colored rugs, cluttered with toys and forgotten garments, to read the Quran. Here, I would stand shoulder to shoulder with my Muslim sisters in prayer on the nights of Ramadan. Here, I would meet the men and women who would become both my close friends and my spiritual guides, although they could not have known I understood them in those terms.

I met and grew to deeply love the Muslims of Edinburgh. I arrived just as Ramadan was about to begin. This holy month is a time of opening and intensity, gravity and community. My heart was wholly open to them, and theirs to me as well. One day, while I was walking out of the mosque, a friend whose uncle and aunt had founded an annual monthlong local radio broadcast, Radio Ramadan Edinburgh, asked me whether I would like to present with her on her afternoon program, "Sister's Sound." I jumped at the chance, and a few times a week I went to the unglamorous basement that served as the studio. Radio Ramadan opened up friendships, in part because I was known to be the only presenter with an American accent. Preparing for prayer one day, the sister next to me asked, "Are you Sara?" She knew me from the program, and we quickly became close friends. This was Edinburgh—openness, friendship, and, from that, guidance.

Despite my blossoming love for the local community, it was sometimes also frustrating to juggle disagreements about the appropriate gender line, which often result in a greater burden for women. A disagreement within the Muslim students' group, for example, proved to be divisive. An e-mail one day from the group's president suggested the executive board consider an addition to the constitution stipulating that only women who wore a headscarf could assume public roles within the organization. The suggestion was absurd, both practically and in principle. The group of active students was already small, and a couple of the most active women happened not to wear a headscarf. More important, the policy felt wrong to me relative to Islam. It was less than a year earlier that I had begun to wear a headscarf, and I felt the choice to be so personal and beautiful that I could not imagine constructing something I saw, and today still see, as coercive. A few of us responded to this proposal in a letter, ultimately presenting each of our points to the group's members. Although the meeting ended with no final decision having been made, I left deflated and confused by the opinions of my counterparts. I felt overwhelmed by the apparent concern with the surface at the risk of ignoring the heart.

One day soon after the meeting, while sitting in the mosque library, I began a conversation with the mosque secretary, a British woman who had converted to Islam years before. She too agreed with the proposed policy, and I began to describe my view to her. Just then, the brother walked in and joined the conversation; though we heartily disagreed with each other, it was ultimately a positive experience. In the weeks that followed, I observed his behavior with less judgment than I had before and saw that same quality that over the years I had come to recognize as *taqwa*—God-consciousness, awe of God—a quality that I forever seek to emulate. It was precisely in being honest to himself and to God that he carried the beliefs he did, and although I could disagree with his reasons, I could only admire their source.

Though many of my friends in college came from various religious (or nonreligious) backgrounds, my closest friends at college were Muslim, and each of them exhibited such excellent behavior. If it was the petty drama of my freshman year that initiated critical introspection, my Muslim friends at college have been the perfect antidote. Despite our incredibly diverse histories and sometimes divergent religious approaches, these men and women, especially my close Muslim sisters, *lived* Islam, and we helped make each other better. My community was my family, and these women my anchor.

Whatever I undertake in life, I want to be useful, and I want to do it with ihsan. As I prepare for future academic studies, I hope to imitate my college mentors with their generosity of mind, time, and spirit. The guidance of one professor in particular, a scholar of Jewish studies and religion, has shaped me in ways it may take me some time to fully understand. With him, I read the words of medieval Muslim sages, postwar German Jewish thinkers, and contemporary Shia philosophers. Learning from him drove home the Islamic imperative to seek knowledge and truth from every source.

My earliest attempts in high school to make sense of myself in the ummah, the global Muslim community, and in the world today take shape now as an interest in political and legal philosophy. I began my postgraduate studies in Berlin by looking at the experience of Muslims in Germany and am now working on a PhD.

My sister half jokingly says that she barely relates to the person she was six months ago and that she will be a stranger to herself just six months from now. This is both the excitement and the struggle of life, when even a word or a glance can move you in yet another possible direction. My self-indulgent reflection and study at college were punctuated every few months with a return home to my parents and my three sisters. When I am home, I immerse myself in the jokes, discussions, and minidramas that occupy our family. We are tender—stopping in the hallway for a hug or reaching for the hand of whoever sits with us in the car. Our home is a sweet place. This is me to the core—my flaws are transparent before them, and they show me what makes me better than I think I am.

Nevertheless, I find comfort in the fact that our family gatherings sometimes involve a brief falling-out and tears because being merely polite would signal a gradual growing apart. Yet, as my own religious consciousness comes into its own, I see each of us inevitably following our own path. This is a reality to which I am still adjusting—although families are built on a common value system, ultimately, in being sincere to our own hearts, we walk in different directions. My sisters have married non-Muslim men. Although marriage outside of the religion is, according to a minority opinion, not forbidden, just discouraged,[1] this choice in a husband signals a gap between us, a gap that is unavoidable yet somehow unexpected—that our choices are not the same, that perhaps Islam will not occupy the primary consciousness of my sisters' families, as I hope it will mine. I'm learning that family love is truly unconditional.

I pray one day to find a Muslim man who will make me a better person simply by being around him. Speaking of mates, God says in the Quran, "They are your garments, and you are their garments" (2:187). Clothing makes you beautiful. It protects you from the cold wind, and shields you from the piercing rays of the sun. My mom says that the people we love most in our lives should be thought of as treasures on loan to us—a treasure that will one day return to its Source, a treasure that ought to be returned, with care, in perfect condition. Though I long for a husband and family, I do not wait for them to give me meaning—meaning is in every moment, with or without that for which we pray.

My ancestry is Afghan, my culture American, my path Islam, and my life—it is to be *authentically* lived. Tariq Ramadan writes:

> Someday we are bound to come back to the beginning. Even the most distant pathways always lead us inward, completely inward, intimacy, solitude between our self and our self—in the place where there is no longer anyone but God and our self.[2]

I inhale, and I am overwhelmed by all the possible paths, by the apparent arbitrariness of the one I journey upon, and how it has been one of ease. I exhale, and I see precisely this thought as bringing me back to *my* history, to *this* me, to *my* authenticity. As a Muslim friend and mentor once wrote, "Emigrate from the place of your heart full of doubt, and you will find that the next step is all that matters." The dynamism of being is what it means to become. So what can I become when I *am* myself? I pray the answer will be "A perfect work of art, a fountain of knowledge, and a channel of grace for the world."[3]

After spending two years studying in Berlin, Sara now lives in Berkeley, where she is working on her PhD in European legal history. In 2012, she celebrated her one-year wedding anniversary with Adam W., with whom she reconnected after their graduation from Dartmouth.

Notes

1. The majority of Muslim scholars conclude that men are permitted to marry non-Muslim women, but Muslim women are not permitted to marry non-Muslim men. A minority take the position I describe above.
2. Tariq Ramadan, *Western Muslims and the Future of Islam* (Oxford: Oxford University Press, 2004), vii.
3. Seyyed Hossein Nasr, *Knowledge and the Sacred* (New York: Crossroad, 1981), 274.

PART V

STRUGGLES WITH FAMILY

13

Tafaoul Abdelmagid   A Child of Experience

I was born in Khartoum, the capital of Sudan, where I grew up among my cousins, aunts, and uncles until the age of ten. Khartoum is a relatively modern city, with gaudy houses and soaring buildings that contrast starkly with the neighboring villages. Temperatures there reach one hundred degrees Fahrenheit for about eight months out of the year. My family had a very stable and comfortable life in Khartoum. I attended an all-girls Catholic private school (yes, in an Islamic country) because it had a rigorous curriculum and provided an excellent education. Education mattered very much to my parents, and I absolutely loved my school for the environment it provided me. It was there among the other girls that I formed my closest friendships and developed my personality. However, this all changed when my father was offered a visa to visit the United States, and my family made the decision to emigrate.

After living in the United States for a few years, I enrolled in a private Islamic high school, where I soon learned the difference between what religious institutions are ideally expected to accomplish and the reality of what actually occurs inside these schools. Ethnic racism is prevalent in North African and Middle Eastern countries, and in my experience, many people from those regions consider black Africans to be inferior to Arabs. Although this ethnic bias is implicit and unspoken, such prejudiced beliefs were present in the classrooms of my Islamic school. As a lower-middle-class Sudanese student, I was viewed as inferior by several of the school's teachers. I became disillusioned with the Islamic school, and during my freshman year I registered at the public high school. My parents initially rejected the idea of enrolling me in a public high school, but there was no other choice for me, other than being homeschooled. They managed their anxiety by trying to find out every detail of my daily life at school. On my return home each day, I was required to give them a detailed report of what had taken place, whom I had spoken to, who spoke to me, whom I sat with during lunch, and so forth. They believed that I needed surveillance and protection from those around me, and even from myself.

As I continued my freshman year at the public high school, I was fearful and felt socially isolated from my classmates. They would talk about the way I looked and give me dirty glances, which made me feel I would never be able to fit in or breach that invisible barrier of communication. I know in retrospect the barrier was caused as much by the prejudice I projected onto my classmates as by their attitudes toward me. But even though I did not seem to belong there, I was determined to carve out a place for myself. At times I did not think I could possibly survive the first year of high school, but every time I earned an excellent grade in one of my courses, my lifeless self was revived.

As the end of freshman year approached, I began selecting challenging courses for my sophomore year. Many of those courses required teacher recommendations or permission, and that posed a great challenge for me. I respected all my teachers and had established decent relationships with them, but I discovered that some of them did not think I was capable of succeeding in advanced courses. My English teacher denied me the right to register for honors English in my sophomore year, claiming that I needed to improve my writing before taking such a challenging course, and my geometry teacher did not approve my selection of an upper-level math course. This discovery that some of the teachers doubted my intellect tore me apart. I talked to my guidance counselor and told her that, despite my teachers' refusal to give me the necessary recommendations, I would not change my selections. The guidance counselor supported my persistence and my desire to challenge myself, and she approved my course selections without the required recommendations. At that point I felt my freshman year had officially ended, and all I now aspired to do was prove my teachers wrong.

Sophomore year of high school passed quickly, and every day of it further strengthened my determination to succeed, to escape by writing, reading, studying. I was becoming less and less tolerant of how much my parents distrusted me, but the more furious I became, the more I channeled my anger into my determination to achieve academically. It was during my sophomore year that I developed a peculiar propensity for writing. I found myself writing everywhere I went, at any time, whether at or outside of school. I wrote and wrote and wrote. Every word, even for my English class essays, was written with fervent emotion, with tears, laughs, anguish, and joy. I realized that I wrote because it made me feel free of any burdens or constraints. I slowly made more friends, none of them Muslim, and started becoming much more receptive to their ideologies, beliefs, and cultural customs.

Surprisingly, at the end of my junior year I was elected vice president of the National Honor Society—something I had never thought possible. The closer senior year came, the more I found myself engrossed in a state of self-reflection and inner confrontation. Suddenly, my faith, principles, and the divergent views I was encountering became tangible subjects that I could discuss inwardly with myself. Somehow I had acquired the courage to confront myself in an internal dialogue that included questions about my beliefs and thoughts: What does it mean for some act to be right or wrong? What does my faith really mean to me? Where do I belong—at school, at home, or inside myself? Who am I? Through these dialogues, I developed the strength to face myself in front of an invisible mirror every time I did something that I knew would be considered culturally unconventional in the eyes of my parents.

I enjoyed every moment of my senior year because I realized that each day took me a step closer to a new beginning in a new place. I was looking forward to a new stage in my life, as things at home were not good. I was silent all the time, and that silence communicated my rebellion to my parents—I honestly didn't know how else to do it. It told my parents that I wanted to be independent, that I was angry and wanted to be away from home. Being silent provided both an escape and temporary relief from confrontations with my parents, but my reticence infuriated them even further. I did my homework in silence, studied in silence, and ate in silence. My silence provoked my parents' suspicion and anger, and rather than encouraging me to continue working hard at school, they began to rebuke me for spending too much time alone and for studying excessively. They repeated over and over that I had become an isolated individual, no longer their radiant, social daughter. "You've become Americanized," they would say, or, "You've changed for the worse." I felt frustrated because I was achieving the academic success they wanted, yet they were not satisfied.

My routine throughout my high-school years consisted of going to school, returning home, and doing homework every night and most weekend days. Doing homework was a way to evade my parents' interrogation and suffocating distrust. As long as I was studying, there was no need for them to question my actions or intentions, and they no longer interrogated me as much because I spent all my time secluded in my little room, studying. Eventually their dissatisfaction and behavior no longer infuriated me and I was able to accept that that was just how they were and may always be. I had a goal, and everything else faded from view.

I began to develop a strong interest in science, especially when we studied anatomy and physiology. My sense of competence, confidence, and passion for learning was evident to my peers and teachers. I also developed strong friendships with a few non-Muslim girls I had known in middle school. I befriended them with a clear caveat in mind: they were my friends during the school day, but never outside the school walls. I knew that I would not be allowed to spend my leisure time with them because they were devout Christians, and I was not allowed to befriend any girl without my mother's approval. She had to meet every one of my potential friends so she could assess their behavior, character, and values. This made it difficult for me to find friends, as it instilled in me a kind of internal filter that prevented me from approaching anyone without first analyzing the person and their intentions. Nevertheless, in time I became closer to a group of girls I had known in middle school, most of whom were Russian or Hispanic immigrants.

None of my closest friends were U.S. citizens or Muslims. There were only two other girls in the school who were Muslim and wore veils, but I never got along with them—I just did not feel comfortable in their presence. Although these two girls were Muslim, they went out with friends all the time, cursed a lot, and even had male friends. They were definitely not the ideal Muslim girls my parents had hoped I would befriend. Everything these girls did at school contradicted what I had been taught about decent Islamic behavior and confirmed my parents' concerns. I felt safer and more comfortable around my Christian friends, who were either devout or otherwise virtuous. While we rarely discussed religion directly, from time to time they would ask me about the purpose of the veil, why I did not eat meat at school, or about my cultural customs in general. By the third year of high school, as some of these friendships grew deeper, I was even allowed to go to their houses—after my mother had completed her multiyear evaluation.

The closer I grew to my friends, the more I understood the core of who I was. Our commonalities brought us closer, and our differences helped me refine my perspective on life and to value my identity. At the same time, I continued to study as hard as I could because I wanted to achieve higher grades than all my classmates. I gained confidence and learned that I could succeed with hard work, diligence, and persistence. My academic achievements and determination to earn the highest grades made me surprisingly popular among my classmates. I earned a reputation as a studious, friendly, yet conservative girl—one who respected herself and never allowed anyone to overstep her boundaries. In a sense, my grades defined me and allowed me to find my place among my classmates and friends. That lonely and unhappy freshman girl bloomed and became a popular student, respected friend, and, without knowing it, a girl who was feared by many boys for her serious demeanor. I cherished my new identity because it was one I had consciously carved into the minds of my fellow students.

At school I was outgoing, vocal, and even strong. I communicated my opinions openly, and I developed the strength to defend my opinions, even if it meant disagreeing with a teacher during a class discussion or with my own friends. Instead of my friends asking me about my religious tenets and customs all the time, I began to ask them about theirs. I wanted to understand why I was different and, surprisingly, I realized that the more I challenged my faith, the more faithful I became. Islam is not simply a religion but a way of life. Its essence is found in everyday things: how I eat, how I act, how I sleep, how I talk, even how I walk. Being able to ask my friends about their own beliefs and outlooks on different issues transformed the way I thought about everything and how I viewed myself. Rather than simply wondering, I asked; instead of feeling confused, I demanded explanations; and instead of being quiet all the time, I had a voice. Over time I formed enduring friendships that were based on both commonalities and a mature appreciation of differences. My friends knew that I did not drink and did not enjoy guy talk or staying out late at night, and they respected me for that. My different way of life did not turn them away.

My French teacher was my favorite. He advised me to apply to all the Ivy League schools and supported me throughout the college application process. He helped me write my personal essay and supplementary application, and never failed to remind me every day to send the required documentation to the colleges on time or to inform me of any scholarships he knew I would qualify for. There are some people who pass by silently in your life, and others who leave a permanent imprint on your heart. This teacher was certainly one of the latter, and I owe him my sincere gratitude and respect, not only as a teacher but as a father figure as well.

I knew that I had to go to college to experience the outside world and leave the bubble of my family life. The idea of attending a college in the United States seemed both menacing and important to my parents. They knew that a college degree from a U.S. institution would open the doors of opportunity for me anywhere in the world, especially in Sudan. Yet at the same time, they feared that the current of U.S. culture and customs would engulf me or even steal me away from them. They undoubtedly feared that I would become like the majority of U.S. youth rather than remain the obedient, modest daughter they had raised. While I understood their fears, I also wanted my freedom. To ensure that they still had a say in my future, my parents made me apply to all the renowned women's colleges: Wellesley, Smith, Mount Holyoke. The mere fact that I had applied to these institutions alleviated their fears. In the end I was able, after much effort, to convince them to let me attend the coed Ivy League school where I was accepted.

The first day I arrived on campus, I felt that I had finally ruptured the bubble around me and entered a new world. I was both excited and terrified. During my freshman year, I was continually overwhelmed with work. I had to learn how to synthesize new ideas and actually apply the information I gathered in lectures, rather than simply regurgitate facts, as I had done to achieve success in high school. It may sound strange, but the more stressed I was, the more spiritual I became. I found myself praying more, and discussing religion more openly and assertively than ever with my non-Muslim friends. I became much more independent. I must say that I owe a lot of my newly invigorated spirituality to the network of Muslim sisters I met. I say "sisters" because of the way they treated me and the strong friendships we developed. We ate together, hung out together, prayed together, studied together—we really became one. I had not had any Muslim friends in high school because I had feared the cultural prejudgments that could taint an attempt at friendship, but in college, the virtuous qualities I found in these girls transcended any personal differences. For the first time in my life, I found older sisters—true friends with whom I could identify as a Muslim woman.

Most of the Muslim friends I made as a college freshman were seniors, so by the end of my freshman year I needed to say good-bye to many of them. Making new friendships outside that strong inner circle seemed impossible. However, I knew that those friends had enabled me to become a stronger, more knowledgeable Muslim girl. They had fortified my spirit and mind through discussions on the role of women in Islam, gender relationships, social roles, independence, professional careers, academia, and our dreams, hopes, and desires. We talked about everything and anything without social constraints or fear, and with a sincere consciousness of God and Islamic teachings. Knowing them also enabled me to become daring enough to form friendships with non-Muslims as well as girls of diverse backgrounds and ethnicities. For once in my life, I was able to feel comfortable being who I am—a Muslim girl—among people who had entirely different views from those I embraced and who came from entirely different backgrounds: white Americans, Mexicans, Russians, Kenyans, Latinas, Nigerians, Somalis, Pakistanis. I no longer feared being labeled as an outlier; in fact, I actually wanted to be known as someone different, not just because I am Muslim but because I am me. I wanted my friends to see me distinctly, and not as just another Muslim girl in a crowd. Through these friendships, I found my inner voice, and rather than simply practicing my religion, I had become an active participant and representative of my faith. I did my best to act, walk, speak, and simply appear like a true, strong Muslim woman. Rather than just letting people see that I wore the veil, I made it a goal for them to understand why. Rather than simply saying that I am Muslim, I allowed my friends to understand what Islam truly is.

Throughout my life, one simple word had fulfilled how I defined myself: Muslim. I am Sudanese by nationality and culture, Arab by language, but above all, I am Muslim. Being Muslim meant that I believed and testified that "there is no God but Allah, and Muhammad is His Prophet and Messenger." I neither cared nor knew about any sects, divisions, or political complications associated with certain Islamic countries. All I knew was that I was Muslim. However, all that changed the day I had a conversation with someone who made me realize that I was ignorant about many aspects of Islam. I had known this person well for a few years, but we had never discussed religion before.

Many people think that Muslims preach about religion all the time, especially Muslim girls, since we wear the veil as an obvious symbol of devotion, but this is not necessarily true. Actually, religion is a topic I typically avoid with my friends, especially my non-Muslim friends. It's not that I'm ashamed to discuss it, but I want to avoid pressuring my friends in any way. Islam is not a religion ruled by an austere set of codes; the real Islam is practiced in the way you interact with others. One day, this person decided to open a rather controversial topic with me: the way the veil is worn. He claimed that he had many close female Muslim friends, some who wore the veil and others who did not. Those who wore the veil, he said, usually wore it with their hair exposed in the front while the back was covered. He alleged that some even revealed their necks. He then asked me quite bluntly, "Why do you wear your veil so tightly in the front?" I replied that each person simply interprets religion in their own way. Unconvinced by my answer, he asked me to prove to him that the veil had to cover the hair and neck completely. I was aware of a verse in the Quran that explicitly states that a Muslim woman should expose only her hands and face. I knew the verse in Arabic, but I could not paraphrase it in English because casual translation of the Quran is not allowed in Islam, and I had not memorized the verse in question from a Quran translated into English. I explained this to him, but he was not convinced. He said very simply, "I don't get it. My other Muslim friend wears her veil half-way, and when I asked her to explain why, she immediately recited a verse in English and took out a translation of the Quran and showed it to me. Looks like you can't do that! See, you can't even prove yourself right!!" That was it: I didn't know how to communicate my knowledge to him, or perhaps I had no true knowledge of my own religion. His blunt censure slashed my heart. I was silent and paralyzed by my shame, and I wished that the earth would open up and swallow me. I couldn't even express anger. I could not blame him because he was right; I was unable to defend my position.

I will never forget his most pointed question: "What's your sect?" I asked, "What do you mean by sect?" He said, "Are you Sunni or Shia?" I knew of these two prominent sects in Islam, but in my eyes, all were Muslim in the eyes of God and under the testimony of Islam, regardless of differences. I replied naively, "I'm Sunni, I guess." "Oh, OK! That's why!!" he replied. "That's why what?!" I asked. "That's why you're so strict. You see, my female friend is Shia, and she's very receptive. She interprets the Quran with flexibility and seems more devoted than you. At least more open-minded! Sunnis are conservative and narrow-minded." He articulated these words with a certainty that terrified me. Is that what other students thought of me?! I couldn't help pondering his words.

After that day, I became more alert to how my fellow students interacted with me. I found myself suddenly "reading between the lines," trying to interpret every smile, every smirk, every glance, at times even every conversation I had with other students. In an attempt to understand why certain students had a misconstrued idea of Sunnis and Shias, I registered for an introduction to Islam course. I wanted to see what it was that these students learned, and to develop a deeper understanding of how they perceived me. Of course, I was the only Muslim student registered in that course. The first day I entered the classroom, heads turned and whispers rippled throughout the room. Their reaction was expected; after all, it was strange to have a Muslim student wearing a hijab in a course that supposedly discussed the basics of her own religion. However, by the end of that semester, I had gained a better understanding of why certain students misjudged Muslims. What we read in textbooks and articles focused only on Shia Islam, not on Islam as an encompassing religion. This reality shocked me, but at the same time it allowed me to present students with a live example of a Sunni Muslim who attended that same class. I educated myself in many aspects of Islam and realized that the more knowledge I shared with others in discussions, the better they understood Islam—and me. This course allowed me to learn more about who I am as a hijabi Muslim girl through my classmates' reflecting glass.

The controversial issue of how the hijab is worn and whether or not it is obligatory, as stated in the Quran, inevitably surfaced during many class discussions. The fact that I was a Muslim girl in the classroom never dissuaded students from making valid comparisons between me and other Muslim girls on campus. I appreciated their avid interest in learning, but at times their questions enlivened my fear of being characterized as narrow-minded. Most questions about the hijab were in fact posed by male students, and in such discussions the conversation often evolved into a different topic: gender relationships in Islam. Most wanted to know how it was possible for a hijabi Muslim girl to express her sexuality when she is forbidden to expose her physical beauty to any man until after marriage. My male classmates respected me and never overstepped my boundaries, and through their interactions with me they learned that I was not just a Muslim classmate but also a friend and a sister. I was able to help them see that, while I revere my religion and the hijab I don, I am also a woman who displays a unique form of beauty. A woman is a woman, whether she wears a miniskirt or is fully clothed with a veil on her head. But there was one topic I often evaded whenever possible in class—marriage.

For most Sudanese girls my age, marriage is a must. It represents the beginning of a new life and the end of girlhood. It's also an end to the days of being lonely. To most girls in Sudanese culture, marriage is the door to another world, the realization of romantic fantasies and the bliss of being with the "right one." However, if that's the enchanting dream that marriage offers, then something is wrong with me, because I have truly never thought about marriage. In high school I would hear my friends talk about all the details of their dream weddings, but those ideas were alien to me. I felt like I was a stranger to the entire concept of marriage. It was enough that I was unlike many girls my age already. I hated makeup—all that disgusting powder, vivid lipstick, and vulgar blush. (No one was ever able to convince me that having bright-red cheeks was attractive!) I despised wearing high heels and never mastered the art of walking in them. Being natural was my adage: God created me as a beautiful person inside and out, so if you don't like what you see, turn around! That was just me, and I'm still that person today, even in college, where girls are supposed to mature into womanhood and adapt to its strange conventions.

From early childhood on, I remember the emphasis that was always placed on becoming a desirable wife. That was every Sudanese mother's dream for her daughter, and at some age, that dream became the daughter's too. It was as if there was nothing else to do in life! I never agreed with any of those beliefs, and I genuinely thought that coming to the United States would mean an end to that narrow definition of being a woman. But that was not the case. I was able to focus on my high-school studies and avoid the entire topic; nevertheless, day after day my mother would bring up the name of a marriage prospect: "He's very respectful, very religious, he can support a family, very educated and open-minded. Oh, and I heard that he comes from a renowned family…" Every time she spoke of a prospect, she made it seem like he was the ONE, the most exceptional of all men. I never really understood how the process of marriage functioned in Sudan until my mother explained it to me when I was sixteen years old. At that time I was a junior in high school and had been living in the United States for about seven years. That was also the year my mother started bringing up these marriage prospects. My response was ALWAYS the same: "No, Mama, I'm still too young and I'm not thinking of getting married now!" While she never forced the idea on me, she also did not ever close the window entirely.

While in college I got more and more marriage proposals. Strangely, I never knew where they came from. When I reached the age of nineteen, I truly became aware of the significance of marriage and its role in my culture and religion. My mother got married when she was only eighteen years old, and she had me, her first child, at the age of nineteen. I could never understand the reality of that, even when I was nineteen years old myself. My mother never exerted any pressure on me or urged me to get married early, but what she did do was emphasize over and over again the need for me to give the topic serious thought, especially since I was getting older; for Sudanese women, age is the factor that determines marriage. In my culture, the older you get, the more unlikely you are to be chosen as a wife. My culture never exalts or even alludes to a woman's right to make her own decision—whether in choosing her partner, when to get married, or even if she wants to get married at all. The entire concept of marriage and its social role seems to have been constructed by the patriarchal ideology of my culture, which I believe is contrary to Islamic teachings.

You would think that living in the United States would allow me to detach myself completely from those conventions and to live my life as I decide. But no, year after year passes and the proposals keep coming. This past summer I received my first serious proposal, one that I could not reject out of hand. I was doing an internship at a clinic for the treatment of pulmonary diseases, hoping to enhance my application to medical school. My youngest maternal aunt had just gotten married and was headed to London for her honeymoon—where she was to meet her husband in person for the very first time. In Sudanese culture, such an arrangement is not unusual. Two weeks into her honeymoon, my aunt started talking to my mother about a guy who happened to be her husband's closest friend. My aunt explained to my mother that this "friend," who was only a few years older than me, was in search of a wife from a decent and respectable family. She said that he happened to see me in one of the photos in her album, which I found rather disturbing and disrespectful, and after many inquiries he insisted on meeting me.

My mother prefaced all this with a long introduction, even though I am sure my aunt got right to the point when discussing it with her. After all, she had to make me sense the urgency of the matter before delivering the shock: "You're getting married!!!" My mother didn't announce it in quite that way, of course, but the message was clear, and she insisted that I give him a chance and not be so antagonistic toward the idea of marriage. It was bad enough that I was out of school for a few months; I now also had to face this revolutionary possibility. I say "revolutionary" because, for the very first time in my life, I did actually begin to think about the idea of marriage. I felt that my parents were truly serious about the matter and I could tell how much they were in favor of allowing the possibility to develop. I felt that I was at a crossroads in my life, one where I had to choose not only which path to follow but also whether I wanted to follow that path alone or with a companion. The thought of being with someone for the rest of my life never really penetrated my mind until that time. I always thought of myself as a student and wanted to be a student for a very long time. The medical field demands focused effort, time, and, quite literally, a life dedicated to the study of the profession. I knew when I entered college that my choice to pursue a medical career would mean making sacrifices, possibly including marriage, family, a personal life— even the simple privilege of being viewed as a woman with human needs.

I have always believed that men are aggressive, callous, insular, and judgmental. This impression is a product of my life experiences. I have never known a happy couple who simply loved each other and lived their life to reflect that love. I have never witnessed a love story in which a man loved a woman for who she was, and not for his image of the "ideal" companion. Not once in my short life have I heard of a real-life "Romeo and Juliet" type of story, where true love has been the weapon through which a man or a woman defended his or her love against the world, against cultural constraints—a love that formed its own unique reality. All I have seen are images that destroy love, that kill its meaning, its purpose, and its blessings. I have heard of so many instances of divorce, of verbal and physical abuse, of injustice, oppression, women being thrown out in the streets by their husbands, of adultery and the impossibility of finding a faithful man, not to mention the exploitation of women by all means, most of all emotionally. God knows how many times I've witnessed women crying before me because their husbands abandoned them or humiliated them for no apparent reason. I was there, even as a child, when my own female relatives spoke of how their husbands treated them like disposable possessions they could disown at will. Pangs of anxiety beset my heart every time I heard stories of the many sacrifices women made for men who proved to be their clandestine enemies—ungrateful, heartless, and selfish. I did not dare envision myself as another of the many such mistreated women in my culture. I did not want to become a mirror image of my mother, my aunts, or my other female relatives. I did not want to become another victim of a generation of voiceless and oppressed women. All that I truly wanted was to be me and to be accepted as an independent, receptive, yet also modest woman. All I wanted was to find a man who would love me for who I am, to live a life of love that God approves of and blesses.

I was expected to talk to this prospective husband, so I started communicating with him over the phone and online from time to time. Every step I took was, of course, with my mother's permission. The relationship developed steadily, although quite frankly I didn't perceive myself as committed to a relationship. I continued to be nonchalant about the entire thing until he started mentioning the idea of our wearing rings and having a wedding. A wedding?! What?!! Hearing of his desire to get engaged filled me with confusion, disbelief, joy, and doubt. Through all of these conflicting feelings, the overriding one was of fear. I was frightened of my destiny, scared of deciding to be with him and then realizing at some future time that we weren't right for each other, yet also fearful of losing this opportunity.

At college, where the topic of relationships and marriage came up often, I tended to discuss my expectations for my "knight in shining armor" in general terms. However, when I realized that many of my Muslim friends were actually getting engaged and forming families, I began to be very specific about what I expected from my future companion and what kind of relationship I actually wanted. It all came down to three simple yet impossible expectations. First, I wanted a man who fears God in everything he does, because by fearing God in all his actions, he will undoubtedly treat me not only as a wife but as a friend. Second, I sought a man who would treat the women in his family decently. Of course, being reared in a patriarchal culture has contaminated my outlook on men, but I tried to remain realistic. Third, I hoped to find a man who would love me for who I am—and I really mean that. I didn't want a man who would try to fit me into *his* image of the ideal partner. I wanted a man who could recognize me for who I was, with all of my attributes and imperfections, and accept me the way I truly was. I wanted a man who would respect my dreams and aspirations and support me throughout my long journey (both through medical school and afterward), who would fully understand my needs or attempt to do so.

So I knew what qualities I was looking for, but now the question before me was whether this suitor would be the right one. Could he truly meet my expectations and accept me and my impulsiveness, my childish ways and independence and determination? Although he seemed like a promising match in some ways, I sensed in him the usual cultural contagion. He projected the image of a modern, progressive, yet God-fearing man, but in reality his thinking reflected the usual mentality of Arab men. He was utterly possessive, which by my standards translated into me becoming his piece of property. I can understand the jealousy a man feels for the woman he loves, but not possessive jealousy. This guy wanted me to tell him where I was going, and for how long, and with whom, while I wanted trust and an understanding of our mutual individuality. I realize that many of the ideas I express may seem radical to other Muslim women, even to my mother sometimes, but I am only voicing the demands of many girls my age. We are looking for a healthy relationship, but also one in which God is at the center, not just an added benefit. So, in the end, I turned him down. He called me "disrespectful" for being so blunt in my refusal and for not explaining why I didn't want to marry him (I can't blame him). I wasn't going to take chances with my matrimonial life, and being blunt was better than being unjust, both to myself and to him. At least that's what I said to myself to justify my actions. As for my family, let's just say that the displeasure of my refusal still lingers. They may never be happy with my choice of a husband, but they can never force me to marry a man I do not want.

Having lived through an unofficial "engagement," I now know one thing for sure: I want to marry a convert to Islam. That idea may give my mother a heart attack, but I know I will never relinquish my will to do so. My reason is that I see conversion as a proclamation that one has understood the essence of Islam, an essence that is unsullied by cultural ideologies, social customs, or materialistic compromises. A convert would be a man who is intrinsically Muslim, not just overtly or superficially a Muslim. Marrying a convert would enable me to practice Islam as it is, not as society and culture want it to be, and to live happily and, most importantly, peacefully alongside a man who believes that Islam is a religion of moderation and rationality, not radicalism. I am looking for a convert because I believe that it is more likely for a converted man to have experienced both the religious and the nonreligious aspects of life. He will allow me to practice my profession as a Muslim female doctor without the constraints of what my culture demands. He would be able to, God willing, comprehend the true Islam that the Prophet (peace be upon him) delivered, rather than abiding by the adulterated version of Islam that patriarchy imposes in the world today. Most important, he will be able to express to me the following: "I love you for who you are, not who I want you to be, and I want to be with you because we're destined for each other, not because our culture declared that we are convenient for each other." He will embody the authentic ideals of Islam, and we will grow together and along the journey. We will learn from one another until we become one.

I have developed into a mature woman who knows what she wants, and I am determined to pursue a life in which I fulfill all my dreams. I may not know what God's plan holds for me, but that's exactly the point; not knowing is a blessing because it allows us humans to thrust our burdens, pains, and troubles on God and to have unwavering faith in His ability to dispose of all our affairs. As to my marriage and whom I'll be with, I ask those who read my story to pray for me and wish me luck. Life is full of surprises, and I am ready to receive them. Whichever direction I choose will be a reflection of God's will. I also know that my experiences, no matter how trivial compared to those of other women, will come in handy someday and fortify me as a Muslim woman.

I am no longer a product solely of my rearing and culture but of experience as well. I was not born the woman I am; I have *become* an independent, determined, strong, and proud Muslim woman. While my time in the United States as a young Muslim woman has thrilled me and granted me countless privileges, I realize that it has not defined me. My identity lies solely and firmly in two essential facts; I am the daughter of my mother, and the child of experience.

Epilogue: Life Goes On

So much has occurred between the time I wrote this essay and my graduation from college. After refusing to marry the suitor my parents presented, I decided that I needed a long hiatus from relationships. I felt unprepared, inexperienced, and certainly reluctant to commit myself to a man. However, I fell in love with an Italian American social worker whom my mother and I had met before I entered college. Although he was a devout Christian at the time, he expressed an avid interest in Islam as a religion and way of life. The fact that he was a Christian made me close my heart to him, even when he relentlessly tried to get closer to me. After all, it was impossible for me to fall in love with a Christian, never mind to marry him!!! So for me he was simply NOT an option.

I didn't know back then that just a few months later that same man would reappear in my life as a devout new convert to Islam. After several conversations with my mother, he openly confessed that he had always thought about me and asked for her permission to speak to me on the phone. My mother didn't entirely approve of this situation, but she grew weary of trying to convince me to get married. He was handsome, cultured, and wealthy, and a convert whom my mother actually respected. I could not shelve that match as unpromising; I believed that shared religious and moral values were the criteria that transcended any cultural or ethnic differences.

Our relationship slowly developed and matured over time, and a few months into it I began to see the true colors of my knight. To my shock, he was chauvinistic, insular, and insecure. What he wanted was a dependent, demure, and selfless partner. My independence appalled him, and my career-oriented mentality and strong will affronted him. To him I was always either too strong-willed or too stubborn, too sociable or too individualistic. I felt that what he truly wanted was a Mother Teresa figure (whom I highly admire but can never match), not a Muslim version of a seemingly Westernized feminist. With all those red flags, I ended my relationship with him, even though we had planned to become officially engaged just a month later.

It took some time to forget him, but I eventually met other men who proved to me that finding the "right one" does not necessarily depend on nationality or conversion to Islam but on a person's innate character. I met Muslim men—men who were willing to convert to Islam for my sake, and others who had recently converted. I returned to Sudan just a few days after my graduation from college, and just three weeks later I got engaged to one of the suitors (a young Sudanese man) who proposed to me. He was just a few years older than me, and he lived and studied in Germany. That engagement didn't last very long, when it became clear he was just not the right fit for me. Of course other men proposed, and I found myself in a rocking boat, unable to decide whether I wanted to sink into marital life or just keep rocking until the right prospect came along.

Well, I did not stay on that boat for very long because right after I ended my engagement, the man I had first rejected in my story, whom my parents had arranged for me to marry, proposed to me—again. It turned out that he had never stopped loving me, even after I had refused him. He prayed for two years that God would destine me to become his wife. I was totally baffled by the fact that a man would pursue me to that extent, and to be honest, I secretly felt flattered. I decided that God must have caused him to resurface in my life for a good reason, so why not give him a chance? However, this time I actually approached the relationship with an open heart, without cultural prejudgments or unrealistic personal expectations. Less than a month from the time we began speaking again, we became happily married.

I realize that my story may seem strange and baffling at times, but in the end, if I had to choose between going back in time to live a different life or to relive mine, I would choose the latter. I wouldn't change a single thing because I know that God put me through trials to test my strength and to bless me with what I deserve at the end. My fairy tale is nothing like *Cinderella* or *Sleeping Beauty*, but more like that of the princess in *Brave*. I never sat and waited for Prince Charming to come and carry me away on his white horse, nor did I spend sleepless nights wondering when my knight in shining armor would appear. I came to view marriage and relationships in general with practicality, yet I never lost sight of my expectations. My acceptance of my husband was not a surrender to my family's demands or to a sense of despair in finding the right one. No! I agreed to marry this man because I felt that he was right for me, but more important because he wanted me to always remain myself. God helped me find a delicate balance between my parents' demands and my own expectations. So, to all you Muslim girls out there, never give up, because the beginning of a new chapter in your life may be just around the corner. But for now, keep chasing life a little.

Tafaoul is still married to the man she rejected at the beginning of her story; he has become her beloved husband and best friend. They now live in the UK, where Tafaoul is pursuing her medical studies.

14

Nasir Nasser A Debt to Those Who *Know* Us

My story begins before *my* story begins. It's a story about my parents. It's a story about my education.

On paper, my parents are quite similar. Both were born and raised in Tanzania and trace their ancestry back to the Kutch district of India. Both are responsible middle-class professionals. Both are Canadian citizens. Both are devout and active Nizari Ismaili Muslims. Both value family and community. Yet live with them, and you soon see that they're an odd couple.

They may both come from Tanzania, but my father—the son of a shop-keeper in the inland town of Dodoma—seems provincial next to my cos-mopolitan mother, who is from the bustling coastal metropolis of Dar es Salaam. For instance, my father watches business news compulsively. When my mother changes the channel—say, to a foreign film—my father quickly loses interest: "It's too slow," he sighs. "This is *culture*. It's *good* for you," my mom scolds. Both my mother and father work nine to five, but while he, an engineering technologist, tinkers with the angles of drain-age pipes on computer-generated maps, she, a rehabilitation consultant, consoles live human beings about their most deeply felt vulnerabilities. The pair differs in their religiosity, too. In contrast to my father's strict regimen—he goes to pray at our *khane* twice a day, every day—my moth-er's attitude is slack. She'll skip khane to watch one of the aforementioned foreign films (hey, it's the only time my dad isn't in the house), but then she'll spend her weekend helping our khane's newly arrived immigrants settle in. My parents even snack differently. My father craves salty foods (potato chips, mostly, with lemon juice and paprika) and my mother likes sweets (white chocolate). But the difference between my parents that weighs heaviest—one I barely sensed when I was growing up—is their feelings about education.

My father was so eager to go to school as a kid that he snuck into the back of his older brother's first-grade classroom. And then his second-grade classroom. And third. I remember hearing that their father bribed the principal to let him stay. It was three years into his education before my father appeared on any official school records. His older brother was always smarter than he was—"Amin was number one in the class," he told me, adding that he wasn't so far behind: "I hovered around fourth or fifth." They were best friends who loved math as much as they loved each other. They both dreamed of one day becoming engineers.

In the early years after independence, the Tanzanian government still forced high schoolers like my parents to sit for the Cambridge O-level exams. Students anxiously prepared for years to take this one test, the results of which determined their futures: Would you get top marks and go on to a local university? Or would your grades fall short, leaving you forever to regret your performance? The grades, which came all the way from England, would be published in the newspaper. Not the Dodoma newspaper—there was none—but the Dar es Salaam newspaper, the *Tanganyika Standard*, which took an extra day to reach the rest of the country. For my father and my uncle, as for all Dodoma teenagers, that extra day was torturous. Less than an hour after the newspaper was published in the city, rumors about the results spread throughout the town. One brother passed, but the other didn't. Nobody knew which was which. It took some time to sort out. To the whole town's surprise, my father passed but his brother didn't. My uncle got top marks in every subject except English, which he failed miserably, pulling down his overall grade. My father was elated. His results seemed to guarantee him access to university.

However, when the government tabulated exam grades to decide which students would get a spot in university, my father came up short. That year, the well-intentioned independent government enacted new racial quotas to ensure that more Africans moved on to higher education. That year, only five of the fifty-five Asians at Dodoma High School were offered spots. Despite his poor exam showing, my uncle was one of the five. My father, ranked seventh, was denied a spot. He didn't get to go to university. He didn't get to study engineering. His heart was broken.

My father was desperate to stay in school, so he went to the only school that accepted him: Egerton Agricultural College near Nakuru, Kenya. The school was founded in colonial times to prepare young male Europeans to till their land. A few years before my father got there, the institution had opened its doors to Asian and African students (East African schools desegregated their schools at about the same time as U.S. schools). My father didn't know a lick about agriculture but, "by elimination," he told me, "there was nothing else left for me." So he spent three years proving his mettle in the hopes that, with his diploma from this vocational school, he could reapply to university and one day study civil engineering. My dad learned to recognize every variety of corn, every breed of cow, every type of irrigation system. It worked. The university offered him a spot, but only in their agricultural engineering program. He reluctantly took it. In order to complete his program he had to log some time on a farm, in his case the Coastal Dairies Industry in Tanzania. But knowing his call to obligatory Tanzanian national military service was less than a month away, my pacifist father dashed back to Kenya. My dad was so worried that he'd be caught, sent back across the border, and forced to serve, that he assumed a false name.

By then, in neighboring Uganda, the dictator Idi Amin had expelled the country's eighty thousand Asians, claiming that they were "bloodsuckers" on the economy. The idealistic yet ill-considered policies of Tanzania's socialist leader Julius Nyerere had the same effect. Nyerere nationalized buildings and land—including the building that doubled as my grandfather's shop and family home. Nyerere also forced relocation to collective farms, known as Ujamaa Villages. My father and his family, along with many fearful Ismaili Muslims across East Africa, packed up their lives and fled to Canada.

Of the two bags my father brought with him, one was filled with thick textbooks on tropical African agriculture. Only after arriving did my father discern what little use these books would be to him in temperate Canada. (The books still sit in a pile in our basement. "Dust collectors, all of them," my father says, rolling his eyes.)

By the time he got to Canada, then in a recession, my father had a hard time finding a job because he lacked Canadian work experience. He went through a string of minimum-wage jobs, all outdoors during a particularly harsh winter. He went from never having seen snow to staring at it for forty-plus hours a week. Employers swindled and exploited him. He once worked full-time for a Dutch landscaping company for a month, saving his paychecks because he knew he'd need the money to sponsor his parents for Canadian citizenship. When he finally went to the bank to deposit his stack of checks, he found out that they all had bounced. He never got the money.

My father found an entry-level engineering job only after a clerk at an employment agency lied on my dad's résumé without his knowledge: his agricultural-school diploma was suddenly transformed into an engineering degree. A decade later, he earned that engineering diploma after years of taking night classes at Ryerson Polytechnic.

Throughout his life, my father never doubted that education—the kind you get in a university—is the most important thing in the world. The more obstacles he came across, the clearer his faith in education became. "Seek knowledge," he quotes the Prophet, "even if you have to go to China."

My mother is more conflicted about education. As a girl, she enjoyed primary school despite her severe British teachers. She recalls that every time her school bus pulled in late, the girls on it—every one of them deemed tardy without exception—had to line up while the principal lashed their calves, one by one, with a ruler. Books were expensive, so each student copied the lesson onto her tiny blackboard with a chalk pen. When my mother went home, her father tutored her in arithmetic, scribbling practice sums in chalk on their living room's cool cement floor. Evidently, she was good enough at it to skip the second grade.

Everything changed for my mother in the seventh grade, after she failed her territorial exams. This failure was public—she was forced to repeat the grade level—and her father, more embarrassed than angry, beat her. Her mother did her best to console her. All of a sudden my mom didn't feel like going to her classes, sewing and cooking in particular. While her classmates hemmed handkerchiefs and baked oatmeal bars, my mom ditched class to play basketball, rounders (a game similar to baseball), and *tikri* (a bit like four square). She often got dragged to the principal's office with a defiant smile on her face.

In the middle of my mother's O-level exam, the principal again pulled her out, this time to break some bad news: "Your mother is sick, she's in the hospital in Upanga." My mother and her younger brother were both sent home, where they sat alone, waiting for news. Late that night, after they had fallen asleep, their uncle woke them, put them in the backseat of his car, and drove them to Upanga. He walked the siblings to a room where their mother lay still on a hospital bed, a white sheet covering her body to the neck. "Kiss your mother," her uncle instructed them both. They did. "Why is she so cold?" my mother thought. They drove home in silence.

It all happened quickly: her mother's funeral (nobody told my mother what to do, so she ran out and played tag with her friends during the ceremony), and then her father's second marriage. "I'm getting married," he told my mother one day over the phone. "To whom?" she asked. "None of your business," he snapped, and hung up the phone. My mother and her brother were sent off to England, where they knew no one and had no place to stay. They were apprehended at customs, detained for ten nightmarish days, and eventually sent back to Tanzania. Once they got back, my mother and her brother severed ties, at least financially, with their father. Still a teenager, my mother became her little brother's de facto guardian.

After just barely finishing her O-levels, my mother went to secretarial school for four months. She used the money she earned from her first job to provide for her brother. The two of them—she, nineteen, her brother, Karim, thirteen—immigrated to Canada around the time my father did and for similar reasons. When they got to Toronto, my mom worked a bevy of temp jobs—mostly secretarial and retail—so that she could keep paying for her brother's studies. He studied during the day and worked all night as a short-order cook at a diner. He slept only on weekends. My mother learned everything she needed to know about the world, not from a school, but from her bosses, her coworkers, and her own struggles to care for her brother better than she had been cared for herself.

After finding a clerical job that she liked at a local hospital, my mother became a career woman. For much of her career, however, she felt cheated: she did more work than her superiors and was often smarter than they were, but without a degree—really only a piece of paper—she would never be promoted.

I remember one time, at age twelve or thirteen, when I was working downtown in the Parliament Building as a legislative page (basically a tuxedoed water boy). A new cabinet minister in charge of education and training had been announced, and the teachers' unions were picketing in protest. One sign read, "John Snobelen didn't even finish high school." I thought it hilarious: an uneducated education minister. When I got home I told my mom, expecting her to laugh, but instead she scolded me: "Education isn't everything. You can't judge people without *knowing* them." It was like a smack in the face.

My own educational history may not be as dramatic as that of my parents, but it does combine elements of both. My parents took out a second mortgage on the house to send my sister and me to private school. The money wasn't enough, however, so they alternated us. In any given year, one of us would be in private school, the other in public. Every few years, we switched. I got better grades than my sister, but that says more about her all-consuming social life than it does about my middling academic record. Whereas my sister belonged to the popular crowd, I was a bit of a loner. I rarely met any of my classmates outside of school, or even after the bell. I was too busy getting an education, I told myself.

In addition to school, my father enrolled me in any and every extra-curricular activity he could. I took lessons in karate, guitar, debate, gymnastics, painting, and platform diving. I participated in math challenges, door-to-door fund-raising drives, speech competitions, spelling bees, and on and on. I was the only boy in my figure-skating class. My dad even signed me up for a month-long information-technology tutorial through the adult-education division of a local community center. Everyone else in the class was middle-aged; I was eleven. Classes were held mostly after school but before khane. Sometime in between we'd hit a drive-through for a fast-food dinner.

On weekends, our neighbor, a retired elementary schoolteacher named Miss Wiggins, taught my sister and me the finer points of English grammar and, now that I think about it, the finer points of just about everything else. She seemed to know it all: from Japanese origami to Greek mythology, from the Berlin Wall to the Great Wall of China. As far as I could gather, she had visited every country in the world. I never asked her, but the scores of newspapers and exotic tchotchkes strewn around her house were proof enough for me.

Every Saturday morning, I attended religious-education classes called *Bait-ul-Ilm* (literally, "house of knowledge"). At ten o'clock in the morning, we'd show up at the Monsignor Percy Johnson Secondary School. There we'd be, learning about Imam Ali with a bronze Christ hanging on the wooden cross just above the door ("It's okay," we'd be told, "Jesus is one of our prophets too"). The teachers, volunteers from khane, were often related to one or another of the dozen students in my class. Usually, that student was me. At different points, my mother, my father, two of my aunts, and one of my uncles were at the head of my class, reading from the syllabus. Even my sister came once as a substitute teacher.

I got away with more than I should have at Bait-ul-Ilm. Until about the third grade, I would openly mock the names of iconic tenth-century missionaries and traditional Muslim scientists (as if my own name is any less awkward than Nasir Khusraw's or Ibn al-Haytham's!). For about five years after that, I would derail theological lessons with blatantly irrelevant questions: "How can someone be a Muslim if they don't speak Arabic?" "When he was in the desert, did Prophet Muhammad wear Chap Stick?" "What time is lunch?" Another game I played was to raise my hand and say the Prophet's name six or so times in a row, forcing everyone else in the room to mutter "Peace be upon him" after every mention. It wasn't that I had dissenting religious opinions or that I wanted to annoy my peers: I was simply bored. I was bored at school, bored with my extracurriculars, and bored in my religious classes. The only time I wasn't bored was when I was with my parents.

The most fun I had was with my father. We'd discuss topics my father deemed important—Christopher Columbus, the stock market, World War II—and spend months trying to make sense of them. We had a ping-pong table in our basement, and he'd make up educational games for us to play on it. "Every time I hit the ball, I'll name one of the fifty states. Every time you hit the ball, you name its capital." Every morning I'd wake up when my father burst into my room with that morning's newspaper headline. Oddly, the morning I best remember was after The Ultimate Warrior beat Hulk Hogan at Toronto's SkyDome. Neither of us knew or cared about wrestling, but my father announced the news with such brio that suddenly The Ultimate Warrior became the most important person in the world.

My mother would take me to the public library—the central branch was near where she worked—and let me loose. We had a canvas bag that was specifically for holding checked-out books. She didn't read so much as sit on a bench and watch me read, mostly Canadian juvenile fiction. The first two adult books I ever read were bought for dimes from the discard section. The first was a schlocky self-help book called *The Monk Who Sold His Ferrari: A Fable about Fulfilling Your Dreams and Reaching Your Destiny* (I liked the title), and the second was *Hamlet* (I wanted to see what all the fuss was about). I'm not sure I understood either. And yet my mother remained encouraging. In the years that followed, she bought me, from that same bin, a philosophy textbook (I liked the 1980s-era cover art) and a novelization of the live-action movie *Teenage Mutant Ninja Turtles* (this should need no explanation). The books did not exactly initiate me intellectually, but they did, in their own strange way, jump-start my curiosity.

Like both of my parents, I left home when I was about sixteen. Unlike their relocations, though, mine was entirely voluntary. When I left, it was for a tiny boarding school in the middle of nowhere. Or, to be more specific, a forested enclave on the southern tip of Vancouver Island (about halfway to China from Toronto, in case the Prophet is keeping tabs). The campus of Pearson United World College of the Pacific was a Shangri-la, secluded to a near-mythic degree from its three neighbors. On one side, a ribbon of lichen-splotched rocks separated us from the vast Pacific Ocean. On another side, armed guards enforced the boundary between us and a low-security prison known as the William Head Institution. On the third side, a faded sign on a flimsy chain-link fence warned us to keep off a patch of Department of National Defense land on which outmoded bombs were detonated (every once in a while a faint "boom" would interrupt English class). Its remoteness made it feel hallowed, but Pearson College was more than just a secluded boarding school.

Pearson College is education at its noblest. The school's guiding philosophy is one line culled from Lester B. Pearson's 1957 Nobel Peace Prize acceptance speech: "How can there be peace without people understanding each other, and how can this be if they don't know each other?" Pearson College plucked two hundred bright students from one hundred different countries and gave each a full scholarship—room, board, airfare, spending money, laundry detergent, everything—and the best education money could buy. The point was to get us, to use Pearson's word, to *know* one another.

To say that I left home because I was offered a spot at Pearson College is to put the cart before the horse: I left for Pearson before I had a spot. I had gone through the application process the year before, and had even been granted an interview, but was later notified that I didn't make the cut. I was listed as an alternate. I was devastated. In an effort to cheer me up, my parents enrolled me in one of the school's ancillary programs—a summer camp for budding activists—as a kind of consolation prize. A week or so into the camp, I realized that I didn't want to leave. Emboldened by new friends and the idyllic campus (picture wild blackberry bushes and the peeling bark of arbutus trees), I walked over to the administration building and knocked on the director's door. I asked him if there was any way he could squeeze me in. "Please," I begged. He told me he couldn't do anything for me. I went back to his office every few days, each time with a new cockamamy proposal. "I don't even have to live in a dorm," I told him. "I can sleep anywhere. Really, *anywhere*." A few days before the end of the camp, I went to his office again. This time he had my application on his desk. Apparently, a student from Burkina Faso couldn't get a visa and was forced to drop out. He had a spot. "Would you like it?" he asked. I nodded, left his office, and sat down on a rock, dizzy. I was in.

Within the week, I had moved in. We lived in stout wooden dorms with giant windows. In my first year, I shared a room with young men from Venezuela, Croatia, and Burma; in my second, with students from Nicaragua, China, and Nigeria. We spoke different languages and had been educated in different ways. We listened to different types of music. (The first time my roommate Ling played a Beijing opera tape, I almost smashed my head through my window. By the end of the year, I'd play it at full blast when he wasn't in the room.) We even brushed our teeth differently: Ling held his toothbrush the way he held chopsticks; as it turns out, I hold mine the way I hold a butter knife.

The school took great pains to include students of different socioeconomic strata. In the dining hall, a Sri Lankan raised in an underfunded rural orphanage could eat her breakfast alongside a Scandinavian prince. A dirt-poor Zimbabwean student used the same library computer as the upper-class Japanese student. We never knew how poor or wealthy any other student was. The subject of money never came up.

The administrators would purposefully pair students from countries in conflict: someone from the United States with an Afghani, an Israeli with a Palestinian, an Indian with a Pakistani. We'd all have to listen to an occasional late-night shouting match through the paper-thin walls. But more often we'd hear the audio tracks of pirated movies, punctuated by raucous laughter. Or karaoke in a language that the singer clearly did not speak. Or, most often, formidable conversations at three in the morning that were about everything and nothing all at once. Whatever our differences—language, money, politics—we shared one circumstance that couldn't be trumped: we were all awkward teenagers far from home. Whether I knew it or not at the time, my move to Pearson was both a journey of rebellion and a journey of imitation. Only by running away from my parents did I sculpt my own story in the image of theirs. I immigrated to a school of immigrants.

The program lasted two years. The first demolished me in a way I assume is familiar to anybody who has left home at a young age. A few weeks into school, I realized that I didn't have to keep praying every day. Just like I didn't have to launder my clothes or cut my hair or eat breakfast or shower daily or finish all my homework. So I didn't. Why should I? I didn't have to do anything I didn't want to do. I didn't have to think anything I didn't want to think. Every tiny action became a tiny decision. I spent the rest of the year slicing into my mind with questions: Why do I think this? Why do I care about that? What should I think about? What should I care about? Does it even matter what I do or think? What does matter? Answers eluded me.

My religion was never any consolation to me. I felt—and still do feel—that it didn't have the right answers, that it wasn't even asking the right questions. It's not that I disbelieved or disparaged the abstract and disembodied notions I had been raised on—God, bipolar morality, the pillars of Islam, our Imam's ancestry—I just didn't think of the world that way.

I could not find the total nourishment in Ismailism that continues to fulfill my parents and the rest of my family. To me, the rituals all felt like chores. The prayers were not in my language (I refer both to the Arabic-Gujrati Du'a, and its stiff, self-serious English translation). Why should I listen to the Imam—a decent enough guy, to be sure, but one who knows nothing about me? I found my religion intellectually and spiritually cumbersome. What I wanted instead was to articulate, as simply as I could, what mattered to me in the world. The task turned out to be far more difficult than I had ever imagined.

I couldn't go home that first summer. I couldn't bear to go back to my suburban khane-going life. Instead, I spent the summer bumming odd jobs at school. For days at a time I was the only person on campus. I ate ramen noodles for breakfast, lunch, and dinner. I'd sit in the biggest lecture hall by myself, desperately looking for meaning, for purpose, for something I could believe in.

As I reflected on my first full year away from home, I thought more than anything of the friends I had made from all over—Ireland and the Bahamas and Kurdistan and Chechnya and Israel and Costa Rica. They had their own baggage, often far weightier than anything I had ever experienced. I remember trying to console a friend from Colombia who was visiting my house over winter break. He had just heard the news that bombs had blanketed his whole region. He was able to contact his parents only days later. These friendships were deeper, more intense than any I had ever had before. I felt bound to these brilliant and beautiful young people because we were all asking the same questions and, moreover, because the answers we had previously been taught were coming up short. Without realizing it, we cobbled together a community.

My first year at Pearson gave me courage to stop seeing the world as an enormous and baffling place. Instead, the world began to look, sound, and feel just like my community. People everywhere, I reasoned, are as human as everyone I know and love—fragile, a little selfish and oblivious, but ultimately sensible and caring. Here I found an elegant answer to my question, what matters to me? People do—more than any religion, more than money, more than power, more than truth, more than beauty. All of a sudden, the world's towering systemic problems— inequality, indignity, and indifference—seemed manageable. If people made it a point to share with one another, to listen to one another, to dignify one another, we'd live in a far better world. Here I found a purpose. I would spend my life appealing to people's empathy, helping them to matter to one another.

In my theater class at the start of second year, our teacher told us that we could write a play for our final project. It had never occurred to me to write one. Late that night, I wrote my first playlet in an e-mail dialogue box and sent it off to her. The play was titled "A Play on Names." It was terrible, yet she responded graciously enough. I was thrilled. Playwriting allowed me to sculpt my own tiny stories in the hope that others would find in them the sincerest version of me, but also something of themselves they hadn't seen before. Every day for the next few months I was in the computer lab printing out the latest draft of my final-project play script, thrusting it on anyone who would agree to read it. I'd sit the reader down with the script in the stairwell, pretend to leave, and peek through the windowed slit in the door. Any and every smile on the reader's face validated the whole world, not to mention my tiny place in it. I had found a way to connect to people: stories. The most meaningful way to know and be known is to swap stories with someone. I still think this is true.

Only years later, after taking three playwriting classes in college, did I get the courage to write a play about my parents. The two-character play chronicled the delicate relationship between an immigrant father and his preteen daughter named Parul. The pair are aliens, each in their own way. He is uneducated, speaks pidgin English, and earns minimum wage. She is socially maladjusted and craves her peers' approval but is unable to win it. Over the course of the play, as he accompanies her to her various daily activities—figure-skating classes in the morning, spelling-bee practice after school, drama class in the evening—she feels more and more alienated. The other girls, with their pristine white figure skates, laugh at the beat-up brown hockey skates that Parul's father bought for her secondhand. She blames her spelling mistakes on her dad's broken English. In her drama class, she is cast in the smallest role, forced to play a waiter. She blames her father for it all:

PARUL. You're so dumb.
PAPA.   Parul.
PARUL. No. You are dumb. You don't understand anything. You never just do stuff properly like every other parent. You can't just get me figure skates like every other girl on the team. You are dumb. Go back to India.

Every one of his attempts to atone simply makes her angrier. He tries to help her practice, but he doesn't quite know how. For instance, when dictating words for her to spell, he pronounces the letters *p* and *b* individually in the word *harrumph*. He tries to make her laugh, but she is never in the mood. Finally, he tries to paint her brown hockey skates white with liquid corrective fluid, a tactic that only calls more attention to them. Parul is Papa's only friend, yet to Parul, Papa is the reason she doesn't have friends.

Papa eventually mollifies his daughter's anger by telling her a story about his own childhood. As a youngster, he also played a bit part in a Gujrati drama, as a guard announcing the entrance of a mythical king. He tells her how he was able to ignore his fellow students when they heckled him: "And even some of the audience, they did ha-rump, ha-rump, but it was fun." Decades later, Papa still remembers his four lines, which he translates for Parul. "From here and there, make respect…" the monologue begins. Eventually, Parul and Papa together decide that Parul should abandon every one of the extracurricular activities that she does not enjoy, like figure skating, and instead try those where "everybody plays together," like hockey. And, of course, she already has the skates. What convinces her is not simply the hope that she'll make new friends but her newfound trust in her father. He *knows* her. He *gets* her in a way that no one else can.

The play was in part a reflection of my own family. Parul is a mash-up of my sister and me, just as Papa is a mash-up of my mother and my father. Her experience with extracurricular activities echoes mine—being alone, being bored, being made fun of. Her father's patience, his carefulness, his attention, his humility, and his sense of humor all came from years of tiny moments shared with my parents. Even the lines that Papa recalls from his own short-lived acting career were ones my father had uttered on a stage about forty years earlier. I know them because he remembers them after all these years.

The final scene of the play is Parul's cameo appearance in her drama-class play. She bobbles her lines owing to nerves. At that moment, Parul makes a decision. She marches to center stage and delivers her lines—not her lines as a waiter, but her father's, in the original Gujrati: "From here and there, make respect…" The gesture is a proud one, a fearless one. Parul refuses to hide behind her submissive and inconspicuous role, and instead claims respect—for her father and for herself. The final stage direction is simple: "PARUL holds the gaze of the audience and starts to smile."

After I finished a solid draft, I submitted the script to my college's annual playwriting competition. To my surprise, it won. The play, titled "From Here and There Make Respect," was to be produced the following term. One of the professors involved in the selection—a distinguished actor and director—would helm the production. We would need students to participate in the process as well—as actors, light and sound technicians, carpenters to build the set, costume designers, and stage and house managers. By the end, we even enlisted a student figure skater to give us some pointers for one of the skating scenes.

As soon as copies of the script were made available from the theater department office, I began receiving e-mails from friends and strangers alike. Most of my friends were surprised. The majority of the plays I had written until then were cerebral comedies, quick and madcap. This one had fewer characters, fewer gimmicks, and fewer punch lines. It was softer, slower, more vulnerable. My friends didn't know I could write that way. Strangers e-mailed me, often Indian or Pakistani Americans who were premed or bound for business school. They had never acted before, but the play resonated with them and they felt deeply for a certain character or other. Would I mind if they auditioned? I was honored.

One by one, actors came in to audition, full of heart and personality. Papa after Papa. Parul after Parul. I was consistently surprised as I heard the lines I had written. At times they were heavier than I had expected, at times lighter; at times faster, at times slower; at times more purposeful, at times more flippant. In the end we decided on two actors, both mature and sensitive.

I e-mailed the script to a bunch of professors and staff I admired—a few theater professors, a physics professor, the draper from the costume shop, an adviser from the History Department. I got much insightful feedback: affirmation but also probing questions and suggestions. One e-mail response I received, though, stood out. It was from an art history professor, a specialist in Indian art. The response was honest and thoughtful, a page or two in length. It was a bold critique of my play. "Perhaps I'm missing something in my reading," she wrote, but "I had a difficult time sympathizing with either character." She compared my play with other works of literature that I quite loved. "When I read Lahiri's recent novels or watch Nair's movies, I am a bit disappointed in the stock material and textbook stereotypical 'quotes' of the immigrant experience. It caters to a western audience and insults the eastern one." To her, my story didn't explore cultural differences on a "meaningful plane" but rather was "any teenager coming-of-age story." *So what?* she seemed to say. "I imagine most teenagers think their parents are awkward or goofy or 'uncool' and would like to distance themselves."

I kept the e-mail to myself for I don't remember how long. I didn't know what to do. I didn't know how to feel. Is my play just a cliché? Is my *life* just a cliché? The rehearsals I loved to sit in on became painful to watch. I read and reread the letter. I needed time to think about it. Could I postpone the show? Or cancel? The production was scheduled; the set was hammered together. I had already invited my parents and my sister. My mother's brother and his family were going to come to New Hampshire with them. I felt rash and presumptuous. Why had I been so quick to submit the play? Who am I to tell my story? Does my story matter? I found myself face-to-face with the sort of crippling questions that I had encountered in high school.

Before I knew it, it was opening night. I ushered my family into the theater: my mother, my father, my sister, my mother's younger brother, his wife, their children. If I hadn't reserved seats for them (near the back, as my dad hates sitting up close), they wouldn't have gotten any. It seemed like everyone I knew was there. Months before, I had invited all my friends and all my professors, including the art historian who had taken the time to give me her feedback. I stood in the back with a few latecomers. I wasn't interested in the play. I had seen the dress rehearsals the previous two nights. Instead, my gaze was glued to the backs of my parents' heads. My parents had seen one other play I wrote—a farce about astronomy—but they didn't like it. (My mom told me all the scientific lingo was over her head. My dad felt ambivalent about the parts he stayed awake for.)

The lights went down and the audience went quiet. The opening lines were Papa's Gujrati monologue announcing the entrance of the mythical king. The second my dad recognized his childhood monologue, he *burst* out laughing. A split second later, a belly laugh followed from my mother, as she lovingly elbowed my father. And then, to my astonishment, even though nobody in the audience understood the Gujrati, the whole audience started laughing. We were less than a minute into the play and we started to build a momentum I've never seen before in a theater. The actor would deliver a line, my parents would recognize it and lose themselves in laughter, and then the whole audience would follow. The actors and technicians adapted, but they wondered, as I did, *how long is this going to last?* We hadn't expected this response. We thought we were doing a serious play. Three minutes in, ten minutes in, the laughter didn't stop. It was an empathetic laughter, an understanding laughter, and it rolled and rolled until the final scene. I could hear in my father's laughter that he was wide-awake, and in my mother's that she was also crying.

I'm not sure whether the laughter changed the play itself or just the way I saw it. I had seen these actors go through these motions a dozen times already, yet this time each moment surprised me. The play became more than a play. It became a sublime moment. It became a living, breathing collaboration between a community of artists and a community of audience members. It became a composite story—a coming-of-age story, sure, but also an intimate family story, an immigrant story, a story about friendship—that the whole audience could share.

As soon as the final scene started, the theater once again went quiet. A stark transition from laughter to nothing. The actor playing Parul marched to center stage and delivered her final lines, underscored with crescendoing Indian music and a crisp spotlight. She scooped up the whole audience into her smiling stare. The world stopped. The moment was bewildering and magical. A character laying herself bare for the world to know her. I looked around the room. I saw friends and strangers, many smiling, others crying. In that moment, everyone involved—the actors, the audience, me—shared something sincere. A vulnerability, a love, a debt to those who raised us, to those who educated us, to those who *know* us.

I couldn't take my eyes off my parents. I could tell, even before they stood to applaud, that they got it. They understood that I wrote this play, this story, *their* story, to thank them. The only way I could thank them. They had driven all the way from Toronto to see this play, but really they had come from much farther.

I looked back up at the stage where my parents' past and my present whorled together. There I saw my education.

Since graduating from Dartmouth in 2008, Nasir has continued on the academic track. He is now a PhD student at Harvard and has found a new outlet for his love of storytelling: contributing to National Public Radio. He goes to Toronto often to visit his family.

About the Editors and Author of the Introduction

Andrew Garrod is a professor emeritus at Dartmouth College, where he previously chaired the Department of Education, directed the Teacher Education Program, and taught courses in adolescence, moral development, and contemporary issues in U.S. education. He currently directs a volunteer-teaching program in the Marshall Islands in the Central Pacific and has conducted a research project in Bosnia and Herzegovina over a number of years. His recent publications include the coedited books *Mi Voz, Mi Vida: Latino College Students Tell Their Life Stories; Balancing Two Worlds: Asian American College Students Tell Their Life Stories; Mixed: Multiracial College Students Tell Their Life Stories;* and the seventh edition of *Adolescent Portraits: Identity, Relationships, and Challenges.* Garrod's chapter on his multiethnic, bilingual production of Shakespeare's *The Tempest* in Bosnia and Herzegovina will be published in the book *The Reflective Teaching Artist: Collected Wisdom from the Drama/Theatre Field.* In 1991 and 2009 he was awarded Dartmouth College's Distinguished Teaching Award.

Robert Kilkenny is a clinical associate in the School of Social Work at Simmons College in Boston. He is coeditor of *Souls Looking Back: Life Stories of Growing Up Black; Balancing Two Worlds: Asian American College Students Tell Their Life Stories; Mi Voz, Mi Vida: Latino College Students Tell Their Life Stories; Mixed: Multiracial College Students Tell Their Life Stories;* and *Adolescent Portraits: Identity, Relationships, and Challenges,* which is in its seventh edition. He is the founder and executive director of the Alliance for Inclusion and Prevention, a public-private partnership providing school-based mental-health, special-education, and after-school programs to at-risk students in the Boston public schools.

Eboo Patel is the founder and president of Interfaith Youth Core (IFYC), a Chicago-based organization building the interfaith movement on college campuses. Author of the book *Acts of Faith: The Story of an American Muslim, the Struggle for the Soul of a Generation,* which won the Louisville Grawemeyer Award in Religion, and *Sacred Ground: Pluralism, Prejudice, and the Promise of America,* Eboo is also a regular contributor to the *Washington Post, USA Today, Huffington Post,* NPR, and CNN. He was named by *U.S. News & World Report* as one of America's Best Leaders of 2009 and served on President Obama's inaugural Advisory Council of the White House Office of Faith-based and Neighborhood Partnerships. Eboo holds a doctorate in the sociology of religion from Oxford University. He lives in Chicago with his wife and their two sons.